Law and Practice
in
Corporate Control

Law and Practice in Corporate Control

BY

CHESTER ROHRLICH

OF THE NEW YORK BAR

BeardBooks

Washington, D.C.

PREFACE

The practice of law always involves the art of prediction and for this reason its successful practice in fields still undergoing modification demands more than the mere knowledge of reported decisions. One cannot chart the probable course of development or predict the outcome of a cause yet to be decided unless knowledge of past decisions is accompanied by an understanding of their background and producing causes, factual, historical and intellectual. Because of this, I have not been content with the recordation of judicial opinions and statutes but have sought for the realities expressed, or concealed, by the words. To help achieve this I have cited, perhaps more than usual, non-judicial dicta from the Law Reviews and elsewhere, and to a lesser extent non-legal writings.

It is surely unnecessary to say, for so small a volume, that it makes no pretense to citing *all* the cases. The treatment is intended to be suggestive rather than exhaustive, but an effort has been made to cite sufficient representative cases and other material on each point to furnish at least a starting place should further research be desired. It is hoped that the volume may prove an adequate survey of the legal aspects of the problem of corporate control and as such a helpful handbook for all who practice in that field.

Much of the material here contained has already appeared, in different form, in various legal periodicals and for permission to use it grateful acknowledgment is made to Cornell Law Quarterly, St. John's Law Review and University of Pennsylvania Law Review.

CHESTER ROHRLICH

New York City, November, 1933.

CONTENTS

CHAPTER I.

PROBLEMS OF CORPORATE CONTROL

The precise nature of the corporate entity is an
eternal subject for disputation among philoso-
phers.[1] One may hold it "real"[2] or a "fiction",[3]
or seek some middle ground.[4] But whatever the
preference the fact remains that beneath the cloak
of the corporate entity there exist the flesh and
blood men interested in it and dependent upon it.[4a]
The public that deals with it is interested in low
prices and fair dealing; the workers want high
wages and good working conditions; the stockholders dividends; the management high salaries; and

[1] Radin, The Endless Problem of Corporate Personality (1932)
32 Columbia L. Rev. 643.

[2] Laski, The Personality of Associations (1916) 29 Harvard L.
Rev. 404; Warren, Corporate Advantages Without Incorporation
(1929); Machen, Corporate Personality (1911) 24 Harvard L. Rev.
253.

[3] Wormser, The Disregard of the Corporate Fiction and Allied
Corporation Problems (1929). *Cf.* Pollock, Has the Common Law
Received the Fiction Theory of Corporations? (1911) 27 Law
Quart. Rev. 219; Machen, *supra*, note 2.

[4] Cohen, Reason and Nature (1931) 386 *et seq.*; Dewey, Philoso-
phy and Civilization (1931) 141 *et seq.*

[4a] "But who is the Company? A mere entity created by law, without body or soul, endowed with capacity to acquire, hold, and dispose of property, in trust for the use and benefit of the natural
persons of whom it is composed in proportion of their several interests therein." Meeker *v.* Winthrop Iron Co., 17 Fed. 48, 50 (C. C.
W. D. Mich. 1883).

1

the creditors certainty of payment.[4b] The conflicts
of interest among these groups is "normally" pas-
sive, probably because the profits of corporate enterprise are sufficiently large to satisfy at least the
minimum demands of the various groups.[5] When
these demands cannot be met, the struggle for control bursts forth into activity, and the resort to the
"law" becomes most frequent.[5a]

Some of the interested groups have as yet
achieved only the barest minimum of legal right to
control.[6] The weakest group is undoubtedly the
wage-earning group.[7] In so far as *direct* control is

[4b] It is not only in corporate enterprises that these divergent interests are present, but this book is concerned only with their corporate phases.

[5] This seems a necessary assumption of capitalism notwithstanding the evidence of the recent depression and the large percentage
of businss failures at all times (Lincoln, Applied Business Finance
(1925) 45). The net income of industrial corporations reporting to
the United States Government swung from a deficit in 1921 to five
and one-half billions in 1929 and back to a deficit of almost two
billions in 1931, The Internal Debt of the United States (Clark, ed.
1933) p. 178.

[5a] Even if the motive be the entirely proper one of holding corporations strictly to the letter of the law, excessive litigiousness may
be an undue burden both upon the courts and the corporations. See
SEARS, THE NEW PLACE OF THE STOCKHOLDER (1929) 199, for cita-
tions of nineteen cases brought by one Clarence H. Venner. The
entire problem of reconciling the right to insist upon the letter of
the bond and the requirements of good morals is an old one still
unsolved. See Graf v. Hope Bldg. Corp., 254 N. Y. 1, 171 N. E.
884 (1930).

[6] See, Dodd, For Whom are Corporate Managers Trustees? (1932)
45 Harvard L. Rev. 1145; Berle, For Whom Corporate Managers
are Trustees (1932) 45 Harvard L. Rev. 1365.

[7] See, O'Leary, Corporate Enterprise in Modern Economic Life
(1933) Chap. V. Employee stock ownership does not affect the
truth of this statement because any power of control thereby acquired is by virtue of stock ownership. On this subject generally, see

concerned, the general public is in no better position.[8] Theoretically, the power of the management to control is based solely upon stock ownership, although there is current a view that it is entitled to substantial rights (chiefly in the profits) by virtue of being the management.[9] By and large the courts consider corporations as existing primarily, if not exclusively, for the benefit of the stockholders,[10] limited only by the rights of creditors. The

Fordham, Some Legal Aspects of Employee Stock Purchase Plans (1930) 8 No. Car. L. Rev. 161; Foerster and Dietel, Employee Stock Ownership in the United States (1926); Employee Stock Purchase Plans in the United States (Natl. Ind. Conf. Board, 1928). See also (Note) Profit Sharing for Executives and Employees (1933) 42 Yale L. J. 419. It has been suggested that the effect upon labor should be considered in determining between immediate liquidation and continued operation by receivers, Douglas and Weir, Equity Receiverships (1930) 4 Conn. B. J. 1, 8–9. This by analogy to the continued operation of utilities for the public's benefit. See *Central Bank & Trust Co.* v. *Cleveland*, 252 Fed. 530, 533 (C. C. A. 4th 1918). But "a devotion to public use does not mean devotion to public consumption or destruction", *Birmingham Trust & Sav. Co.* v. *Atlanta, B. & A. Ry. Co.*, 271 Fed. 731, 738 (D. C. N. D. Ga. 1921). *Cf.* Bankruptcy Act, Sec. 77 (o) (p) (q); National Industrial Recovery Act, Sec. 3(a).

[8] The public at large does of course ultimately control through the machinery of the political state.

In April 1933, New York Railways Corporation and Fifth Avenue Coach Company, in order to increase their "good will", elected to their boards "public directors". The compulsory election of "public directors" has been suggested as a remedy for certain corporate abuses, Wormser, Frankenstein, Incorporated (1931) 137–139.

[9] Manton, C. J., in *Rogers* v. *Hill*, 60 F. (2d) 109, rev'd. 289 U. S. 582, 53 S. Ct. 731, 77 L. Ed. 945 (1933); O'Leary, *supra* note 7, chap. III; Berle and Means, The Modern Corporation and Private Property (1932) 342–344. See also (Note) Profit Sharing For Executives and Employees, *supra* note 7, for a discussion of the relative positions achieved by the workingmen and by the executives.

[10] "A business corporation is organized and carried on primarily for the profit of the stockholders. The powers of the directors are

traditional division of rights between stockholders and creditors is becoming increasingly unreal as applied to the holders of long-term evidences of indebtedness. The former are becoming more and more "investors" rather than entrepreneurs,[11] and the latter less and less inclined, or able, to stand on the letter of their bond. The identity of their interests is tending to overshadow the technical divergence which exists,[12] for in the last analysis both are dependent upon the success of the corporation as a going concern.[13]

Even when dealing with the conflicts of which it has already taken cognizance, the law is limited not only by the human and economic materials with which it must deal but also by its own history.

to be employed for that end. The discretion of directors is to be exercised in the choice of means to attain that end and does not extend to a change in the end itself, * * *", Dodge v. Ford Motor Co., 204 Mich. 459, 507, 170 N. W. 668 (1919).

[11] This seems to be true even of employee stockholders, see Employee Stock Purchase Plans, *supra* note 7, at p. 155.

[12] Berle and Means, *supra* note 9, p. 278 *et seq.*; Isaacs, Business Security and Legal Security (1923) 37 Harvard L. Rev. 201, 210. *Cf.* Berl, The Vanishing Distinction Between Creditors and Stockholders (1928) 76 U. of Pa. L. Rev. 814, where any tendency to "permit investors to be treated as creditors for the purposes of security and as stockholders for the purposes of profit" is decried. See, Warren v. King, 108 U. S. 389, 399, 2 S. Ct. 789, 27 L. Ed. 769 (1883); Hamlin v. Toledo, St. L. & K. C. R. Co., 78 Fed. 664, 670–671 (C.C.A. 6th 1897); *In Re* Lathrop, 61 F. (2d) 37 (C.C.A. 9th 1932). See also (Note) Protective Devices Available to the Preferred Stockholder (1927) 27 Columbia L. Rev. 587.

[13] The idea is not new. Almost forty years ago it was said (Greene, The Commercial Basis for Railway Receiverships (1894) 33 Amer. Law Reg. & Rev. 417, 425): "Railway mortgages are not sacred because of the strong legal terms in which they are drawn, but are dependent upon success in the business of transportation * * *".

Probably the most significant psychological factor that complicates the problem of corporate control is the feeling which corporate executives have that the investors—stockholders as well as creditors—are without any moral right to control or even to share in the profits beyond the minimum necessary to procure their capital contribution.[14] Justified by this attitude they frequently become "ingenious in devising methods to evade and avoid corporate responsibilities."[15] The problem is essentially one of so dividing the responsibilities and profits as to afford sufficient inducement to the managers and yet leave sufficient to attract the necessary funds.[16]

Another psychological force of no slight influence in corporate affairs is the social opprobrium which seems to attach to the dissenter. One hesitates to be called a "striker". This influence is chiefly felt in reorganizations where it tends to give complete sway to the majority committees organized by the "insiders".[17]

Lawyers are prone "to exaggerate their own importance and the significance of their legal machinery" and to overlook the fact that their devices are primarily determined by the economic factors.[18]

[14] See description of Mr. Ford's attitude in *Dodge* v. *Ford Motor Co.*, *supra* note 10 at p. 505.

[15] *Godley* v. *Crandall & Godley Co.*, 212 N. Y. 121, 105 N. E. 818 (1914).

[16] See, Payne, Corporation Salaries and Bonuses, 42 Annalist 605 (1933) ; also *supra* note 9.

[17] See, Dewing, The Financial Policy of Corporations (1926) 973; Isaacs, *supra* note 12, at pp. 208-9.

[18] Dewing, *supra* note 17, at p. 932.

The overwhelming power of economics over law is most sharply illustrated by the inability of creditors to enforce the letter of their contract and legal rights whenever economic conditions are not auspicious.

The historical development of the corporation combines with economic fact to render the present legal approach to problems of corporate control inadequate in many particulars.

Originally, a small group were able, by negotiation, to procure from the State a charter granting corporate existence and the privilege to engage in a particular line of activity. These charters were granted by special legislative enactments, each limited to a single corporation.[19] This genesis of the corporation has left an imprint on corporation law which persists even under the wholly different system of incorporation under general statutes which prevails today. The charter may have been a real contract;[20] today, it is still considered a "contract".[21] The "consent" to the terms of the charter

[19] For early history of corporations, see Davis, Essays in the Earlier History of American Corporations (1917); Williston, History of the Law of Business Corporations before 1800 (1888) 2 Harvard L. Rev. 105; Mr. Justice Brandeis' dissenting opinion in Louis K. Liggett Co. v. Lee, 288 U. S. 517, 53 S. Ct. 481, 77 L. Ed. 553 (1933). In England, prior to the American Revolution, corporations were generally created by royal charter rather than by Act of Parliament, Warren, Safeguarding the Creditors of Corporations (1923) 36 Harvard L. Rev. 509, 515.

[20] Trustees of Dartmouth College v Woodward, 4 Wheat. 518 (U. S. 1819).

[21] "The charter of a corporation having a capital stock is a contract between three parties, and forms the basis of three distinct contracts. The charter is a contract between the state and the cor-

imposed on stockholders and others is almost always based upon a legal fiction and not upon an intelligent consent in fact.[22] Also, because the earliest corporations were public in character—municipalities and universities—and had very definite, direct and personal relations with the sovereign, the courts, by the indiscriminate application to private business corporations of analogies drawn from the law of public corporations,[23] foisted theories of voting rights and limitations upon stockholders quite inconsistent with their private profit-making motives, with resultant inconsistencies in the law as well as in practice. These, and other historical vestiges have made difficult a wholly realistic approach to the problems of corporate control.

The first private business corporations were intended to permit a few to pool a part of *their* resources in a venture without risking all, but

poration; second, it is a contract between the corporation and the stockholders; third, it is a contract between the stockholders and the state", Cook, Corporations (8th Ed. 1923) Sec. 492.

[22] See *Katz* v. *DeWolf*, 151 Wis. 337, 344, 138 N. W. 1013, 1015 (1912); *Ripin* v. *U. S. Woven Label Co.*, 205 N. Y. 442, 447, 98 N. E. 855, 856 (1912); Note (1931) 44 Harvard L. Rev. 442. As to constructive notice to the public of the contents of certificates of incorporation and by-laws, see Stevens, A Proposal as to the Codification and Restatement of the Ultra Vires Doctrine (1927) 36 Yale L. J. 297, 326–327; Uniform Business Corporations Act, Sec. 10.

[23] *E.G.*, *Cone* v. *Russell & Mason*, 48 N. J. Eq. 208, 21 Atl. 847 (1891). In the early days, little attention was given to the distinction between public and private corporations (see Williston, *supra* note 19, at pp. 149, 156) and many inconsistencies in modern corporation law can be traced to this early confusion. See *Gold Bluff Mining & Lumber Corp.* v. *Whitlock*, 75 Conn. 669 (1903); Bergerman, Voting Trusts and Non-Voting Stock (1928) 37 Yale L. J. 445; Note (1931) 44 Harvard L. Rev. 442. Perhaps the distinction is only one of degree, *infra* p. 10, *cf. infra* p. 19, note 26.

soon, taking advantage of the limited liability afforded them,[24] more and more recourse was had to borrowed funds.[25] The problem of "safeguarding the creditors of corporations" thus became a vital one.[26]

 A much more significant change resulting from the desire of incorporators to venture further and further with less and less of their own funds was the enlargement of the number of stockholders.[27] Not only did the aggregate number of stockholders increase but concurrently the number of shares owned by each stockholder decreased.[28] The inevitable consequence was the separation between those who actively controlled and operated the corporation and those who passively awaited dividends. This division brought in its wake many problems centering on the respective rights and obligations of the "majority" and "minority".[29]

 In the immediate future, it would seem, more attention must be given to the increasing separa-

[24] "At common law no individual liability was imposed upon the members or stockholders of a corporation", *Hoffman* v. *Worden Co.*, 2 F. Supp. 353, 354 (D. C. N. D. Cal. 1933) ; Warren, *supra* note 19, at pp. 518–522.

[25] The long-term debt of American industrial corporations represents one-fifth of their tangible assets and of railroad and public utility corporations about one-half, The Internal Debt of the United States, *supra* note 5 at pp. 182, 101, 143.

[26] Warren, *supra* note 19.

[27] This tendency was of course also a manifestation of the development of large-scale industry and was largely accelerated by the invention of expensive machinery necessitating large investments.

[28] *Infra* p. 46, note 69.

[29] "Majority" and "minority" are used in deference to customary usage. As we shall later point out control is not in fact necessarily vested in the "majority".

tion that exists between ownership and control. In the past, decisions have been strongly influenced by the fact that the majority which controlled also had the largest financial interest in the corporation.[30] This is frequently no longer true,[31] but it does not necessarily follow that a reversal of any principle is called for. There are counter-balancing factors. For instance, investment bankers controlling the management *may* have a very real and substantial interest in the success of the corporation because the good-will of their customers is dependent upon it even though they may not directly own any of its securities.[32]

To what extent will the law tolerate the deliberate deprivation of any power of control? What disclosures can the minority compel? And to what extent will the courts intervene to control the management of a corporation? Must not the law also recognize the fact that the average stockholder when he becomes distrustful of the management prefers to sell his stock rather than litigate? If this form of extra-legal redress is to be available stockholders must be assured of a ready market and a fair market.[33] Thus, the questions of corpo-

[30] Robotham *v.* Prudential Insurance Co., 64 N. J. Eq. 673, 53 Atl. 842 (1903); Barnes v. Brown, 80 N. Y. 527, 537 (1880); Thalmann v. Hoffman House, 27 Misc. 140, 58 N. Y. S. 227 (1899); Shaw v. Davis, 78 Md. 308, 328–9, 28 Atl. 619 (1894); Cone *v.* Russell & Mason, *supra* note 23.

[31] Because of the use of bonds, non-voting classes of stock, scattered stock ownership, and the use of various devices to keep control regardless of the investment. *Infra* pp. 46–53.

[32] See New Jersey National Bank & Trust Co. *v.* Lincoln Mortgage & Title Guaranty Co., 105 N. J. Eq. 557, 561, 148 Atl. 618 (1930).

[33] The existence of such a market may be legally recognized. It has

rate publicity and of stock exchanges become relevant to the subject of corporate control.[34]

The large "publicly" owned corporations involve all the problems we have suggested plus the fact that their very size [35] renders them fit subjects for government regulation and control. Nor can such control continue to be limited to "businesses affected with a public interest",[36] if that phrase is to be defined solely by precedent. "What large business is there in which the public has not a real interest?" [37]

Not all corporations are large. Despite the historical trends which we have noted, the number, if not the individual wealth, of small, close corporations continues to be very great.[38] Their problems are quite distinct from those which beset the national corporations each with its thousands of

been in determining whether the court should compel the declaration of a dividend—see, *Raynolds* v. *Diamond Mills Paper Co.*, 69 N. J. Eq. 299, 309–310, 60 Atl. 941, 945 (1905) ; *Hiscock* v. *Lacy*, 9 Misc. 578, 30 N. Y. Supp. 860 (1894)—and the sale of corporate assets for securities having a ready market has been treated as the equivalent of a sale for cash—*Geddes* v. *Anaconda Min. Co.*, 254 U. S. 590, 598, 41 S. Ct. 209, 65 L. Ed. 425 (1921). The existence of a ready market is a contributing factor to disinterest in management.

[34] This function of the stock exchange has received scant attention. See Berle and Means, *supra* note 9, pp. 289–331.

[35] As of January 1, 1930, the 200 largest non-banking corporations in the United States had assets of $81,000,000,000, being about one-half of the total corporate wealth of the country, the other half being owned by about 300,000 corporations, the aggregate representing at least 78 per cent of the total business wealth of the nation. Berle and Means, *supra* note 9, pp. 19, 28, 31.

[36] *Infra* p. 18, note 25.

[37] Cohen, Law and the Social Order (1933) 59.

[38] *Supra* note 35.

stockholders. In so far as close corporations are concerned, the major, special problem is the reconciliation of corporate immunity as to outsiders with an internal arrangement analogous to a partnership.

Beneath and beyond all technical considerations is the obligation of the law adequately to protect the minority against illegality, fraud and unfairness without encouraging the "striker" or unduly litigious stockholder and without hampering honest management. The courts are alert to the problem.[39]

[39] "In proper cases courts protect minorities, even minorities of one, against the oppression of the majority of stockholders and boards of directors. It sometimes happens, however, that a minority institute 'strike' suits and seek to oppress majorities and to involve the corporation itself in disaster for purposes of their own and for reasons not always revealed. So that there are cases in which courts are compelled to protect minorities against majorities and majorities against minorities." Staats v. Biograph Co., 236 Fed. 454, 457 (C. C. A. 2d, 1916).

CHAPTER II.

GOVERNMENT CONTROL

It seems prerequisite to any study of the subject of corporate control [1] to examine the external control exercised by the state over the corporate entity *because it is a corporation.* [2]

Requiring "some positive governmental authorisation" [3] as a condition of their being, corporations

---

[1] In its usual connotation this phrase refers to the conflicts between majority and minority stockholders with which this book is primarily concerned. It seemed appropriate however to touch upon the external control exercised by the state and hence this chapter.

[2] This is something quite different from the very popular subject of government control of *business.* There is an extensive literature on that subject. The newly enacted National Industrial Recovery Act, approved June 16, 1933, provoked considerable material. See, Handler, The National Industrial Recovery Act (1933) 19 A. B. A. J. 440; Wahrenbrock, Federal Anti-Trust Law and the National Industrial Recovery Act (1933) 31 Michigan L. Rev. 1009; Corwin, Social Planning Under the Constitution (1932) 26 American Pol. Sci. Rev. 1; Marshall and Meyers, Legal Planning of Petroleum Production (1931) 41 Yale L. J. 33; Fuchs, Legal Technique and National Control of the Petroleum Industry (1931) 16 St. Louis L. Rev. 189. For reviews of the older forms of government control (*i.e.*, anti-trust laws, trade, commerce and utility commissions) see the lectures by Wickersham, Montague, Coleman, Guthrie and Hines, reprinted in Some Legal Phases of Corporate Financing Reorganization and Regulation (1917 and 1931), also Mosher and Crawford, Public Utility Regulation (1933); The Federal Anti-Trust Laws (Handler, ed. 1932). See also Keezer and May, The Public Control of Business (1930); Cheadle, Government Control of Business (1920) 20 Columbia L. Rev. 438, 550.

[3] Freund, The Police Power (1904) 356.

12

are subject to governmental domination by the very act of their creation.[4] The earliest method of controlling corporations was the imposition of limitations and conditions in the charter.[5] Construed as a contract,[6] the state lost all future power to impose new or different limitations upon the corporation once the charter was granted and accepted. This loss of control was overcome by the device of reserving the power of alteration, amendment and repeal—a reservation of power now universal.[7] This reservation gives the legislature no greater legislative power than would without it be vested

[4] "A corporation being the mere creature of the Legislature, its rights, privileges and powers are dependent solely upon the terms of its charter. Its creation (except where the corporation is sole) is the investing of two or more persons with the capacity to act as a single individual, with a common name, and the privilege of succession in its members without dissolution, and with a limited individual liability". *Horn Silver Mining Co.* v. *State of New York*, 143 U. S. 305, 312–313, 12 S. Ct. 403, 36 L. Ed. 164 (1892). The common-law characteristic of non-individual liability (*Hoffman* v. *Worden Co.*, 2 F. Supp. 353, 354—D. C. N. D. Cal. 1933) may be abrogated or modified by statute, see, *Bissell* v. *Heath*, 98 Mich. 472, 478–480 (1894) ; *Thomas* v. *Matthiessen*, 232 U. S. 221, 34 S. Ct. 312, 58 L. Ed. 577 (1914).

[5] From this source flows the entire doctrine of ultra vires. For collection of cases see 3 Cook, Corporations (8th Ed. 1923) Sec. 669. As a result of increasingly liberal general corporation statutes and the use of the broadest possible terminology in certificates of incorporation, the problem of ultra vires is now of slight importance. See (1932) 45 Harvard L. Rev. 1393. For a succinct resume of some of the earlier limitations see the dissenting opinion of Mr. Justice Brandeis in *Louis K. Liggett Co.* v. *Lee*, 288 U. S. 517, 53 S. Ct. 481, 77 L. Ed. 553 (1933).

[6] *Trustees of Dartmouth College* v. *Woodward*, 4 Wheat. 518 (U. S. 1819).

[7] That is, in the United States. "It is a sort of proviso peculiar to American legislation, growing out of the decision in the Dartmouth College case", Mr. Justice Bradley in *Sinking Fund Cases*, 99 U. S. 700, 748 (1878).

in it under the constitution—the effect of the reservation is to retain, not to create, legislative control over charters.[8] And it is limited to control over the charter, giving the state no greater power than it would have without it in so far as the corporation's property is concerned.[9] Under the guise of repeal or amendment, the state may not take or destroy vested property rights.[10] Although the limitation to the effect that amendments under the reserved power must not be "basic" still persists,[11] it is without importance today in view of incorporation under general laws permitting the filing of certificates authorizing the doing of "any lawful business."[12] Such certificates of incorporation may

[8] Opinion of the Justices, 66 N. H. 629 (1891); Bradley, J. dissenting in the *Sinking Fund Cases, supra* note 7.

[9] *County of Santa Clara* v. *So. Pac. Ry. Co.,* 18 Fed. 385 (C. C. Cal. 1883), *affd.* 118 U. S. 394, 6 S. Ct. 1132, 30 L. Ed. 118 (1886).

[10] *Chicago, M. & St. P. RR. Co.* v. *Wisconsin,* 238 U. S. 491, 35 S. Ct. 869, 59 L. Ed. 1423 (1915); *People* v. *O'Brien,* 111 N. Y. 1, 18 N. E. 692, *cf. Greenwood* v. *Freight Co.,* 105 U. S. 13 (1881). Exemption from taxation is not a vested right, *Tomlinson* v. *Jessup,* 15 Wall. 454 (U. S. 1872). Certain voting rights in a business corporation may be deemed vested property rights, *Miller* v. *The State,* 15 Wall. 478 (U. S. 1872); *Lord* v. *Equitable Life Assur. Society,* 194 N. Y. 212, 87 N. E. 443 (1909); *cf. Matter of Mount Sinai Hospital,* 250 N. Y. 103, 164 N. E. 871 (1928). But an amendment providing for cumulative voting is valid, *Looker* v. *Maynard,* 179 U. S. 46, 21 S. Ct. 21 (1900), *cf. Smith* v. *Atchison, T. & S. F. R. Co.,* 64 Fed. 272 (C. C. Kan. 1894); *In Re Newark Library Assn.,* 64 N. J. L. 265, 45 Atl. 622 (1900); *Comm. ex rel.* v. *Flannery,* 203 Pa. 28, 52 Atl. 129 (1902).

[11] *Hollender* v. *Rochester Food Products Corp.,* 242 N. Y. 490, 493, 152 N. E. 402 (1926); *Zabriskie* v. *Hackensack & N. Y. RR. Co.,* 18 N. J. Eq. 178 (1867). *Cf. Interstate Commerce Comm.* v. *Oregon-Washington RR. Co.,* 288 U. S. 14, 53 S. Ct. 66, 77 L. Ed. 310 (1933). See also 2 Cook, Corporations (8th Ed. 1923) 1657.

[12] See Brandeis, J. *supra* note 5. We are here concerned only with the power of the state to impose an amendment upon an unwilling

not be amended by special acts of the legislature but only by general acts.[12a] Under the prevailing system almost all charters are initially acquired by the *ex-parte* act of the incorporators acting under general statutes, and amendments thereto are voluntarily adopted by the majority stockholders under permissive statutes. The important questions raised are therefore those involving the right of the minority to resist.[13]

In the exercise of its police power [14] a state may

corporation. See also, Stern, The Limitations of the Power of a State Under a Reserved Right to Amend or Repeal Charters of Incorporation (1905) 53 Univ. of Pa. L. Rev. 1, 73, 145; Ohlinger, Some Comments on the Reserved Power to Alter, Amend and Repeal Charters (1931) 29 Mich. L. Rev. 432.

[12a] *E.g.*, Delaware Constitution, Article IX, Section 1.

[13] *Infra* p. 128.

[14] In a sense the reserve power of amendment was an early substitute for the "police power". See, Ohlinger, *supra* note 12; Schoetz, Can a State More Effectively Regulate Corporations Under the Reserve Clause of its Constitution than Under its Police Power (1922) 7 Marquette L. Rev. 69. Courts have sustained under the reserve power statutes which were essentially police regulations and which they were not prepared to sustain under the "police power". See, *Berea College* v. *Kentucky,* 211 U. S. 45, 29 S. Ct. 33, 53 L. Ed. 81 (1908) ; *People* v. *Beakes Dairy Co.,* 222 N. Y. 416, 119 N. E. 115 (1918). "It is hardly possible to overestimate the theory that corporate existence depends on positive sanction as a factor in public and legislative policy. . . . So far as the business of banking and insurance have been carried on under corporate charters they have been the subject of thorough and detailed regulation, while private banking and the unincorporated form of fraternal insurance remain to the present day in the main unregulated and uncontrolled. Railroads have been built and operated from the beginning by corporate enterprise; thus legislation was called for and was made the instrument of exercising public power over operation, service, and in some cases over rates; the express business, on the other hand, which happened to be carried on chiefly by unincorporated concerns, or at least did not seek special charters, practically escaped regulation . . . ; this tends to show that it was not merely the fact of being a

prohibit corporations from engaging in certain activities, *e.g.*, the practice of the learned professions,[15] and may withhold the privilege of doing business from foreign corporations.[16] It may, on the other hand, insist that only corporations engage in certain lines of business.[17]

common carrier subject to special power, but more particularly the fact of being a corporation asking for powers, which subjected the railroad company to the extensive and intensive legislative regime which it has experienced . . . In the case of a corporation it will also often be possible to construe charter limitations in conformity to public policy, and thus to identify injury to public interests with illegality; . . . Altogether, if there lurks in corporate organization a special danger to the public, it also affords the legal ways and means for public control of exceptional strength", Freund, Standards of American Legislation (1917) 40–42.

[15] *State Electro-Medical Institute* v. *State of Nebraska*, 74 Neb. 40, 103 N. W. 1078 (1905); *Matter of Co-operative Law Co.* 198 N. Y. 479, 92 N. E. 15, 32 L. R. A. (N. S.) 55 (1910); *Meisel & Co.* v. *Natl. Jewelers Board of Trade*, 90 Misc. 19, 152 N. Y. Supp. 913 (1915); *Thompson Optical Institute* v. *Thompson*, 119 Ore. 252, 264, 237 Pac. 965 (1925). Cf. *Matter of Dr. Bloom Dentist, Inc.* v. *Cruise*, 259 N. Y. 358, 361, 182 N. E. 16 (1932), app. dis. 288 U. S. 588, 53 S. Ct. 320, 77 L. Ed. 408 (1933).

[16] *Railway Express Agency, Inc.* v. *Virginia*, 282 U. S. 440, 51 S. Ct. 201, 75 L. Ed. 450 (1931); *Hemphill* v. *Orloff*, 277 U. S. 537, 548, 48 S. Ct. 577, 72 L. Ed. 978 (1928); *Pembina Cons. S. Mining & M. Co.* v. *Pennsylvania*, 125 U. S. 181, 184–5, 8 S. Ct. 737, 31 L. Ed. 650 (1888). But foreign corporations may not be denied resort to the courts, *Kentucky Finance Corp.* v. *Paramount Auto Ex. Corp.*, 262 U. S. 544, 43 S. Ct. 636, 67 L. Ed. 1112 (1923). See also *Power Mfg. Co.* v. *Saunders*, 274 U. S. 490, 47 S. Ct. 678, 71 L. Ed. 1165 (1927). See generally, Henderson, The Position of Foreign Corporations In American Constitutional Law (1918).

[17] *North Dakota ex rel. Goodhill* v. *Woodmansee*, 1 No. Dak. 246, 11 L. R. A. 420 (1890) banking; *Commonwealth* v. *Vrooman*, 164 Pa. 306, 25 L. R. A. 250 (1894) insurance. See also Noble State Bank v. *Haskell*, 219 U. S. 104, 31 S. Ct. 185, 55 L. Ed. 112, rehearing denied 219 U. S. 575, 31 S. Ct. 299, 55 L. Ed. 341 (1911). As to whether the state can compel incorporation of "ordinary business vocation," see Drucklieb v. Harris, 209 N. Y. 211, 102 N. E. 599 (1913).

Corporations are "subject to the same legislative control that natural persons are under like circumstances",[18] for "the chartered rights of a corporation are not more sacred than the individual's rights of person and property, and all must give way to any legislative exercise of the police power of the state".[19] They are subject to the penal law,[20] to the power of eminent domain,[21] and are liable for their torts.[22]

All businesses, hence all business corporations, are subject to some degree of governmental control,[23] but in this Country, perhaps only because of an "historical error"[24] there is a vast distinction —at least in the absence of an emergency[24a]—between the degree of regulation to which businesses "affected with a public interest" and those not so

[18] *Ward* v. *Farwell,* 97 Ill. 593, 608 (1881).

[19] *Kansas Pac. Ry. Co.* v. *Mower,* 16 Kan. 573, 581 (1876); *Hammond Packing Co.* v. *Arkansas,* 212 U. S. 322, 345, 29 S. Ct. 376, 53 L. Ed. 530 (1909). The police power is of course exercised not only by the legislature directly but also by the executive and judicial departments of the government. See *State ex rel. Cuppel* v. *Milwaukee Chamber of Commerce,* 47 Wis. 670, 679–680, 3 N. W. 760 (1879).

[20] 1 Cook, Corps. (8th Ed. 1923) 121–124; *People* v. *Canadian Fur Trappers Corp.,* 248 N. Y. 159, 161 N. E. 455 (1928).

[21] *West River Bridge Co.* v. *Dix,* 6 How. 507 (U. S. 1848).

[22] 1 Cook, Corps. (8th Ed. 1923) 112–120.

[23] *New State Ice Co.* v. *Liebman,* 285 U. S. 262, 273, 302, 52 S. Ct. 371, 76 L. Ed. 747 (1932).

[24] Brandeis, J. dissenting in *New State Ice Co.* v. *Liebman, supra* note 23, at p. 302. See also, McAllister, Lord Hale and Business Affected with a Public Interest (1930) 43 Harvard L. R. 759.

[24a] See, *Southport Petroleum Co.* v. *Ickes,* 1 U. S. Wkly. L. J. 473 (D. of C. Aug. 17, 1933); *Tyson & Bro.* v. *Banton,* 273 U. S. 418, 437, 47 S. Ct. 426, 71 L. Ed. 718 (1927); *McCarthy* v. *Prudence-Bonds Corp.,* 149 Misc. 13, 266 N. Y. S. 629 (1933); Mott, due Process of Law (1926) 344–360.

affected may be constitutionally subjected.[25]
Whatever criteria may be adopted for determining whether or not a particular business is one

[25] It is beyond the scope of this book to examine this distinction.
Attention should however be called to the danger of regarding "precedent" alone as a sufficient criterion. This is sharply illustrated by
two decisions rendered within one month (June-July 1933). One
sustained price fixing of milk (People v. Nebbia, 262 N. Y. 259,
186 N. E. 694); the other refused to sustain price fixing of petroleum (H. Earl Clack v. Public Service Commission, — Mont. —, 22
Pac. (2d) 1056). See also, Mr. Justice Brandeis' dissenting opinion in
New State Ice Co. v. Liebman, supra note 23, at pp. 284, 301, 303;
Keezer and May, supra note 2, chap. V; Cheadle, supra note 2,
at pp. 584–5, where the contention is advanced that the determination
whether a business is "affected with the public interest" is primarily a legislative and not a judicial function. It is however
well-settled that "the mere declaration by the legislature that a
particular kind of property or business is affected with a public
interest is not conclusive". Tyson & Bro. v. Banton, supra note
24a, at p. 431. The practical consequence is that the determination has become a judicial question. See Hairston v. Danville
& W. Ry. Co., 208 U. S. 598, 606, 28 S. Ct. 331, 52 L. Ed. 637
(1908). It has been said that "the decisions of Public Service Commissions as to what constitutes a public use in those businesses
admitting of both a public or private calling have been almost unani-
mously contra to the decisions of the courts," (Note) What Constitutes a Public Use (1918) 32 Harvard L. Rev. 169, 171. The distinction between businesses affected with a public interest and others is
most sharply illustrated in cases involving the right to fix prices
(See, Tyson & Bro. v. Banton, supra; Public Service Comm. v.
Great Northern Utilities Co., 289 U. S. 130, 53 S. Ct. 546, 77 L. Ed.
135 (1933); Finkelstein, From Munn v. Illinois to Tyson v. Banton:
A Study In the Judicial Process (1927) 27 Columbia L. Rev. 769;
Rottschaefer, The Field of Governmental Price Control (1926) 35
Yale L. J. 438; Hamilton, Affectation with Public Interest (1930) 39
Yale L. J. 1089), or wages (see, Wilson v. New, 243 U. S. 332, 37
S. Ct. 298, 61 L. Ed. 755 (1917); Wolff Co. v. Industrial Court, 262
U. S. 522, 43 S. Ct. 636, 67 L. Ed. 1103 (1923); Powell, The Supreme
Court and the Adamson Law (1917) 65 Univ. of Pa. L. Rev. 607;
Kales, 'Due Process', the Inarticulate Major Premise and the Adam-
son Act (1917) 26 Yale L. J. 519), or to insist upon a certificate of
public convenience and necessity as a condition precedent to doing
business (see, New State Ice Co. v. Liebman, supra note 23).

"affected with a public interest", it is clear that the character of the owner, that is, whether a corporation or an individual, is not a permissible one.[26] "Of course, corporations may not arbitrarily be selected in order to be subjected to a burden to which individuals would as appropriately be subject. Classification must be reasonable."[27] Discrimination is not *per se* unconstitutional; the question for judicial determination is whether the particular discrimination complained of is arbitrary and unreasonable.

The prohibitions against the deprivation of life, liberty and property without due process of law contained in the Fifth and Fourteenth Amendments to the Federal Constitution may be invoked by corporations as well as by individuals in the defense of their property.[28] Similarly, corporations

[26] *People* v. *Budd,* 117 N. Y. 1, 21, 22 N. E. 670, 682, 5 L. R. A. 559 (1889) *affd.* 143 U. S. 517, 12 S. Ct. 468, 36 L. Ed. 247 (1892). It has been held that mere size is not a sufficient test, *Tyson & Bro.* v. *Banton, supra* note 24a; *Williams* v. *Standard Oil Co.,* 278 U. S. 235, 47 S. Ct. 115, 73 L. Ed. 287 (1929); *cf.* Brandeis, J. dissenting in *Louis K. Liggett Co.* v. *Lee, supra* note 5; *infra* p. 23, note 46.

[27] *Mallinckrodt Chem. Works* v. *Missouri,* 238 U. S. 41, 55, 35 S. Ct. 671, 59 L. Ed. 1192 (1915). Conversely, individuals may not be unreasonably discriminated against in favor of corporations, *Frost* v. *Corporation Commission,* 278 U. S. 515, 49 S. Ct. 235, 73 L. Ed. 483 (1929).

[28] See, *County of Mateo* v. *So. Pac. R. Co.,* 13 Fed. 145, 151 (C. C. Cal. 1882); *The Railroad Tax Cases,* 13 Fed. 722, 746–747 (C. C. Cal. 1882), app. dis. 116. U. S. 138, 6 S. Ct. 317, 29 L. Ed. 589 (1885); *Liggett Co.* v. *Baldridge,* 278 U. S. 105, 49 S. Ct. 57, 73 L. Ed. 204 (1928). Compare as to "liberty", *Northwestern Natl. Life Ins. Co.* v. *Riggs,* 203 U. S. 243, 27 S. Ct. 126, 51 L. Ed. 168 (1906); *Western Turf Association* v. *Greenberg,* 204 U. S. 359, 27 S. Ct. 384, 51 L. Ed. 520 (1907).

are entitled to the protection against unreasonable searches and seizures afforded by the Fourth Amendment.[29] On the other hand, corporations have been denied the right to avail of the privilege against self-incrimination granted by the Fifth Amendment.[30] Nor are corporations "citizens" whose "privileges and immunities" are protected against abridgment by the Fourteenth Amendment.[31] They are, however, "citizens" of the incorporating state within the meaning of Section 2 of Article 3 of the Constitution defining the jurisdiction of the Federal courts.[32]

Blue Sky laws are inherently corporate regula-

[29] *Silverthorne Lumber Company, Inc.* v. *United States*, 251 U. S. 385, 40 S. Ct. 392, 64 L. Ed. 319 (1920); *Federal Trade Commission* v. *P. Lorillard Co.*, 283 Fed. 999, *aff'd.* 264 U. S. 298, 47 S. Ct. 336, 68 L. Ed. 696 (1924). See, (Note) The Fourth and Fifth Amendments and the Visitorial Power of Congress over State Corporations (1930) 30 Columbia L. Rev. 103.

[30] *Essgee Co.* v. *United States*, 262 U. S. 151, 43 S. Ct. 514, 67 L. Ed. 917 (1923); *United States* v. *Fifty-Eight Drums, etc.*, 38 F. (2d) 1005 (D. C. W. D. Pa. 1930). "This is involved in the reservation of the visitorial power of the State, and in the authority of the National Government where the corporate activities are in the domain subject to the power of Congress," *Wilson* v. *U. S.*, 221 U. S. 361, 382, 31 S. Ct. 538, 55 L. Ed. 771 (1911). For a criticism of the rule, see Proskauer, Corporate Privilege Against Self-Incrimination (1911) 11 Columbia L. Rev. 445.

[31] *Selover, Bates & Co.* v. *Walsh*, 226 U. S. 112, 33 S. Ct. 69, 57 L. Ed. 146 (1912); Liberty Warehouse Co. v. Burley Tobacco Growers, 276 U. S. 71, 48 S. Ct. 291, 72 L. Ed. 473 (1928).

[32] Louisville, C. & C. RR. Co. v. Letson, 2 How. 497, 11 L. Ed. 353 (U. S. 1844); Puerto Rico v. Russell & Co., 288 U. S. 476, 479–480, 53 S. Ct. 447, 77 L. Ed. 594 (1933). For a criticism of this rule, see U. S. v. Mayor, etc. of Hoboken, 29 F. (2d) 932, 937–938 (D. C. N. J. 1928) and the material there cited. See also Warren, Corporations and Diversity of Citizenship (1933) 19 Va. L. Rev. 66; Yntema, The Jurisdiction of the Federal Court in Controversies Between Citizens of Different States (1933) 19 A. B. A. J. 71, 149, 265.

tions.[33] Their constitutionality was sustained by the Supreme Court as a proper exercise of the police power to prevent fraud.[34] An earlier lower Federal Court has however suggested that such statutes are valid only when applied to corporations selling their own securities.[35] A recent case,[36] speaking of the California statute, says:

"The Corporate Securities Act was enacted for the purpose of protecting the general public, not only against fraudulent or unlawful stock schemes, or enterprises, but likewise to give to the state authority to regulate and control the class and character of securities or investments that might be offered to the public

[33] See, Brown, A Review of the cases on "Blue Sky" Legislation (1923) 7 Minn. L. Rev. 431; Meeker, Preventive v. Punitive Security Laws (1926) 26 Columbia L. Rev. 318; Ashby, The Influence of Securities Regulation upon Standards of Corporation Financing (1928) 26 Mich. L. Rev. 880 (1928); Dalton, The California Corporate Securities Act (1930) 18 Calif. L. Rev. 115, 255, 373; Bitker, Blue Sky Law in Wisconsin, (1931) 15 Marquette L. Rev. 158; Simpson, The New York Blue Sky Law and the Uniform Act (1931) 8 N. Y. U. L. Q. 465. The latest venture in the field is the [Federal] Securities Act of 1933, approved May 27, 1933. See, Tracy, The New Federal Securities Act (1933) 31 Mich. L. Rev. 1117, also, Washburn and Steig, Control of Securities Selling (1933) 31 Mich. L. Rev. 768, 775. We are not here distinguishing between the different types of regulatory laws, see Breed, Public Regulation in Origination and Distribution of Securities (1933), an address, reprinted in Investment Banking, February 21, 1933.

[34] The Blue Sky Cases, 242 U. S. 539, 559, 568, 37 S. Ct. 217, 224, 227, 61 L. Ed. 480, 493, 498 (1917).

[35] *Bracey* v. *Darst*, 218 Fed. 482 (D. C. N. D. W. Va. 1914). See also People v. Pace, 73 Cal. App. 548, 238 Pac. 1089 (1925).

[36] *Hayden Plan Co.* v. *Friedlander*, 97 Cal. App. 12, 275 Pac. 253 (1929).

for purchase." [37]

Discrimination between corporations and individuals with respect to anti-trust laws has been sustained.[38] So much of the Clayton Act [39] as applies only to corporations and not to individuals is not for that reason unconstitutional.[40] State statutes requiring the filing of affidavits of non-violation of anti-trust laws by corporations but not by individuals or partnerships also have been held valid.[41]

In determining the form of corporate activities heed must of course be given to taxing statutes,[42] but in being obliged to consider the incidence of taxation corporations are in no substantially different position than the other forms of business organizations. The leading case holding a tax invalid because of discrimination is *Quaker City Cab Co. v. Pennsylvania,*[43] where the Supreme Court

[37] *Cf.* People v. Beakes Dairy Co., *supra* note 14, *pp.* 427–428.

[38] See *Crescent Cotton Oil Co.* v. *Mississippi,* 257 U. S. 129, 42 S. Ct. 42, 66 L. Ed. 166 (1921).

[39] 15 U. S. C. A. Sec. 18.

[40] *Swift & Co.* v. *Federal Trade Comm.,* 8 F. (2d) 595 (C. C. A. 7th 1925), rev'd on other grounds 272 U. S. 554, 561, 47 S. Ct. 175, 178, 71 L. Ed. 405 (1926).

[41] *Mallinckrodt Chemical Works* v. *Missouri, supra* note 27; *People* v. *Butler Street Foundry,* 201 Ill. 236, 66 N. E. 349 (1903). See also, *Hammond Packing Co.* v. *Arkansas, supra* note 19.

[42] See, Eisner, Taxation Affecting Corporate Reorganization, and Ballantine, Valuation for Income Tax Purposes, both printed in Some Legal Phases of Corporate Financing Reorganization and Regulation (1931). Note also Section 104 of the Revenue Act of 1932 imposing a penalty tax on corporations aiding their shareholders to escape surtaxes. See, Smith, Legislation to Prevent Corporate Evasion of Taxes (1933) 7 St. John's Law Rev. 361.

[43] 277 U. S. 389, 48 S. Ct. 553, 72 L. Ed. 927 (1928).

held invalid a State statute taxing the gross receipts of transportation corporations but which did not tax like receipts of individuals or partnerships engaged in the same business. With this exception the courts seem to have interfered but little with the legislative taxing powers over corporations because of alleged discrimination.[43a] States may tax the franchise of a corporation even though it is engaged in interstate commerce.[44] And a tax imposed by Congress on corporate income (denominated by it as a "special excise tax") was sustained by the Supreme Court even before the Sixteenth Amendment went into effect.[45]

It seems that it may be permissible to distinguish in taxation between large and small corporations [46] but not between domestic and foreign corporations validly within the state.[47]

[43a] See generally 14 Fletcher, Cyclopedia of Corporations (Perm. Ed. 1932) § 6925.

[44] *Kansas City, F. S. & M. R. Co.* v. *Kansas*, 240 U. S. 227, 36 S. Ct. 261, 60 L. Ed. 617 (1916).

[45] *Flint* v. *Stone Tracy Co.*, 220 U. S. 107, 31 S. Ct. 342, 55 L. Ed. 389 (1911). *Cf. Pollock* v. *Farmers Loan & Trust Co.*, 157 U. S. 429, 15 S. Ct. 673, 39 L. Ed. 759, 158 U. S. 601, 15 S. Ct. 912, 39 L. Ed. 1108 (1895). The Sixteenth Amendment became effective in 1913 but it had already been submitted to the States for ratification at the time of the Flint decision.

[46] *Citizens' Telephone Co.* v. *Fulder*, 229 U. S. 322, 33 S. Ct. 833, 57 L. Ed. 206 (1913), but note remarks at p. 332 of opinion. See also *Tax Commissioners* v. *Jackson*, 283 U. S. 527, 51 S. Ct. 540, 75 L. Ed. 1248 (1931). *Cf. supra* note 26.

[47] *Hanover Fire Ins. Co.* v. *Harding*, 272 U. S. 494, 47 S. Ct. 179, 71 L. Ed. 372 (1926). *Cf. Northwestern Life Ins. Co.* v. *Wisconsin*, 247 U. S. 132, 38 S. Ct. 444, 62 L. Ed. 1025 (1918); *Cheney Bros. Co.* v. *Massachusetts*, 246 U. S. 147, 38 S. Ct. 295, 62 L. Ed. 632 (1918); *Kansas City, M. & B. RR. Co.* v. *Stiles*, 242 U. S. 111, 37 S. Ct. 58, 61 L. Ed. 176 (1916). See also *supra* note 16.

Among the "discriminatory" taxing statutes sustained as valid by the Supreme Court are: (a) taxing stock owned by domestic corporations in other domestic corporations but not taxing like stock owned by individuals;[48] (b) taxing the income of resident individuals resulting from activities outside the State but not like income of domestic corporations;[49] and (c) providing for a special method for reassessing and collecting back taxes from corporations but not from individuals.[50]

Many efforts have been made to protect employees by legislation aimed exclusively at corporate employers. The question of the validity of such legislation is frequently tied up with the related one of the validity of discrimination between different types of business and it is ordinarily difficult to segregate the influence of these two different factors on the decision. The Supreme Court[51] has left open the question whether legislation modifying the common-law liabilities of employers for injuries sustained by employees may validly discriminate between corporate and individual employers regardless of the character of the business.

[48] *Fort Smith Lumber Co.* v. *Arkansas,* 251 U. S. 532, 40 S. Ct. 304, 64 L. Ed. 396 (1920).

[49] *Lawrence* v. *State Tax Comm.,* 286 U. S. 276, 52 S. Ct. 556, 76 L. Ed. 1102 (1932). *Cf. Royster Guano Co.* v. *Virginia,* 253 U. S. 412, 40 S. Ct. 560, 64 L. Ed. 989 (1920), holding invalid a statute which taxed the entire income of domestic corporations excepting only those which did no business in the State.

[50] *White River Lumber Co.* v. *Arkansas,* 279 U. S. 692, 49 S. Ct. 457, 73 L. Ed. 963 (1929).

[51] *Aluminum Co.* v. *Ramsey,* 222 U. S. 251, 32 S. Ct. 76, 56 L. Ed. 185 (1911).

There seems to be a tendency on the part of the Federal Courts to sustain such discrimination [52] and on the part of the State Courts to hold it unconstitutional. [53] Statutes prescribing the time and mode of payment of wages by corporations have been sustained, [54] as have acts requiring the payment of earned wages on the day of termination of employment, [55] even where such legislation was held unconstitutional when applied to individual employers. [56] An act requiring corporations to give letters to their discharged or resigned employees setting forth the nature and duration of the employment has been sustained by the Supreme Court. [57]

Even in the procedural aspects of litigation attempts have been made to place corporations on a different plane than individuals. In *Kentucky Finance Corporation* v. *Paramount Auto Exchange*

---

[52] *Missouri Pacific R. Co.* v. *Mackey,* 127 U. S. 205, 8 S. Ct. 1161, 32 L. Ed. 107 (1888) ; *Cincinnati, H. & D. R. Co.* v. *Thiebaud,* 114 Fed. 918 (C. C. A. 6th 1900).

[53] *Bedford Quarries Co.* v. *Bough,* 168 Ind. 671, 80 N. E. 529, 14 L. R. A. (N. S.) 418 (1907) ; *Ballard* v. *Mississippi Cotton Oil Co.,* 81 Miss. 507, 34 So. 533, 62 L. R. A. 407 (1903).

[54] *N. Y. C. & H. R. R. Co.* v. *Williams,* 199 N. Y. 108, 92 N. E. 404 (1910) ; *Erie RR. Co.* v. *Williams,* 233 U. S. 685, 34 S. Ct. 761, 58 L. Ed. 1155 (1914). *Cf. Braceville Coal Co.* v. *People,* 147 Ill. 66, 35 N. E. 62, 22 L. R. A. 340 (1893) ; *Johnson* v. *Goodyear Mining Co.,* 127 Cal. 4, 59 Pac. 304, 47 L. R. A. 338 (1897).

[55] *St. Louis, I. M. & S. R. Co.* v. *Paul,* 64 Ark. 83 (1897) app. dis. 173 U. S. 404, 19 S. Ct. 419, 43 L. Ed. 746 (1899).

[56] *Leep* v. *Railway Co.,* 58 Ark. 407 (1894), app. dis. 159 U. S. 267, 15 S. Ct. 1042, 40 L. Ed. 142 (1894).

[57] *Prudential Ins. Co.* v. *Cheek,* 259 U. S. 530, 42 S. Ct. 516, 66 L. Ed. 1044 (1922).

Corporation,[58] a statute which required foreign corporations to submit to examination before trial within the state but applied to non-resident individuals only when served within the state was held unreasonably discriminatory. It is, however, permissible for the legislature to give effect to essential differences between individuals and corporations. Thus, it is constitutional to proceed against corporations for violations of the penal law by bill of ouster in equity even though individuals must be proceeded against by indictment and criminal trial.[59]

[58] *Supra* note 16.
[59] *Standard Oil Co. v. Tennessee,* 217 U. S. 413, 30 S. Ct. 543, 54 L. Ed. 817 (1910).

CHAPTER III.

CORPORATE VOTING: MAJORITY AND MINORITY CONTROL *

The simple corporate set-up is based upon the democracy of the dollar—one share, one vote; majority control.[1] None of the cynicism towards the importance of corporate voting [1a] elsewhere rampant has entered the courts. In the opinions of the judges the right to vote is "a property right," "a

* Part of this chapter was published in St. John's Law Review for May, 1933 (Vol. 7, p. 218).

[1] State v. Gray, 20 Ohio App. 26, 153 N. E. 187 (1925). The use of no par stock in part destroys this concept because, unless otherwise expressly provided, each share of stock is entitled to one vote regardless of its par value, State v. Kinkead, 113 Ohio St. 487, 149 N. E. 697 (1925). The original common law view that each stockholder is entitled to only one vote regardless of the number of shares owned by him (Taylor v. Griswold, 14 N. J. L. 222 (1834); Matter of Rochester Dist. Tele. Co., 40 Hun 172 (N. Y. 1886); Commonwealth v. Conover, 10 Phila. 55 (Pa. 1873) was abandoned in the earliest days of business corporations, but such voting may still be permissible, Op. Atty. Gen. (N. Y. 1910) 406; North Dakota Civil Code, § 4534; Washington, Rem. Code, § 3812. The move away from the man to his investment was also marked by the allowance of proxy voting which is now universal but which was not permitted at common law, Bowditch v. Jackson Co., 76 N. H. 351, 82 Atl. 1014 (1912); Commonwealth v. Bringhurst, 103 Pa. 134 (1883). The practice of proxy-voting has become so intrenched that an agreement on the part of stockholders not to vote by proxy has been described as "pernicious." Fisher v. Bush, 35 Hun 641, 644 (N. Y. 1885).

[1a] Unless otherwise noted, the discussion of "voting" in this chapter is confined to voting for directors. Stockholders also vote on other matters; these are discussed primarily in Chap. VI.

27

vested interest," "a vital right," "an inherent right," "an essential attribute" of the stock itself, a right of "substantial value," indeed, the stockholder's "supreme right and main protection." [2] Notwithstanding the broad sweep of the language quoted, it is not surprising in view of the statutory nature of the modern corporation itself [3] that statutory restrictions upon voting rights have been sustained. [4] It has been held that the majority do not have such a vested right in their voting power as to invalidate a statutory amendment providing for cumulative voting designed to give the minority representation upon, the board of directors. [5] Conversely, the minority do not have such a vested right in the benefits of cumulative voting sufficient to prevent an amendment to the charter

[2] Stokes v. Continental Trust Co., 186 N. Y. 285, 78 N. E. 1090 (1906); Lord v. Equitable Life Assur. Society, 194 N. Y. 212, 87 N. E. 443 (1909); Kinnan v. Sullivan County Club, 26 App. Div. 213, 50 N. Y. Supp. 95 (1st Dept. 1898); Page v. Amer. & Br. Mfg. Co., 129 App. Div. 346, 113 N. Y. Supp. 734 (1st Dept. 1908); State v. Greer, 78 Mo. 188 (1883); Hays v. Commonwealth, 82 Pa. St. 518 (1876); Baker's Appeal, 109 Pa. St. 461 (1885).

[3] Prior to the American Revolution, corporations were generally created by royal charter rather than by Act of Parliament. See Warren, *Safeguarding the Creditors of Corporations* (1923) 36 HARV. L. REV. 509, 515.

[4] *E.g.*, limiting voting power to residents, State v. Hunton, 28 Vt. 594 (1856); limiting number of votes to be cast by any one stockholder, Mack v. DeBardeleben Coal & Iron Co., 90 Ala. 396, 8 So. 150 (1890); *cf.* Miller v. Farmers Milling & Elevator Co., 78 Neb. 441, (1907) holding invalid a *by-law* limiting the number of shares which may be owned by one person.

[5] Atty. Gen. v. Looker, 111 Mich. 498, 69 N. W. 929 (1897), *aff'd.*, *sub-nom* Looker v. Maynard, 179 U. S. 46, 21 Sup. Ct. 21 (1900); *cf.* Hays v. Commonwealth; Baker's Appeal; State v. Greer, all *supra* note 2; Commonwealth v. Butterworth, 160 Pa. St. 55, 28 Atl.

abolishing it [5a] or to prevent a reduction in the number of directors which would make it necessary for more shareholders to combine in order to obtain representation on the board.[6]

The corporation itself may not change voting rights as fixed by statute.[7] Where the statute provides that the directors shall be elected by the stockholders, a vote may not be given to bondholders.[8] Nor may a statutory provision that such election be by a plurality vote be changed by a charter provision requiring a unanimous vote.[9] And where the statute provides for annual elections of directors, the charter may not create a permanent, self-perpetuating board.[10]

In *Lord* v. *Equitable Life Assurance Society*,[11] the certificate of incorporation gave each stock-

507 (1894); Dick v. Lehigh Valley R. R. Co., 4 Pa. Dist. 56 (1894); Commonwealth v. Flannery, 203 Pa. St. 28, 52 Atl. 129 (1902); Smith v. Atchison, T. & S. F. R. Co., 64 Fed. 272 (C. C. Kan. 1894). For an explanation of "cumulative voting," see Pierce v. Commonwealth, 104 Pa. St. 150 (1883).

[5a] Maddock v. Vorclone Corp., 147 Atl. 255 (Del. Ch. 1929).

[6] Bond v. Atlantic Terra Cotta Co., 137 App. Div. 671, 122 N. Y. Supp. 425 (1st Dept. 1910). The court distinguished the *Page* case, *infra* note 15, by emphasizing the fact that the minority stockholder had no vested right in the possibility of other minority stockholders joining with him.

[7] Brewster v. Hartley, 37 Cal. 15 (1869).

[8] Pollitz v. Wabash R. R. Co., 167 App. Div. 669, 152 N. Y. Supp. 803 (1st Dept. 1913); Durkee v. People, 155 Ill. 354, 40 N. E. 626 (1895). See also, Holt v. California Development Co., 161 Fed. 3 (C. C. A. 9th 1908). *Cf.* State v. McDaniel, 22 Ohio St. 354 (1872); Ecker v. Kentucky Ref. Co., 144 Ky. 264, 138 S. W. 264 (1911).

[9] Matter of Boulevard Theatre & Realty Co., 195 App. Div. 518, 186 N. Y. Supp. 430 (1st Dept. 1921), *affd.*, 231 N. Y. 615, 132 N. E. 910 (1921).

[10] State v. Anderson, 31 Ind. App. 34, 67 N. E. 207 (1903).

[11] *Supra* note 2.

holder one vote for each share owned and provided
that the directors might grant one vote to each pol-
icyholder insured for not less than $5,000. Some
years later, the legislature enacted a law providing
that the directors with the consent of a majority of
the stockholders might confer upon policyholders
the right to vote for all or any lesser number of
directors. Thereupon the directors with the necessary concurrence of stockholders sought to confer
upon the policyholders the right to vote for 28 out
of 52 directors and to limit the stockholders to
the right to vote for 24 directors. The court held
the legislative act valid in view of the "mutualiza-
tion" features contained in the original certificate
of incorporation but held the action taken thereunder as invalid because it construed the statute as
permitting the granting of a vote to policyholders
but not as authorizing the denial of any vote to the
stockholders.[12]

A corporation may not issue all of its stock without voting powers, vesting such power in another
body,[13] or stipulate in advance the manner in which

[12] The Company was thereafter completely mutualized. The Charter was first amended to permit policyholders and stockholders to
vote for all directors and then the stock was purchased and can-
celled, leaving the sole voting power with the policyholders, see
Royal Trust Co. *v.* Equitable Life Assurance Society, 247 Fed. 437
(C. C. A. 2d, 1917).

[13] Lebus v. Stansifer, 154 Ky. 444, 157 S. W. 727 (1913). Corpo-
rations with self-perpetuating boards may of course be created by
the legislature. This was done in the case of N. Y. Life Ins. & Trust
Co. (N. Y. March 9, 1830). The Charter is still being used—now by
Bank of New York and Trust Company. See also Reynolds, The
Legal Structure of the Bank for International Settlements, 19 A. B.
A. J. 289, 292 (1933).

stockholders shall vote on matters submitted to them.[14] And when voting power has once attached to stock its relative voting strength may not be reduced by the corporation without its consent.[15]

Under the arrangement thus far discussed, it is assumed that the majority stockholders control the corporation. But despite their power ultimately to change the management, the very existence of the board of directors serves sharply to delimit their powers. Stockholders may not control (that is, directly and avowedly, as by agreement) the directors in the exercise of the discretion vested in them as to the ordinary business of the corporation or with respect to powers directly conferred upon them by statute.[16] This result follows from the fact

[14] McNulta v. Corn Belt Bank, 164 Ill. 427, 45 N. E. 954 (1897), holding void a by-law requiring stockholders to vote in favor of proposals to increase capital made by directors. *Cf.* Elger v. Boyle, 69 Misc. 273, 126 N. Y. Supp. 846 (1910), sustaining a provision in a will directing executors to vote stock in a corporation as directed by its directors. But see Randall & Sons, Inc. v. Lucke, 123 Misc. 5, 205 N. Y. Supp. 121 (1924). See also *"Validity and Effect of Provision in Will to Control Voting Power of Corporate Stock"* (1920) 9 A. L. R. 1242, (1922) 17 A. L. R. 238.

[15] Page v. Amer. & Br. Mfg. Co., *supra* note 2, holding illegal reduction in power of common stock resulting from attempted change of capital from 80,000 shares common and 20,000 shares preferred to 20,000 shares of each where both classes were entitled to vote. See *supra* note 6.

[16] Manson v. Curtis, 223 N. Y. 313, 119 N. E. 559 (1918); Fells v. Katz, 256 N. Y. 67, 175 N. E. 516 (1931); Rush v. Aunspaugh, 179 Ala. 542, 60 So. 802 (1912); Jackson v. Hooper, 76 N. J. Eq. 592, 75 Atl. 568 (1910). *Cf.* Wabash Ry. Co. v. Amer. Ref. T. Co., 7 F. (2d.) 335 (1925) cert. den. 270 U. S. 643 (1926), where an agreement by *all* the stockholders with the corporation as to the distribution of its profits was held valid; contra: Dejonge v. Zentgraf, 182 App. Div. 43, 169 N. Y. S. 377 (1918). Such agreements may be binding on the parties even if not on the corporation, Lorillard v.

that the statutes confer certain powers directly upon the directors and such powers may not therefore be regarded merely as delegated to the directors by the stockholders,[17] and from the view that directors are fiduciaries for *all* the stockholders and may not therefore assume inconsistent obligations to some of them.[18]

In the absence of express authorization in the statutes or the charter, directors may not be removed during their term of office by the stockholders except for cause.[19] Nor in the absence of such authorization may the board remove a director.[20] Where sufficient cause exists, the right of removal is inherent in the stockholders.[21] Directors may not

Clyde, 86 N. Y. 384 (1881). See also Fitzgerald v. Christy, 242 Ill. App. 343 (1926). Contra: Seitz v. Michel, 148 Minn. 80, 181 N. W. 102 (1921) holding such contracts void as against public policy.

[17] Manson v. Curtis, *supra* note 16; Bechtold v. Stillwagon, 119 Misc. 177, 195 N. Y. Supp. 66 (1922), holding invalid by-law vesting election of officers in stockholders; State v. Daubenspeck, 189 Ind. 243, 123 N. E. 402 (1920), denying right of stockholders to interfere with directors' by-law-making power.

[18] Singers-Biggers v. Young, 166 Fed. 82 (C. C. A. 8th 1908); 3 FLETCHER, CYC. CORPS. (Perm. ed.) § 838.

[19] Toledo T. L. & P. Co. v. Smith, 205 Fed. 643 (D. C. N. D. Ohio 1913); People *ex rel.* Manice v. Powell, 201 N. Y. 194, 94 N. E. 634 (1911); Matter of Korff, 198 App. Div. 553, 190 N. Y. Supp. 664 (1st Dept. 1921); Walsh v. State, 199 Ala. 123, 74 So. 45 (1917). *Query*, whether such power may be given by the by-laws, see Matter of Automotive Mfg. Assn., Inc., 120 Misc. 405, 199 N. Y. Supp. 313 (1923).

[20] Raub v. Gerken, 127 App. Div. 42, 111 N. Y. Supp. 319 (2d Dept. 1908). The Raub case (dicta) and Matter of Schwartz, 119 Misc. 387, 196 N. Y. Supp. 679 (1922) hold valid a by-law adopted by the stockholders vesting such power in the board. But see Laughlin v. Geer, 121 Ill. App. 534 (1905).

[21] Matter of Koch, 257 N. Y. 318, 178 N. E. 545 (1931); Templeman v. Grant, 75 Colo. 519, 227 Pac. 555 (1924); Brush v. Natl. Gtee. Credit Corp., 13 Del. Ch. 180, 116 Atl. 738 (1922). As to what

extend their own term by changing the date of election.[22] Controlling stockholders do, however, possess a method of procuring a favorable board even between regular elections. They may increase the number of directors and forthwith proceed to elect the new additional directors.[23]

The proper procedure [24] to test the validity of corporate elections and title to corporate office is by *quo warranto*,[25] and mandamus is ordinarily the

constitutes sufficient cause, See Matter of Koch, *supra;* SPELLMAN, CORPORATE DIRECTORS (1931) § 108. (Many of the cases cited by Spellman do not involve removal by the corporation.) Where the power to remove exists, judicial review thereof will be limited to ascertaining whether it has been exercised "fairly and in good faith" and whether the removed director was given notice and an opportunity to be heard in his own defense, State v. Brost, 98 W. Va. 596, 127 S. E. 507 (1925). The procedural requirements of due process may be waived, Matter of Koch, *supra.* Judicial procedure for the removal of directors for misconduct is sometimes provided by statute (*e.g.,* N. Y. GEN. CORP. LAW (1929) § 60), but in the absence thereof courts have no inherent jurisdiction to remove corporate officers, Johnstone v. Jones, 23 N. J. Eq. 216 (1872); Whyte v. Faust, 281 Pa. 444, 127 Atl. 234 (1924).

[22] Walsh v. State, *supra* note 19.

[23] *In re* Griffing Iron Co., 63 N. J. L. 168, 41 Atl. 931 (1898), *aff'd,* 63 N. J. L. 357, 46 Atl. 1097 (1899); Gold Bluff Mining & Lumber Corp. v. Whitlock, 75 Conn. 669 (1903). But a reduction in the number of directors does not serve to remove those in office. Matter of Manoca Temple Assn., 128 App. Div. 796, 113 N. Y. Supp. 172 (3d Dept. 1908).

[24] Except as modified by statute; *e.g.,* N. Y. GEN. CORP. LAW (1929) § 25.

[25] Hartt v. Harvey, 32 Barb. 55 (N. Y. 1860); Brooks v. State *ex rel.* Richards, 29 Del. 1, 79 Atl. 790 (1911); Deal v. Miller, 245 Pa. 1, 90 Atl. 1070 (1914). In Massachusetts, *quo warranto* may not be used in private corporations, Haupt v. Rogers, 170 Mass. 71, 48 N. E. 1080 (1898). For collection of cases, see *"Quo Warranto, or Information in Nature of Quo Warranto, To Test Title to Office in Private Corporation,"* Note (1914) 51 L. R. A. (N. S.) 1126.

proper method to compel the holding of elections in accordance with the governing law.[26] Mandamus will also issue to inspectors of election directing them to receive votes entitled to be cast.[27]

However, when a suit is properly pending in equity the court will determine all questions of title to office or validity of elections which may incidentally arise therein or the determination of which is necessary to enable it to do complete justice.[28] Ordinarily, equity prefers to give redress against specific wrongs and not interfere with corporate voting *per se*,[29] but it has acted directly in a large number of cases by injunction. Thus: Corporations have been restrained from voting majority stock held *ultra vires* in rival competing corporations;[30] voting on stock title to which, or the

[26] People *ex rel.* Miller v. Cummings, 72 N. Y. 433 (1878); Walsh v. State, *supra* note 19; Bassett v. Atwater, 65 Conn. 355, 32 Atl. 937 (1894); Cella v. Davidson, 304 Pa. 389, 156 Atl. 99 (1931); *cf.* Lutz v. Webster, 249 Pa. 226, 94 Atl. 834 (1915).

[27] Matter of Young v. Jebbett, 213 App. Div. 774, 211 N. Y. Supp. 61 (4th Dept. 1925). Inspectors of election are ministerial officers, Matter of Cecil, 36 How. Pr. 477 (N. Y. 1869); Gow v. Consolidated Coppermines Corp., 165 Atl. 136 (Del. Ch. 1933). Mandamus may also lie to compel persons wrongfully claiming office to deliver up books, American Railway-Frog Co. v. Haven, 101 Mass. 398 (1869).

[28] Deal v. Miller, *supra* note 25; Chicago Macaroni Mfg. Co. v. Baggiano, 202 Ill. 312, 67 N. E. 17 (1903); West Side Hospital v. Steele, 124 Ill. App. 534 (1906); Mechanics Natl. Bank v. Burnet Mfg. Co., 32 N. J. Eq. 236 (1880). The mere allegation of a substantial equitable action is insufficient if the court does not hear or act on it but confines itself to the incidental question, Cella v. Davidson, *supra* note 26.

[29] Davidson v. American Blower Co., 243 Fed. 167 (C. C. A. 2d, 1917).

[30] Steele v. United Fruit Co., 190 Fed. 631 (C. C. E. D. La. 1911), *aff'd*, 194 Fed. 1023 (C. C. A. 5th, 1912); Milbank v. N. Y., L. E. & W. R. R. Co., 64 How. Pr. 20 (N. Y. 1882); George v. Central R. R.

voting power of which, is in dispute has been restrained *pendente lite*[31] but not necessarily in
every case where the plaintiff claims the stock
from the defendant;[32] registered holders not entitled to vote have been restrained from doing so.[33]

& Bkg. Co., 101 Ala. 607, 14 So. 752 (1893); Memphis & Charles-
ton R. Co. v. Woods, 88 Ala. 630, 7 So. 108 (1889); Dunbar v. Amer.
Tel. Co., 224 Ill. 9, 79 N. E. 423 (1906). But an injunction will not
be granted where the stock is legally held merely because of possible
danger to the minority, Oelbermann v. N. Y. & N. Ry. Co., 77 Hun
332, 29 N. Y. Supp. 864 (1894); Bigelow v. Calumet & Hecla Min.
Co., 167 Fed. 721 (C. C. A. 6th, 1909); Toledo T. L. & P. Co. v.
Smith, 205 Fed. 643 (D. C. N. D. Ohio 1913).

[31] Harvey v. Harvey, 290 Fed. 653 (C. C. A. 7th, 1923); Harper
v. Smith, 93 App. Div. 608 (1st Dept. 1904); Stewart v. Pierce, 116
Iowa 733, 89 N. W. 234 (1902). The voting of issued but unauthor-
ized stock may also be enjoined, Haskell v. Read, 68 Neb. 107, 93
N. W. 997 (1903), rehearing denied, 68 Neb. 107, 96 N. W. 1007
(1907). The stockholder is a necessary party to an injunction suit
against his stock being voted, General Inv. Co. v. Lake Shore & M.
S. Ry. Co., 250 Fed. 160 (C. C. A. 6th, 1918); Talbot J. Taylor Co.
v. Southern Pacific Co., 122 Fed. 147 (C. C. W. D. Ky. 1903); Jones
v. Nassau S. H. Co., 53 Misc. 63, 103 N. Y. Supp. 1089 (1907);
Bouree v. Trust Francais, 14 Del. Ch. 332, 127 Atl. 56 (1924). Where
the stock in question represents control, an injunction may be obtained not only by its claimants but also by minority stockholders,
the minority, however, being restrained from holding elections while
such injunction against the majority stock is in force, Villamil v.
Hirsch, 138 Fed. 690, 143 Fed. 654 (C. C. S. D. N. Y. 1905-6).

[32] Lucas v. Milliken, 139 Fed. 816 (C. C. So. Car. 1905), action for
specific performance of agreement to sell; Maine Products Co. v.
Alexander, 115 App. Div. 112, 100 N. Y. Supp. 711 (1st Dept. 1906),
action to rescind sale but injunction against resale by defendant
granted.

[33] Pledgees: Haskell v. Read, *supra* note 31; McHenry v. Jewett,
26 Hun 453 (N. Y. 1882); *cf.* Granite Brick Co. v. Titus, 226 Fed.
557 (C. C. A. 4th, 1915). Voting rights as between pledgor and
pledgee are now frequently regulated by statute, *e.g.,* N. Y. Stock
Corporation Law (1930) § 47. Escrow Agent: Butler v. Standard
Milk Flour Co., 146 App. Div. 735, 131 N. Y. Supp. 451 (1st Dept.
1911). See also Com. *ex rel.* Langdon v. Patterson, 158 Pa. 476, 27
Atl. 998 (1893).

And the injunctive powers of equity are broad enough to meet special situations that may arise.[34] Occasionally equity will even use its powers in order to direct the manner in which votes shall be cast and to control the subjects submitted to stockholders for action. In *Byington* v. *Piazza,*[35] persons holding stock under an agreement whereby they were required to vote in favor of the re-election of the "present Board of Directors" were restrained *pendente lite* from voting to increase the board from five to seven.[36] The submission to a stockholders' meeting of a proposed by-law which would be illegal has been enjoined as has been the submission of a resolution providing for an issue of stock where the only effect of an affirmative vote would be a waiver on the part of the voting stockholder

[34] Graselli Chemical Co. v. Aetna Explosives Co., 252 Fed. 456 (C. C. A. 2d, 1918), stockholders restrained from voting while corporation in hands of equity receiver. Millspaugh v. Cassedy, 191 App. Div. 221, 181 N. Y. Supp. 276 (2d Dept. 1920) is a very special case. There the certificate of incorporation filed in 1908 failed to exclude the preferred stock from voting power but the by-laws did in accordance with the understanding of the incorporators. The preferred stockholders did not claim the right to vote for twenty years and then when they did the Court made a decree directing the stockholders to amend the certificate of incorporation.

[35] 131 App. Div. 895, 115 N. Y. Supp. 918 (1st Dept. 1909). See also Ripin v. U. S. Woven Label Co., 205 N. Y. 442, 98 N. E. 885 (1912).

[36] *Cf.* Lersner v. Adair Mach. Co., 137 N. Y. Supp. 565 (1912), where the Court refused to restrain the majority stockholder from voting to decrease the board and then ousting the plaintiff merely because of the probability that such new board might release the majority stockholder from certain claims. "It is an unheard-of thing that stockholders of a corporation can be enjoined from voting on the ground that the persons they may vote for to manage it may possibly abuse their trust," Lucas v. Milliken, *supra* note 32, at 833.

of his preemptive rights and the notice of the meeting did not advise the stockholders of the effect of their voting in favor thereof.[37]

One of the extraordinary powers of equity with respect to corporate elections is the power to appoint special masters to conduct them.[38] The power will be exercised when sufficient reason is shown for anticipating that a fair and honest election cannot be held because of the danger of fraud, violence or other unlawful conduct.[39]

No court decree may justify the voting of stock in a manner contrary to statute.[40]

Under the traditional system of corporate voting there is ever present the danger (largely theoretical, as we shall see) that the management may be changed at each annual meeting of the stockholders. It therefore, very early in the history of corporations, became common for an existing majority to enter into contracts restricting their future discretion as to voting. Since "it is not illegal

[37] Scott v. P. Lorillard Co., 108 N. J. Eq. 153, 154 Atl. 515 (1931), aff'd, 109 N. J. Eq. 417, 157 Atl. 388 (1931).

[38] This power may, of course, be limited by statute or rule, see Yetter v. Delaware Vy. R. R. Co., 206 Pa. 485, 56 Atl. 57 (1903); cf. Deal v. Erie Coal & Coke Co., 248 Pa. 48, 93 Atl. 829 (1915).

[39] Bartlett v. Gates, 118 Fed. 66 (C. C. Colo. 1902); Tunis v. Hestonville, M. &. F. P. R. R. Co., 149 Pa. 70, 83, 24 Atl. 88 (1892); Deal v. Erie Coal & Coke Co., supra note 38; Dick v. Lehigh Valley R. R. Co., 4 Pa. Dist. 56 (1895). For the powers of such master, see In re Petition of Gulla, 13 Del. Ch. 23 (1921).

[40] People v. Burke, 72 Colo. 486, 212 Pac. 837 (1923). This is an extreme case (30 A. L. R. 1100) and held that a decree carrying into effect an agreement whereby the stockholders of a corporation undertook to elect to its board certain nominees of another corporation was void and subject to collateral attack.

or against public policy for two or more stockholders owning the majority of the shares of stock
to unite upon a course of corporate policy or action, or upon the officers whom they will elect",[41]
agreements to vote for certain persons as directors
are valid.[42] And an agreement substantially giving
one stockholder a veto power has been held valid,
at least where *all* the stockholders were parties to
it.[43] An agreement whereby the parties agreed to
vote as determined by a majority of them has been
sustained.[44] There is, however, a reluctance spe-

[41] Manson v. Curtis, *supra* note 16.

[42] Bonta v. Gridley, 77 App. Div. 33, 78 N. Y. Supp. 96 (4th
Dept. 1902); McQuade v. Stoneham, 230 App. Div. 57, 242 N. Y.
Supp. 548 (1st Dept. 1930); Harris v. Magrill, 131 Misc. 380, 226
N. Y. Supp. 621 (1928); Weber v. Della Mt. Min. Co., 14 Idaho
404, 94 Pac. 441 (1908); Venner v. Chicago City Ry. Co., 258 Ill.
523, 101 N. E. 949 (1913); Thompson v. Thompson Carnation Co.,
279 Ill. 54, 116 N. E. 648 (1917); Winsor v. Commonwealth Coal
Co., 63 Wash. 62, 114 Pac. 908 (1911); *cf.* Cuppy v. Ward, 187
App. Div. 625, 176 N. Y. Supp. 233 (1st Dept. 1919), *aff'd,* 227
N. Y. 603, 125 N. E. 915 (1919). *Contra:* Morel v. Hoge, 130 Ga.
625, 61 S. E. 487 (1908). But such an agreement "must be construed
as an obligation to retain him only so long as he keeps the agreement on his part faithfully to act as a trustee for the stockholders,"
Fells v. Katz, 256 N. Y. 67, 175 N. E. 516 (1931). *Cf.* Hellier v.
Achorn, 255 Mass. 273, 151 N. E. 305 (1926).

[43] Fitzgerald v. Christy, *supra* note 16. But see other cases there
cited.

[44] Smith v. San Francisco & N. Pac. Ry. Co., 115 Cal. 584, 47
Pac. 582 (1897); *cf.* Morel v. Hoge, *supra* note 42; Sullivan v.
Parkes, 69 App. Div. 221, 74 N. Y. Supp. 787 (1st Dept. 1902).
Agreements such as in the Smith case must be sharply distinguished
from "irrevocable proxies." It is well settled that a proxy to vote
stock, not "coupled with an interest," may be revoked even though
it purports to be irrevocable, 3 COOK, CORPORATIONS (8th ed. 1923)
2136; 14 C. J. 911; Schmidt v. Mitchell, 101 Ky. 570, 41 S. W. 929
(1897); Luthy v. Ream, 270 Ill. 170, 110 N. E. 373 (1915); Randall
& Sons, Inc. v. Lucke, *supra* note 14; Woodruff v. Dubuque & S.
C. R. Co., 30 Fed. 91 (S. D. N. Y. 1887).

cifically to enforce contracts involving corporate control even when the contracts are held valid.[45] In its eagerness to protect the sanctity of the corporate ballot-box, the law has not been content to prevent the involuntary taking away of a stockholder's vote (once attached) but has gone further and imposed limitations even on his own right to deal with it.

The stockholder may not, of course, be compelled to exercise his voting right,[46] but, on the other hand, he will not be permitted to sell his vote to another.[47] Thus, it is said that a stockholder may not, for a consideration private and personal to himself and to which the corporation is a stranger,

[45] Gage v. Fisher, 5 N. D. 297, 65 N. W. 809 (1895); Foll's Appeal, 91 Pa. St. 434 (1879). In McQuade v. Stoneham, *supra* note 42, a complaint asking for specific performance of an agreement by stockholders to "use their best endeavors" to continue certain named persons (3 out of 7) as directors and the plaintiff as treasurer was sustained, but, after trial, the Court refused specific performance and granted damages (also asked for in the complaint)—142 Misc. 842, 256 N. Y. Sup. 431 (1932). But in Harris v. Magrill, *supra* note 42, a motion to restrain plaintiff's removal as director and officer in violation of agreement was granted. See also Byington v. Piazza, *supra* p. 36.

[46] See Vandenburgh v. Broadway Ry. Co., 29 Hun 348 (N. Y. 1883); Schmidt v. Mitchell, *supra* note 44.

[47] This common law rule is sometimes embodied in statute, *e.g.*, N. Y. Stock Corporation Law (1930) § 47, New York Penal Law (1909) § 668. The New York statutory provision that proxies are revocable (N. Y. GEN. CORP. LAW [1929] § 19) has, in view of the foregoing, been construed to prevent the creation of a proxy "coupled with an interest," Matter of Germicide Co., 65 Hun 606, 20 N. Y. Supp. 495 (1892). See also, Matter of Glen Salt Co., 17 App. Div. 234, 45 N. Y. Supp. 568 (3d Dept. 1897), *aff'd*, 153 N. Y. 688, 48 N. E. 1105 (1897). The proposed Uniform Business Corporations Act, expressly limits the provision that proxies are revocable to such as are "not coupled with an interest" (art. 27IV).

agree to cast his vote in a certain prescribed way.[48] Agreements whereby one of the parties undertakes to vote in a particular manner in consideration of his employment by the corporation, accordingly have been held invalid.[49] There is considerable confusion in the cases and it seems futile to attempt any detailed analysis of them in the hope of reconciling them on the basis of "distinguishing" facts. In preference we shall comment on the underlying attitudes.

The courts which sustain agreements such as here under discussion are impressed with the importance of the right freely to contract.[50] They have not as yet sought support in frank recognition of the fact that most stockholders purchase stock for financial return and that it is entirely in

[48] Brady v. Bean, 221 Ill. App. 279 (1921); Gilchrist v. Hatch, 100 N. E. 473 (Ind. 1913); Guernsey v. Cook, 120 Mass. 501 (1876); Woodruff v. Wentworth, 133 Mass. 309 (1882); Palmbaum v. Magulsky, 217 Mass. 306, 104 N. E. 746 (1914); Wilbur v. Stoeppel, 82 Mich. 344, 46 N. W. 724 (1890); Scripps v. Sweeney, 160 Mich. 148, 125 N. W. 72 (1910); Stott v. Stott, 258 Mich. 547, 242 N. W. 747 (1932); Dieckmann v. Robyn, 162 Mo. App. 67, 141 S. W. 717 (1911).

[49] Hellier v. Achorn, supra note 42, refusing to recognize a distinction in fact that employment was to continue only so long as plaintiff "did his best"; Cone v. Russell & Mason, 48 N. J. Eq. 208, 21 Atl. 847 (1891); Kreisel v. Distilling Co., 61 N. J. Eq. 5, 47 Atl. 471 (1900). The two last-cited cases recognize that a stockholders' pooling agreement would be valid if intended to carry out some corporate policy for the benefit of all stockholders. See also Rigg v. Railway Co., 191 Pa. 298, 43 Atl. 212 (1899). An agreement between stockholders that one of them would be employed by the corporation may be binding on the other parties to the agreement even if it is not binding on the corporation, Drucklieb v. Harris, 209 N. Y. 211, 102 N. E. 599 (1913). See also supra note 16.

[50] E.g., Smith v. San Francisco & N. Pac. Ry. Co., supra note 44.

harmony with their attitude to leave control to others.[51] Courts which have invalidated such agreements have done so because of a refusal to recognize "sterilized" boards of directors [52] or because of a refusal to permit the so-called separation of voting power from beneficial ownership. It is difficult to understand how the voluntary separation of voting power from beneficial ownership can be deemed contrary to "public policy" in states which permit the issuance of non-voting stock or the use of voting trusts.[53] The doctrine against the "sale" of votes [54] is, it is submitted, equally at variance with other principles of corporation law. The horror with which courts view such transactions is undoubtedly directly attributable to their drawing analogies from public law with its views as to the duties of citizens and public officials.[55] If there was any validity to the analogy when corporations were created by special charters establishing certain definite relations between the corporators and the sovereign, it vanished when it came to pass that a certificate of incorporation could be obtained by any one upon the filing of a document in a public office.[56] Although the "policy" behind it may pos-

[51] *Infra* p. 46, note 70; p. 107, note 24.

[52] *Supra* pp. 31–32.

[53] Of course, in those states where voting trusts are authorized by statute, there are certain safeguards such as the requirement that the agreement be open to all stockholders. It may be desirable that all agreements among stockholders as to voting should be filed with the corporation, open to inspection by all stockholders, in order to be valid. See also *infra* note 92.

[54] See *supra* notes 47–49.

[55] *Supra* p. 7, note 23.

[56] See Ripin v. U. S. Woven Label Co., *supra* note 35; Katz v.

sibly be sound,[56a] the reasons for the doctrine given by many courts do not withstand, it seems, close analysis. It is surely illogical to conclude, as some opinions do, that a stockholder may not agree with another how he will vote because he may "vote as he pleases." The only effect of recognizing the validity of a sale of stock for the purpose of selling control[57] and invalidating a "sale" of a vote seems to be to make the purchase of control more expensive in those cases where the control is not already separated from ownership by the use of various legal devices which are recognized as valid.[58] The writer is at a loss for a sound reason why a stockholder should not be permitted to own a share of common stock, as an investment, free to dispose of its vote, *if* corporations are at liberty to sell non-voting securities.[59] *If* investors are able to buy non-voting securities, ordinarily in ignorance of the governing voting provisions, it ought to follow that

DeWolf, 151 Wis. 337, 138 N. W. 1013 (1912) ; Note (1931) 44 HARV. L. REV. 442.

[56a] *Infra* p. 53, note 94.

[57] Doherty & Co. v. Rice, 186 Fed. 204 (C.C.M.D. Ala. 1910; Barnes v. Brown, 80 N. Y. 527 (1880) ; Stanton v. Schenck, 140 Misc. 621, 251 N. Y. Supp. 221 (1931) ; Beitman v. Steiner Bros., 98 Ala. 241, 13 So. 87 (1892) ; Smith v. Gray, 50 Nev. 56, 250 Pac. 369 (1926) ; Keeley v. Block, 91 N. J. Eq. 520, 111 Atl. 22 (1920) ; No. Cent. Ry. Co. v. Walworth, 193 Pa. 207, 44 Atl. 253 (1899) ; *cf*. McClure v. Law, 161 N. Y. 78, 55 N. E. 388 (1899) ; Jacobus v. Diamond S. W. M. Co., 94 App. Div. 366, 88 N. Y. Supp. 302 (1st Dept. 1904) ; Commonwealth T. & T. Co. v. Seltzer, 227 Pa. 410, 76 Atl. 77 (1910) ; Porter v. Healy, 244 Pa. 427, 91 Atl. 428 (1914) ; Foll's Appeal; Gage v. Fisher, both *supra* note 45.

[58] *Infra* pp. 47–52.

[59] *Infra* p. 51, note 89.

they may *voluntarily* buy stock with voting rights and then, in the exercise of *their* own discretion, contract with respect to its voting power even to the extent of "selling" the voting power, for limited periods, to others for a consideration.[60] This would merely be a frank judicial recognition of the fact that "control" has a financial value.[61] It might enable corporations to get the benefit of the higher prices for which voting stock can be issued in comparison with non-voting stock and might enable small investors to realize upon the value of "control" which they do not exercise or even desire. Conversely, it might possibly check the resort to schemes designed to deprive stockholders of their votes against their will.[62]

[60] It may possibly be argued that stockholders, like infants, should be protected against their own acts, but if that is to become the guiding principle in corporation law, in order to render it effective, the state must go very much further than it has. Professor Wormser has said (FRANKENSTEIN, INCORPORATED—1931, p. 159): "If stockholders refuse or neglect to protect themselves * * * the State must take up the cudgels in their behalf." The opposite point of view was recently expressed by Mr. William C. Breed (an address, reprinted in Investment Banking Feb. 21, 1933), as follows: "The theory of State-constituted guardianship of investors should be abandoned, * * *. It is an exercise of the sovereign authority in a manner which tends to prevent the development of that caution, sagacity and character which an investing public must possess if it is to avoid unnecessary loss." Although not unmindful of the fact that "the truth may lie between the two extremes" (Andrews, *The Decisions of the Court of Appeals in Recent Years and How They Have Affected Substantive Law* (1927) 12 CORN. L. Q. 433, 435, 452), the present writer nevertheless deems it appropriate to call attention to the lack of consistency and of policy in the present state of the law on this subject.

[61] See Royal Trust Co. v. Equitable Life Assurance Society, *supra* note 12 at 441; Elliott v. Baker, 194 Mass. 518, 80 N. E. 450 (1907).

[62] It would also accelerate the development of a professional man-

The original justification for holding that a stockholder should not be permitted to barter his vote for a private consideration was the notion that every stockholder was entitled to the honest and unbiased judgment of every other stockholder.[62a] This view is at variance with the well settled principle that a stockholder is not disqualified from voting merely because he is personally interested and that he may vote so as to best serve his personal interests.[63] It has become so completely un-

agerial class. The more completely management is subjected to the obligations of fiduciaries the less danger there is in non-voting stock. It is in the temper of the times to impose such obligations upon those who handle "other peoples' money." See President Roosevelt's Message to Congress, March 29, 1933. There has, however, developed no greater tolerance for non-voting stock. The EMERGENCY BANK-ING LAW of March 9, 1933, seems to contemplate that the preferred stock to be issued by national banks shall have voting powers (§ 302a) and the form of by-law drafted by the Comptroller of the Currency thereunder so provides.

[62a] See Stott v. Stott, *supra* note 48.

[63] Du Pont v. Du Pont, 251 Fed. 937 (D. C. Del. 1918), *aff'd* (except as to costs) 256 Fed. 129 (C. C. A. 3rd. 1919), *cert. den.* 249 U. S. 599, 39 S. Ct. 492 (1919); Gamble v. Queens C. W. Co., 123 N. Y. 91, 25 N. E. 91 (1890); Socorro M. M. Co. v. Preston, 17 Misc. 220, 40 N. Y. S. 1044 (1896); Gen. Inv. Co. v. American H. & L. Co., 97 N. J. Eq. 807, 54 Atl. 1 (1903). A court will not inquire into a stockholder's motives for voting as he does. Ervin v. Oregon Ry. & Nav. Co., 20 Fed. 577, app. dis. 136 U. S. 645 (1890) s. c. 27 Fed. 625 (C. C. S. D. N. Y. 1886); Du Pont v. Du Pont, *supra;* Chicago Macaroni Mfg. Co. v. Baggiano, *supra* note 28. A stock-holder may not be deprived of his vote because he proposes to vote in a manner which the other stockholders deem detrimental to the corporation. Walsh v. State, *supra* note 19; Holcomb v. Forsyth, 216 Ala. 486, 113 So. 516 (1927); Albert E. Touchet, Inc. v. Touchet, 264 Mass. 499, 163 N. E. 184 (1928); Camden & Atlantic R. R. v. Elkins, 37 N. J. Eq. 273 (1883); Elevator Supplies Co. v. Wylde, 106 N. J. Eq. 163, 150 Atl. 347 (1930). There are however equitable limitations upon the rule stated in the text, see Chap. VI. Query, whether the election of directors may not be considered as the

realistic that the courts are abandoning it.[64] Much of the confusion in the cases is due to a failure to distinguish between agreements made by stockholders *qua* stockholders and those made by directors *qua* directors.[65] It is clear that elected directors should not be permitted to assume in consideration of a secret profit private obligations to certain stockholders which may be inconsistent with the trust duties which they owe to all the stockholders,[66] but it does not follow that stockholders are necessarily subject to the same limitations.[66a] In their case, their agreements as to voting should be "valid and binding if they do not contravene any express charter or statutory provision or contemplate any fraud, oppression or wrong against other stockholders or other illegal object." [67]

exercise of a corporate function vested in the stockholders by statute and hence as one in the exercise of which stockholders are "trustees" for each other, see *infra* p. 109.

[64] "The old theory which seemed to dominate the earlier writers, to the effect that every stockholder in a corporation is entitled to have the benefit of the judgment of every other stockholder in the selection of a board of directors, has necessarily been rendered obsolete because of our modern business being conducted by large corporations located in all parts of the country." Mackin v. Nicollet Hotel, Inc., 25 F. (2d) 783, 786 (C. C. A. 8th, 1928), *cert. den.*, 278 U. S. 618, 49 Sup. Ct. 22 (1928). The use of uninstructed proxies necessarily involves an abandonment of the notion. See *supra* note 1. See Gow v. Consolidated Coppermines Corp., *supra* note 27, for an indication of the powers vested by a general proxy in the attorney.

[65] *E.g.*, West v. Camden, 135 U. S. 507, 10 Sup. Ct. 838 (1890); Snow v. Church, 13 App. Div. 108, 42 N.Y. Supp. 1072 (2d Dept. 1897); Haldeman v. Haldeman, 176 Ky. 635, 197 S. W. 376 (1917); Creed v. Copps, 103 Vt. 164, 152 Atl. 369 (1930).

[66] Singers-Biggers v. Young, *supra* note 18.

[66a] See *infra* pp. 104–109.

[67] Manson v. Curtis, *supra* note 16.

We have thus far written *as if* the important corporations of today were in fact controlled by majority stockholders. This is not the fact.[68]

Such factors as widespread ownership,[69] inertia and distinterest in management,[70] and inaccessible places of meeting[71] have combined to render the "privilege of voting" largely "theoretical"[72] with the result that control is ordinarily exercised, even in corporations having only voting stock, by the owners of a minority thereof.[73]

---

[68] Only 22 of the 200 largest corporations in the United States are controlled by majority owners, Berle and Means, The Modern Corporation and Private Property (1932) 94.

[69] At the end of 1931, over 4,000,000 persons owned the common stock of the 65 leading corporations listed on the New York Stock Exchange. Some average individual holdings were: U. S. Steel, 49.9 shares; Amer. Tel. & Tel. Co., 29 shares; General Motors Corp., 14.7 shares. See N. Y. Times, Feb. 7, 1932, Part 2, at 9. The first indication of a check in the trend towards widespread stock ownership occurred during the third quarter of 1932 when U. S. Steel, General Motors, and other large corporations showed the smallest increase in number of common stockholders experienced since 1928 (N. Y. Times, Oct. 9, 1932, Part 4, at 1, Dec. 14, 1932, at 16) but even at that time it was estimated that 88 per cent of the owners of common stock in 48 representative American corporations owned less than 100 shares each (*ibid.*).

[70] The average stockholder in the large corporations is primarily interested in financial return; when apprehensive of the management he sells his stock. This seems to be true even of employee stockholders, see Employee Stock Purchase Plans in the United States (Natl. Ind. Conf. Board, 1928) 155. See also Kline, *infra*, p. 107, note 24.

[71] Stockholders' meetings are generally held in the state of incorporation but that state is not usually chosen because it is the place of residence of most stockholders. See, Flynn, Why Corporations Leave Home (1932) 150 Atlantic Monthly 268; "WHY CORPORATIONS LEAVE HOME" (The Corporation Trust Company, 1929).

[72] DEWING, THE FINANCIAL POLICY OF CORPORATIONS (1926) 628; see also Andrews, *Our "Voting" Stock* (1932) 8 VA. Q. REV. 400.

[73] 134 of the 200 largest corporations in the United States are

The technique of retaining control by virtue of the factors just mentioned without the aid of legal devices is simple and well-established. With the notice of annual meeting, a request for the execution and return of an enclosed proxy by stockholders "unable to attend" is transmitted. The proxy ordinarily runs in favor of one or more persons selected by the board of directors. The return is almost automatic.[74]

This practice of proxy solicitation by the board of directors is tolerated by the courts, at least until there is an active contest for control and so long as the expense to the corporation is small.[75]

The weakness of this method of self-perpetuation from the point-of-view of the management is that the *power* to control continues to reside with the majority and at times of stress this power, normally quiescent, may assert itself in full vigor.[76] Various legal devices have been developed to protect the management against ouster.

First came the voting trust.[77] The fundamental

controlled by the management and by minority stockholders, Berle and Means, *supra* note 68.

[74] It is reported that a small minority stockholder once obtained control of a large corporation by the expedient of mailing *stamped* return envelopes with the proxies he solicited whereas those in control sent out unstamped return envelopes. The Autobiography of Lincoln Steffens (1931) 533.

[75] Lawyers' Adv. Co. v. Consolidated Ry. L. & R. Co., 187 N. Y. 395, 80 N. E. 199 (1907); Bounds v. Stephenson, 187 S. W. 1031 (Texas 1916).

[76] The New York World-Telegram has published (October 31-November 5, 1932) a series of short articles on some noteworthy proxy battles.

[77] There is an extensive literature on the subject. See Lilienthal,

differences between a proxy and a voting-trust have been summarized thus,[78]

"The usual proxy merely establishes a relation of principal and agent terminable by the principal at will either through revocation or through sale of his stock. The voting trust agreement vests in the trustee an interest in the stock which the original owner obviously is unable to nullify by any sale of the stock and which he cannot otherwise cancel except through an attempted breach of contract. The holder of a proxy has no control over the stock itself, while the voting trustees have the possession of the stock as well as the legal title to it. The proxy creates a relation of a temporary character under a restrictive statutory authority; the voting trust is created without the need of statutory license[79] and confers not a

Corporate Voting and Public Policy (1887) 10 HARV. L. REV. 428; Baldwin, *Voting Trusts* (1892) 1 YALE L. J. 1; Moore, *Voting Trusts in Corporations* (1902) 36 AM. L. REV. 222; Rogers, *Pooling Agreements Among Stockholders* (1910) 19 YALE L. J. 345; Wormser, *Legality of Corporate Voting Trusts and Pooling Agreements* (1918) 18 COL. L. REV. 123; Smith, *Limitations on the Validity of Voting Trusts* (1922) 22 COL. L. REV. 627; Finkelstein, *Voting Trust Agreements* (1926) 24 MICH. L. REV. 344; CUSHING, VOTING TRUSTS (2d ed. 1927), having in mind Matter of Morse, 247 N. Y. 290, 160 N. E. 374 (1928); Bergerman, *Voting Trusts and Non-Voting Stock* (1928) 37 YALE L. J. 445; Bernays, The Validity of Voting Trusts of the Stock of National Banks (1928) 22 Illinois L. Rev. 587; Comment (1932) 5 So. Cal. L. Rev. 214.

[78] Cushing, *supra* note 77, at pp. 162–3. See Matter of Application of Chilson Re Public Industrials Corp., 168 Atl. 82 (Del. Ch. 1933).

[79] This statement is not universally true; the common law of voting-trusts is uncertain. As to the effect of the enactment of voting-

revocable authority upon an agent but a qualified title upon a transferee of property."

The law of voting-trusts has been many years in the making. Early decisions date from a period when the nature of business corporations (at least as now known) was little understood and even less sympathized with.[80] Voting-trusts also labored under the odium which at one time attached to the use of "trusts" as means of achieving business monopolies. The result has been a vast accumulation of learning and precedent, with its inevitable burdens as well as benefits.

The general problems involved in determining the validity of voting-trusts have been indicated in the foregoing discussion of the validity of the less formal agreements among majority stockholders.[81] The important fact today is that the voting-trust is not deemed a sufficient means of perpetuating control.[82] Among the causes contribut-

trust statutes upon the common law, see Matter of Morse, *supra* note 77; Mackin v. Nicollet Hotel, *supra* note 64. The OHIO GENERAL CORP. ACT (1927) permitting voting trusts, expressly provided that the rights conferred were "in addition to rights at common law" § 34.

[80] Prof. Wormser, (Frankenstein, Inc., at p. 48) fixes 1875 as the year when "the modern American law of corporations was well under way". Even at that early date the voting trust was already in use (see Cushing, *op. cit. supra* note 77, at 4 *et seq.*) and a decision with respect to a very similar instrument was rendered as early as 1867, Brown v. Pacific Mail S. S. Co., Fed. Cas. No. 2,025, 4 Fed. Cas. 420 (C. C. S. D. N. Y. 1867).

[81] *Supra* pp. 37–45.

[82] Its primary function today seems to be to insure continuity of management for a relatively short period of time and is therefore most frequently used after reorganization. In close corporations its aim is to protect the minority.

ing to this feeling may be enumerated: (A) doubt as to its validity in certain states; (B) its limited duration; (C) the need for designated trustees with fixed obligations; and (D) the necessity for initial ownership of majority stock.

A. The trend of judicial decisions has been definitely in favor of the validity of voting-trusts,[83] and this trend has been accelerated by the adoption of permissive statutes in a number of important states.[84]

B. Most statutes authorizing voting-trusts limit their duration, usually to five or ten years, and even in the absence of statute there seems to be a common-law requirement that a voting-trust to be legal must be for a definite, and not unreasonable, length of time.[85]

C. "It may be accepted as true that a voting trust is a trust in the accepted equitable sense and is subject to the principles which regulate the administration of trusts." [86] Accordingly, the trustees

[83] See, Carnegie Trust Co. v. Security Life Ins. Co., 111 Va. 1, 68 S. E. 412 (1910); Mackin v. Nicollet Hotel, *supra* note 64. The trend can be readily noted by reading the material cited under note 77 chronologically.

[84] New York was the first in 1901; the latest is California in 1931. At least 10 states have such statutes, including, in addition to those named, Delaware, New Jersey, and Ohio. The Uniform Business Corporation Act permits voting trusts (Sec. 29). New York limited its statute (Stock Corporation Law, § 50) in 1925 by making it inapplicable to banks (Laws of 1925, Chap. 120).

[85] See, Thibodeau v. Lake, 40 Idaho 456, 234 Pac. 456 (1925); Canda v. Canda, 113 Atl. 503, 513-514, *affd*. 92 N. J. Eq. 423, 112 Atl. 727 (1921).

[86] Chandler v. Bellanca Aircraft Corp., 162 Atl. 63, 67 (Del. Ch. 1932). It was there held that under the Delaware statute permitting the voting by proxy of stock held by voting trustees they may only

named in the voting-trust agreement are clearly under fiduciary obligations to the certificate holders,[86a] but, it is not as yet definitely established that those who control corporations by virtue of other devices are under trust obligations to the other security holders.[87]

D. A voting-trust agreement is entered into by stockholders and in order to be effective beyond doubt there must be deposited thereunder a majority of the voting stock. This means that those desirous of perpetuating their control with the aid of a voting-trust must first acquire either from the corporation or from others a majority of the voting stock.[88]

Non-voting stock avoids these difficulties. Most corporation statutes are so phrased as to allow charter provisions for non-voting stock.[89] The is-

delegate the ministerial act of voting to a proxy but not the discretion as to how to vote, but that such delegation of discretion may be validly permitted by the voting trust agreement.

[86a] Voting trustees are not necessarily liable for the misfeasance or non-feasance of the directors or officers. See Lawrence v. Curtis, 191 Mass. 240, 77 N. E. 314 (1906); Loughery v. Bright, 267 Mass. 584, 166 N. E. 744 (1929); infra pp. 107–109.

[87] Infra p. 104. It must also be noted that under the other devices it is not as easy as under the voting trust to determine who in fact controls.

[88] This requirement is not serious where no-par stock can be acquired as an original issue by the promoters of a newly-organized corporation.

[89] Randle v. Winona Coal Co., 206 Ala. 254, 89 So. 790 (1921); General Investment Co. v. Bethlehem Steel Corp., 87 N. J. Eq. 234, 100 Atl. 347 (1917); People v. Koenig, 133 App. Div. 756, 118 N. Y. Supp. 136 (1909); Miller v. Ratterman, 47 Ohio St. 141, 24 N. E. 496 (1890); cases cited 21 A. L. R. 643 (1922). It is an open question whether non-voting stock may be issued under a constitutional provision that "every shareholder shall have the right to vote." See

suance of preferred stock without voting rights is an old practice.[90] Taking advantage of the readiness of "investors" to purchase stocks without thought of participating in the management, promoters extended the old practice and began issuing "Class A" stocks which had no voting rights and very slight preferences and little junior capital. From this it was but a short step to provide for a small class of "management" stock in which all voting rights are centered and to issue the remaining common stock without any preference or junior capital and without any vote. It was this development that provoked a storm of criticism.[91] However, the law, speaking broadly, has given no heed to these objections,[92] beyond imposing to some ex-

Brooks v. State, 29 Del. 1, 79 Atl. 790 (1911); People v. Emmerson, 302 Ill. 300, 134 N. E. 707 (1922); State v. Swanger, 190 Mo. 561, 89 S. W. 872 (1905). The Delaware constitutional provision considered in the Brooks case was repealed in 1903.

[90] See Miller v. Ratterman, *supra* note 89. It is usual to provide that after default in the payment of preferred dividends for a certain period the preferred stock acquires voting rights. The order may be reversed so as to give the common stock the vote only after the preferred dividends have been paid. See Mackintosh v. Flint & P. M. R. Co., 32 Fed. 350, 34 Fed. 582 (C. C. E. D. Mich. 1887-8).

[91] See, Nickel-Plate Unification, 105 I. C. C. 425, 444 (1926); Stevens, Stockholders' Voting Rights and the Centralization of Voting Control (1926) 40 Quar. Jour. of Economics 353, 382, *et seq.;* Ripley, Main Street and Wall Street (1927) Chap. IV. It would seem that the criticisms are not directed towards the use of preferred stock. For instance, the rules of the New York Stock Exchange provide that "no non-voting stocks [of investment trusts] will be listed *unless substantially preferred as to both dividends and assets.*" In Hamlin v. Toledo, St. L. & K. C. R. Co., 78 Fed. 664, 671 (C. C. A. 6th. 1897), the Court speaking of non-voting preferred stock said that it was "perhaps valid" but "of doubtful public policy."

[92] The law at present not only recognizes the validity of separa-

tent fiduciary obligations on the holders of voting stock in favor of the holders of non-voting securities.[93] Whether it should raises basic social and economic questions as to the extent to which separation of ownership from control ought to be permitted as a matter of policy.[94]

By whatever the means,[95] the result has been the division of the body of stockholders into two groups, one vested with the management and control of the corporation and the other entirely dis-

tion of ownership from control resulting from the use of non-voting stock and voting trusts, but in many other ways, see Benkard v. Leonard, 231 App. Div. 625, 248 N. Y. Supp. 497 (1st Dept. 1931), holding that the personal representative of a deceased settlor, who had reserved the voting rights of trusteed stock, succeeded thereto in preference to the trustee in whom legal title was vested; Davis v. Rossi, 326 Mo. 911, 940, 34 S. W. (2d) 8 (1930) holding valid a trust of stock although the settlor reserved the voting power; Buffalo Electro-Plating Co. v. Day, 151 App. Div. 237, 135 N. Y. Supp. 1054 (4th Dept. 1912), holding that a director does not forfeit his office by selling all his stock. A director need not be a stockholder (e.g., N. Y. STOCK CORP. LAW (1930) § 55). See Matter of Ringler & Co., 204 N. Y. 30, 97 N. E. 593 (1912) as to nominal stockholders serving as directors). A holder of non-voting stock may be a director (Matter of Haecker, 212 App. Div. 167, 207 N. Y. Supp. 561 (2d Dept. 1925). See also, In Re Newcomb, 18 N. Y. Supp. 16 (1891).

[93] Kidd v. Traction Co., 74 N. H. 160, 66 Atl. 127 (1907); Bates Street Shirt Co. v. Waite, 130 Me. 352, 156 Atl. 293 (1931); Uniform Business Corporations Act, Sec. 28II; Berle, Non-Voting Stock and "Bankers' Control" (1926) 39 Harvard L. Rev. 673.

[94] See, Bergerman, supra note 77; Berle and Means, supra note 68.

[95] In addition to the devices here touched upon, the holding company (pyramiding) affords a method for controlling large enterprises with small investments, but legally the set-up, at least so far as the base corporation is concerned, must involve one or more of the other factors here treated. See, Bonbright and Means, The Holding Company (1932); Powell, Parent and Subsidiary Corporations (1931); Berle, Studies in the Law of Corporate Finance (1928) Chap. VIII.

associated from such management and control and having, in substance, only a financial interest in the corporation. This development, at variance with the traditional view of corporation law, has forced upon the courts the necessity of formulating principles to regulate this relationship, called for convenience that of the majority and the minority.

CHAPTER IV.

THE STOCKHOLDER'S RIGHT TO INFORMATION

While knowledge may not be power in corporate affairs, it is beyond dispute that without adequate knowledge of the corporation's affairs a stockholder or creditor is in no position successfully to assert any legal rights or even wisely to exercise any non-legal right—such as the sale of his shares or bonds.

As a member of the general public, a corporate security-holder has access to such information as the corporation makes public voluntarily or pursuant to the requirements of the blue-sky laws to which it may be subject,[1] or pursuant to any listing agreements with stock exchanges to which it may be a party.

But what are a stockholder's legal rights[2] to

---

[1] Certain states have statutes requiring the filing of reports as to the consideration received by the corporation for issued stock. *Cf.* Delaware General Corporation Law, Sec. 23.

[2] Only a stockholder of record—*Matter of Reiss*, 30 Misc. 234, 62 N. Y. S. 145 (1900); *Mateer* v. *N. J. Tel. Co.*, 136 Atl. 317 (N. J. 1927)—or the legal representative of one—*Feick* v. *Hill Bread Co.*, 91 N. J. L. 486, 103 Atl. 813, *affd.*, 92 N. J. L. 513, 105 Atl. 725 (1918); *cf. Chas. Hegewood Co.* v. *State*, 149 N. E. 170 (Ind. 1925) —can enforce such rights. A registered holder who has parted with title may not, *S. F. Bowser & Co.* v. *State*, 192 Ind. 462, 137 N. E. 57 (1922); *In Re Gaines*, 180 N. Y. S. 191, *affd.*, 190 App. Div. 941, 179 N. Y. S. 922 (1920). Nor will an inspection be granted on the

55

compel disclosure of corporate affairs by virtue of his stock-ownership ? [3]
Unlike a director—even a "dummy" director [4] —who has an absolute right to examine the books and records [5] of his corporation,[6] the stockholder, exclusive of statute, has but a qualified right which will be judicially enforced only for a "proper" purpose.[7]

application of one who holds stock for the benefit of a corporation which is without power to own it, *Richmond* v. *Hill,* 148 Ill. App. 179 (1909). Query whether a pledgee of untransferred stock may compel disclosure, see, *In re Citizens Savings & Trust Co.,* 156 Wis. 277, 145 N. W. 646 (1914).

[3] For an unusual case where a stockholder attempted to *prevent* disclosure to another stockholder, see, *Mercantile Trading Co.* v. *Rosenbaum Grain Corp.,* 154 Atl. 457 (Del. 1931).

[4] *People ex rel. Stauffer* v. *Bonwit Bros.,* 69 Misc. 70, 125 N. Y. S. 958 (1910).

[5] The principles here discussed with respect to "books and records" seem to be equally applicable to the right to inspect the corporation's tangible property. See, *Hobbs* v. *Tom Reed Gold Mining Co.,* 164 Cal. 497, 129 Pac. 781 (1913).

[6] *Lawton* v. *Bedell,* 71 Atl. 490 (N. J. 1908) ; *People ex rel. Leach* v. *Central Fish Co.,* 117 App. Div. 77, 101 N. Y. S. 1108 (1907) ; *Matter of Wilkins* v. *Ascher Silk Corp.,* 207 App. Div. 168, 201 N. Y. S. 739, *aff'd.,* 237 N. Y. 574, 143 N. E. 748 (1924). *cf., People ex rel. Bellman* v. *Standard Match Co.,* 202 N. Y. S. 840 (1924) dissolved corporation.

[7] *Guthrie* v. *Harkness,* 199 U. S. 148, 26 S. Ct. 4, 50 L. Ed. 130 (1905) ; *Matter of Steinway,* 159 N. Y. 250, 53 N. E. 1103 (1899) ; *State ex rel. Miller* v. *Loft,* 156 Atl. 170 (Del. 1931). The stockholder may have the benefit of a presumption of propriety and good faith. *Hauser* v. *York Water Co.,* 278 Pa. 387, 123 Atl. 330 (1924) ; *Development Co.* v. *Kennedy,* 121 Ohio 582, 170 N. E. 434 (1930) ; *Bernert* v. *Multnomah L. & B. Co.,* 119 Ore. 44, 247 Pac. 155, 248 Pac. 156 (1926). The burden of pleading and proving bad faith or an improper motive is upon those who resist the inspection. *Dreyfuss & Sons* v. *Benson,* 239 S. W. 347 (Texas 1922) ; *Burns* v. *Drennen,* 220 Ala. 404, 125 So. 667 (1930) ; *Outjes* v. *Harrer,* 208 Iowa 1217, 277 N. W. 101 (1929) ; *Orlando* v. *Reliance Homestead Ass'n.,* 171 La. 1027, 132 So. 777 (1931). There are cases which

Except as modified by statute,[8] the number of shares owned by the petitioner is immaterial.[9] Nor will the inspection be denied merely because the corporation is successful [10] or because there is no pending specific controversy or dispute [11] or because the epithet "fishing expedition" can be applied to the inspection.[12] The fact that the corporation sends out annual statements,[13] or is under the supervision of a government department whose reports are public,[14] or offers to furnish a statement [15] or to permit an audit by an accountant

hold that the petitioner must disclose his purpose. See, *Bruning* v. *Hoboken P. & P. Co.*, 67 N. J. L. 119, 50 Atl. 906 (1902). Of course, petitioner may not obtain a peremptory writ of mandamus in the first instance where issues of fact are raised. 38 C. J. 929, § 708.

[8] *E.g.*, New York Stock Corp. Law, Sec. 10.

[9] *Richmond* v. *Hill, supra* note 2; *Matter of Steinway, supra* note 7; *Matter of Hitchcock*, 157 App. Div. 328, 142 N. Y. S. 247 (1913); *Matter of O'Neil*, 47 Misc. 495, 95 N. Y. S. 964 (1905). *Cf., Lyon* v. *American Screw Co.*, 16 R. I. 472, 17 Atl. 61 (1889). As on many other discretionary applications (*infra* pp. 151-2, note 147), the courts are influenced by the smallness of petitioner's holdings in determining his "good faith". See, *In Re De Vengoechea*, 86 N.J.L. 35, 91 Atl. 341 (1914); *Dines* v. *Harris*, 88 Colo. 22, 35-36, 291 Pac. 1024 (1930).

[10] *Matter of Rogers* v. *American Tobacco Co.*, 143 Misc. 306, 257 N. Y. S. 321, *aff'd.* 233 App. Div. 708, 249 N. Y. S. 993 (1931).

[11] *Varney* v. *Baker*, 194 Mass. 239, 80 N. E. 524 (1907). *Cf., Lyon* v. *American Screw Co., supra* note 9.

[12] *Dines* v. *Harris, supra,* note 9, at p. 34.

[13] *Feick* v. *Hill Bread Co., supra,* note 2.

[14] *Burns* v. *Drennen, supra* note 7. The fact that there is no public source of information may be a make-weight argument in granting an inspection in the case of a close corporation. See, *Matter of Wygant*, 101 Misc. 509, 513-4, 167 N. Y. S. 369 (1917). But see, *People ex rel. Clason* v. *Nassau Ferry Co.*, 86 Hun 128, 33 N. Y. S. 244 (1895) to the effect that a stockholder should first exhaust other methods of obtaining information before asking for mandamus; *cf. infra,* note 17.

[15] *Matter of Wygant, supra,* note 14.

mutually satisfactory,[16] is not sufficient reason for denying a stockholder's petition for an inspection.[17] Nor is it a sufficient answer to the petition that the petitioner is hostile to the managing officers,[18] or that he is a stockholder in a competing corporation,[19] or that the corporation has offered to buy his stock.[20]

The most frequently avowed purpose of a desired inspection successfully to pass judicial scrutiny is the ascertainment of the real value of the petitioner's stock.[21] The desire to ascertain the names and addresses of fellow-stockholders so as to

[16] *Kulbach* v. *Irving Cut Glass Co.*, 220 Pa. 427, 69 Atl. 981 .(1908).

[17] *Cf., State ex rel. Miller* v. *Loft, Inc., supra* note, 7. It must, of course, appear that there has been a prior demand and refusal before a court will intervene, *Matter of Latimer* v. *Herzog Teleseme Co.*, 75 App. Div. 522, 77 N. Y. S. 714 (1902). The failure to attend a stockholder's meeting where the books were open for inspection does not bar relief, *State ex rel. Bank* v. *J. & M. Paper Co.*, 27 Del. 248, 88 Atl. 449 (1913). See also supra, note 14 and text.

[18] *Matter of O'Neil, supra,* note 9. *Cf., Matter of Rehe,* 136 Misc. 136, 239 N. Y. S. 41 (1930).

[19] *Kublach* v. *Irving Cut Glass Co., supra,* note 16; *State ex rel. English* v. *Lazarus,* 127 Mo. App. 401, 105 S. W. 780 (1907); *People ex rel. Ludwig* v. *Ludwig & Co.,* 126 App. Div. 696, 111 N. Y. S. 94 (1908). *Contra, Matter of Kennedy,* 75 App. Div. 188, 77 N. Y. S. 714 (1902); *People ex rel. Britton* v. *American Press Association,* 148 App. Div. 651, 133 N. Y. S. 216 (1912); see, also, *Matter of Rehe, supra,* note 18. Even where the inspection is granted it may be limited so as to preclude disclosure of trade secrets, *State ex rel. English* v. *Lazarus, supra.*

[20] *Kublach* v. *Irving Cut Glass Co., supra,* note 16; *State ex rel. Wilson* v. *St. Louis & S. F. R. Co.,* 29 Mo. App. 301 (1888).

[21] *State ex rel. Brumley* v. *J. & M. Paper Co.,* 24 Del. 379, 77 Atl. 16 (1910); *State ex rel. Rogers* v. *Sherman Oil Co.,* 117 Atl. 122 (Del. 1922); *State ex rel. English* v. *Lazarus, supra,* note 19; *Garcin* v. *Trenton Rubber Mfg. Co.,* 60 Atl. 1098 (N. J. 1905); *Matter of Wygant, supra,* note 14.

communicate with them for the purpose of calling their attention to grievances or to solicit proxies has also been frequently sustained as a "proper" purpose.[22] Occasionally, petitioners are more explicit as to their real purposes. Inspection has been granted to enable the petitioner to ascertain whether the corporation had been purchasing property at more than fair value,[23] or to ascertain why no dividend had been paid on the stock and whether the corporation had received full consideration for its issued stock.[24] As is to be expected when the test is nothing more definite than "propriety", there are decisions quite to the contrary. One court held that it was not "laudable" for a stockholder to seek information as to whether the corporation was meeting its fixed charges out of capital for the purpose of laying the matter before the Attorney General, and therefore denied an inspection for such purpose.[25] The court justified its holding by arguing *inter alia* that the proposed inspection could not "enhance or protect" the value of petitioner's securities. While it seems in order for a court to conjecture as to the probable effect

---

[22] *Drovin* v. *Lehigh Coal & Nav. Co.,* 265 Pa. 447, 109 Atl. 128 (1919); *Hauser* v. *York Water Co., supra,* note 7; *Grayburg Oil Co.* v. *Jarratt,* 16 S. W. (2d) 319 (Texas 1929). *Cf., Matter of Rehe, supra,* note 18.

[23] *Matter of Hitchcock, supra,* note 9.

[24] *Matter of Colby* v. *Imbrie & Co., Ltd.,* 126 Misc. 457, 214 N. Y. S. 53, *aff'd.,* 216 App. Div. 713, 214 N. Y. S. 819 (1926).

[25] And to ascertain whether the corporation was selling its product below cost, *Matter of Pierson,* 44 App. Div. 215, 60 N. Y. S. 671 (1899). See, also, *People ex rel. McElwee* v. *Produce Exchange Trust Co.,* 53 App. Div. 93, 65 N. Y. S. 926 (1900).

of an inspection on the whole body of stockholders,[25a] it appears to be rather assuming the role of parent with a vengeance to deny an application for the petitioner's own good.

Ordinarily the courts will direct inspection where the petitioner suspects mismanagement and the inspection is desired as a preliminary to a stockholder's suit in equity;[26] but not when the court is satisfied that the proposed suit is calculated solely to harass the defendants into purchasing petitioner's stock.[27]

The courts are divided as to whether a stockholder is entitled to an inspection for the purpose of enabling him to obtain evidence against third persons.[28]

It seems that in the absence of a compelling

[25a] See Tachna v. Pressed Steel Car Co., 112 N. J. Eq. 411, 164 Atl. 413 (1933).

[26] *Commonwealth ex rel. Sellers* v. *Phoenix Iron Co.*, 105 Pa. 111 (1884); *Kulbach* v. *Irving Cut Glass Co.*, *supra*, note 16; *State ex rel. Humphrey* v. *Monida & Y. Stage Co.*, 110 Minn. 193, 124 N. W. 971 (1910). The fact that petitioner makes public his findings or the existence of litigation is not sufficient reason to deny him inspection, *People ex rel. Ludwig* v. *Ludwig & Co.*, *supra* note 19. Whether mandamus for an inspection in aid of a lawsuit should be granted may involve consideration of the adequacy of other available methods for obtaining evidence. See, *State ex rel. Watkins* v. *Donnell Mfg. Co.*, 129 Mo. App. 206 (1908); *Matter of Rogers* v. *American Tobacco Co.*, *supra*, note 10.

[27] *State ex rel. Linihan* v. *United Brokerage Co.*, 6 Boyce 570, 29 Del. 570 (1917).

[28] See, *Woodworth* v. *Old Second National Bank*, 154 Mich. 459, 117 N. W. 893, 118 N. W. 581 (1908) granted; *White* v. *Manter*, 109 Me. 408, 84 Atl. 890 (1912) granted; *Matter of Taylor*, 117 App. Div. 348, 117 N. Y. S. 1039 (1907) denied; *In Re Gaines*, *supra*, note 2, denied.

statutory mandate to the contrary,[29] the courts are inclined to deny relief to one who acquires a minimum number of shares to be held for a very brief period for the sole purpose of obtaining the stock list for use in his securities or similar business.[30] The inspection must, of course, be conducted in a reasonable manner [31] and at a reasonable time,[32] but this does not mean that the right of inspection may be exercised only once.[33] It may be exercised through an agent,[34] but the court may disqualify

[29] *Shea* v. *Parker*, 234 Mass. 592, 126 N. E. 47 (1920); *Lawshe* v. *Royal Baking Powder Co.*, 54 Misc. 220, 104 N. Y. S. 361 (1907). *Cf.*, New York Stock Corporation Law, Secs. 10, 113.

[30] *Day & Co., Inc.* v. *Booth*, 123 Me. 443, 123 Atl. 557 (1924); *Shea* v. *Sweetser*, 119 Me. 400, 111 Atl. 579 (1920); *People ex rel. Althouse* v. *Giroux Cons. M. Co.*, 122 App. Div. 617, 107 N. Y. S. 188 (1907); *American Mortgage Co.* v. *Rosenbaum*, 114 Ohio 231, 151 N. E. 122 (1926); *State ex rel. Theile* v. *Cities Service Co.*, 115 Atl. 773 (Del. 1922). *Cf.*, *Lawshe* v. *Royal Baking Powder Co.*, *supra*, note 29. See, also, New York Stock Corporation Law, *supra*, note 29, evidencing a similar attitude on the part of the legislature.

[31] *Conerty* v. *Butler County Oil Ref. Co.*, 301 Pa. 417, 152 Atl. 672 (1930); *State ex rel. Wilson* v. *St. Louis & S. F. R. Co. supra*, note 20; *Furst* v. *Rawleigh Med. Co.*, 282 Ill. 366, 118 N. E. 763 (1918).

[32] *Conerty* v. *Butler County Oil Ref. Co.*, *supra*, note 31; *Furst* v. *Rawleigh Med. Co.*, *supra*, note 31; *Breslauer* v. *S. Franklin & Co.*, 205 Ill. App. 372 (1917).

[33] *Cincinnati Volksblatt Co.* v. *Hoffmeister*, 62 Ohio 189, 199, 56 N. E. 1033 (1900).

[34] *People ex rel. Poleti* v. *Poleti, Coda & Rebecchi, Inc.*, 193 App. Div. 738, 184 N. Y. S. 368 (1920) accountant; *Cincinnati Volksblatt Co.* v. *Hoffmeister*, *supra*, note 33; *Varney* v. *Baker*, *supra*, note 11; *State ex rel. Johnson* v. *St. Louis Transit Co.*, 124 Mo. App. 111, 100 S. W. 1126 (1907) stenographer; *Feick* v. *Hill Bread Co.*, *supra*, note 2, accountant; *People ex rel. Clason* v. *Nassau Ferry Co.*, *supra*, note 14, attorney; *Conerty* v. *Butler County Oil Ref. Co.*, *supra*, note 31. *Cf.*, *Garcin* v. *Trenton Rubber Mfg. Co.*, *supra*, note 21; *S. F. Bowser & Co.* v. *State*, *supra*, note 2.

improper persons.[35]

The matter of stockholders' inspection of corporate books and records is now very widely covered by statute. They are very seldom construed as restrictive of the common-law [36] and are most frequently held to be either declaratory thereof [37] or as granting to the stockholder an absolute right to inspect *the books designated in the statute* regardless of his purpose or motive.[38] But even under "absolute" statutes some courts have insisted upon their discretionary right to deny mandamus.[39]

A stockholder's right of inspection may not, by by-law, be made dependent upon the grace of the directors,[40] although the by-laws may prescribe

---

[35] *People ex rel. Poleti* v. *Poleti, Coda & Rebecchi, Inc., supra,* note 34, employee of competitor; *State ex rel. Humphrey* v. *Monida & Y. Stage Co., supra,* note 26, hostile former director.

[36] *Matter of Steinway, supra,* note 7; *People ex rel. Stobo* v. *Eadie,* 63 Hun 320, 18 N. Y. S. 53, *aff'd.,* 133 N. Y. 573, 30 N. E. 1147 (1892).

[37] *O'Hara* v. *National Biscuit Co.,* 69 N. J. L. 198, 54 Atl. 241 (1903).

[38] *Pfirman* v. *Success Mining Co., Ltd.,* 30 Idaho 468, 166 Pac. 216 (1917); *Johnson* v. *Langdon,* 135 Cal. 624, 67 Pac. 1050 (1902); *Cobb* v. *Lazarde & Sons,* 129 Ala. 488, 30 So. 326 (1900); *Furst* v. *Rawleigh Med. Co., supra,* note 31; *Cincinnati Volksblatt Co.* v. *Hoffmeister, supra,* note 33; *White* v. *Manter, supra,* note 28; *Palmer* v. *Diel,* 233 Ill. App. 508 (1924); *Cooper* v. *Nutt,* 254 Ill. App. 445 (1929).

[39] *People ex rel. Britton* v. *American Press Association, supra,* note 19; *State ex rel. Theile* v. *Cities Service Co., supra,* note 30; *Shea* v. *Sweetser, supra,* note 30; *Dines* v. *Harris, supra,* note 9; *Bernert* v. *Multnomah Lumber & Box Co., supra,* note 7; *Slay* v. *Polonia Publishing Co.,* 249 Mich. 609, 229 N. W. 434 (1930); *People ex rel. Hunter* v. *Natl. Park Bank,* 122 App. Div. 635, 94 N. Y. S. 173 (1907). See, also, *People ex rel. Hatch* v. *Lake Shore & M. S. R. R. Co.,* 11 Hun 1, app. dis., 70 N. Y. 220 (1877).

[40] *State ex rel. Brumley* v. *J. & M. Paper Co., supra* note 21;

reasonable regulations as to inspection of books by stockholders.[41] It has even been held that the right may not be unreasonably restricted by a provision in the certificate of incorporation.[42] The usual procedure for compelling access to corporate books and records is by mandamus.[43] The common-law redress for a wrongful refusal to permit an inspection of corporate books is an action for damages.[44] Certain statutes authorize

Klotz v. *Pan-American Match Co.,* 221 Mass. 38, 108 N. E. 764 (1915). See, also, *Hodgens* v. *United Copper Co.,* 67 Atl. 756 (N. J. 1907). Such a by-law is not even binding on a stockholder who voted for it, *Commonwealth ex rel. Wilde* v. *Penn. Silk Co.,* 267 Pa. 331, 110 Atl. 157 (1920). The usual by-law "closing" books for a period before annual meetings closes them only for transfer purposes and not so as to preclude inspection during the period, *State ex rel. Wilson* v. *St. Louis & S. F. R. Co., supra,* note 20.

[41] *Klotz* v. *Pan-American Match Co., supra,* note 40.

[42] *State ex rel. Cochran* v. *Penn-Beaver Oil Co.,* 143 Atl. 257 (Del. 1926). See, also, *Hodgens* v. *United Copper Co., supra,* note 40. *Hauser* v. *York Water Co., supra,* note 7, seems to recognize the validity of charter limitations. See, also, *Ranger* v. *Champion Cotton-Press Co.,* 51 Fed. 61 (C. C. So. Car. 1892).

[43] *Maeder* v. *Buffalo Bill's Wild West Co.,* 132 Fed. 280 (C. C. N. J. 1904); *Fuller* v. *Hollander & Co.,* 61 N. J. Eq. 648, 47 Atl. 646 (1900); *Stettauer* v. *New York & S. C. C.,* 42 N. J. Eq. 46, 6 Atl. 303 (1886); *Matter of Steinway, supra,* note 7; *Commonwealth ex rel. Sellers* v. *Phoenix Iron Co., supra* note 26. *Cf., Ranger* v. *Champion Cotton-Press Co., supra,* note 42; *Weir* v. *Bay State Gas Co.,* 91 Fed. 940 (C. C. Del. 1898); *Huylar* v. *Cragin Cattle Co.,* 40 N. J. Eq. 392, 2 Atl. 274 (1885); *State ex rel. Rosenfeld* v. *Einstein,* 46 N. J. L. 479 (1884); *Cincinnati Volksblatt Co.* v. *Hoffmeister, supra,* note 33.

[44] *Boardman* v. *Marshalltown Grocery Co.,* 105 Iowa 445, 75 N. W. 343 (1898); *Bourdette* v. *Sieward,* 107 La. 258, 31 So. 630 (1902). The existence of such an action is no reason for denying mandamus, *Johnson* v. *Langdon, supra,* note 38. Costs and attorneys' fees can only be allowed pursuant to statute, *State ex rel. Charvat* v. *Sage,* 119 Neb. 374, 229 N. W. 118 (1930); *Clason* v. *Nassau Ferry Co.,* 20 Misc. 315, 45 N. Y. S. 675, *affd.,* 27 App. Div. 621, 50 N. Y. S. 160 (1898).

the recovery of penalties.[45] A stockholder is not entitled to the appointment of a receiver merely because the directors denied him the right of inspection.[46]

Although the question is not universally free from doubt, the general rule is that mandamus will issue for the inspection of books and records of foreign corporations whenever the writ can be effectively and conveniently enforced.[47]

[45] *E.g.*, New York Stock Corporation Law, Secs. 10, 113. The wrongful denial of inspection may be made a penal offense, see, New York Penal Law, Sec. 665(4).

[46] *Ridpath* v. *Sans Poil & C. R. F. & T. Co.*, 26 Wash. 427, 67 Pac. 229 (1901). It would seem that an inspection may be had even when the corporation is in the hands of a receiver, *State ex rel. Burleigh* v. *Miller*, 266 S. W. 985 (Mo. 1924), *cf., Davis* v. *Cambria Title, S. & T. Co.*, 304 Pa. 32, 155 Atl. 108 (1931), corporation in hands of state banking department.

[47] See, *Matter of Rogers* v. *American Tobacco Co., supra,* note 10; *Conerty* v. *Butler County Oil Ref. Co., supra,* note 31. See, also, New York Stock Corporation Law, Sec. 113, and *infra*, p. 160. The earlier cases are collected in 18 A. L. R. 1399–1402.

CHAPTER V.

PROTECTIVE COMMITTEES*

One of the significant results of wide-spread ownership of corporate securities [1] is utter powerlessness on the part of a lone security-holder to participate effectively in corporate matters. Ordinarily he recognizes and accepts this state of affairs. He makes no pretense of exercising any power of ownership theoretically his. In a recent popular book [2] the author, a professor of law, remarks:

"Stockholders, especially small ones, are surprisingly indifferent to all corporate ills and abuses, especially while dividends are being paid. The lack of participation by stockholders in the actual management and control of their corporations is itself perhaps the worst corporate evil. The enormous number of shareholders may be in part responsible for this. . . . When corporations have stockholders numbering in the many thousands, it becomes impossible to hold corporate meetings which amount to anything. . . . The growing tendency to corporate control by a small

* The substance of this chapter was published in the University of Pennsylvania Law Review for March, 1932 (Vol. 80, p. 670).
[1] *Supra* p. 46, note 69.
[2] WORMSER, FRANKENSTEIN, INCORPORATED (1931), 156 *et seq.*

group, which in turn often is controlled by one man, has given rise to a reign of corporate oligarchy. The many have been drowned out by the few. The shareholders have become an empty cipher."

However, there are times when these stockholders, and holders of other classes of corporate securities, are eager to influence the course of corporate affairs. The possible issues are multifarious and not confined to the financial reorganization of insolvent companies.[3]

Illustrative of such issues are questions of policy with respect to the merger or sale of the company or with respect to dividends.

A recent *cause celebre* was the ill-fated Youngstown-Bethlehem merger. Immediately upon announcement by the directors of Youngstown of the proposed merger, its stockholders split into hostile camps. Proxy committees, *pro* and *con*, were organized[4] and these carried on intensive campaigns for proxies wherein every conceivable method was employed.[5] The struggle was carried to the courts where the battle was equally intense;[6] the decision was unfavorable to the proponents of the merger and the result was its abandonment.[7]

[3] See Chapters VI and VII hereof.

[4] New York Times, March 14, 1930, at 28.

[5] New York Times, March 19, 1930, at 38; March 20, 1930, at 44; March 21, 1930, at 38; March 23, 1930, pt. ii, at 16, pt. iii, at 2.

[6] New York Times, Jan. 8, 1931, at 36; Jan. 25, 1931, at 26.

[7] New York Times, Oct. 16, 1931, at 34. It was later held that the minority stockholder had no cause of action, Wick v. Youngstown Sheet & Tube Co., 12 Ohio L. Abs. 355 (1932).

A somewhat unique problem faced the security-holders of the privately owned transit lines in New York City as a result of attempts made for their "unification".[9] One of the companies, The Interborough Rapid Transit Company, was controlled by voting-trustees acting under a voting-trust agreement of 1922, and certain holders of voting-trust certificates, having different views than the trustees concerning the proper method of dealing with the situation, organized a Protective Committee [10] under a deposit agreement [11] which provided for the deposit with the committee of both voting-trust certificates and shares of capital stock which had not been deposited under the voting-trust. The object of the organization of this Protective Committee was to give these security-holders direct representation in negotiations with the City.

An interesting controversy over dividend and capital policies faced the Northern Pipe Line a few years ago. A group of stockholders felt that the company had cash in excess of its business requirements and that this excess should be distributed to stockholders. Unable to persuade the management of the soundness of their opinion, they organized a proxy-committee which carried the issue directly to the stockholders.[12] The proxies obtained enabled this committee to elect two out of

[9] A similar situation existed in Chicago. There too Protective Committees were organized (1930).

[10] New York Times, March 15, 1930, at 4.

[11] Dated, March 15, 1930.

[12] New York Times, Dec. 29, 1927, at 38.

five directors at the next annual meeting of the company.[13] This was followed by a cash distribution of $2,000,000.[14]

It is obvious that upon such occasions the individual security-holder must find his lone efforts doomed at the outset to futility. Equally obvious is it that union with other security-holders of like mind affords a remedy for the individual's weakness.

The random illustrations of internal corporate controversies adverted to have indicated three devices in use for the effectuation of such unions: the proxy-committee,[15] the voting-trust,[16] and the protective committee.[16a] While they have much in common they also have very substantial differences.

The limitations of the proxy-committee method are inherent in the law of the subject. By reason of the revocability of proxies, the proxy-committee has no assurance that before it acts its proxies will not be revoked, either by express revocation, the execution of a later proxy to another, or by the personal attendance of the stockholder at the meeting.[16b] Because of this factor, the proxy-committee as a means of corporate control may be used effec-

[13] New York Times, Jan. 20, 1928, at 28.

[14] New York Times, March 29, 1928, at 39; June 14, 1928, at 38; June 16, 1928, at 28.

[15] *Supra* p. 47.

[16] *Supra* pp. 47–51.

[16a] Another possible device is indicated by the recently incorporated (Ill. Aug. 1933) "Montgomery Ward Stockholders Association," a non-profit corporation.

[16b] See Matter of Application of Chilson Re Public Industrials Corp., 168 Atl. 82 (Del. Ch. 1933),

tively only in short contests. Furthermore, the method affords no means for raising funds whereby prolonged investigation or litigation may be conducted.[17]

To achieve "irrevocable proxies", the voting-trust was developed.[18]

Standing halfway, in more than one sense, between the proxy and the voting-trust is the protective committee. Despite the close relationship of all three, the protective committee differs fundamentally from both the proxy-committee and the voting-trust. Before entering upon the detailed study of the protective committee, it is well to note these basic differences.

Of the three, the protective committee alone is suited for use by the holders of non-voting securities, such as bonds or non-voting classes of stock.[19] Both proxy-committees and voting-trustees must, in general, achieve their ends by the election of a favorable board of directors and then through that board. This feature is dominant in the very definition of a voting trust. "A voting trust agreement accumulates in the hands of a person or persons shares of several owners, in trust for the purpose of voting them, in order, through the selection and

---

[17] In practice, an opposition proxy-committee may itself initially represent such substantial financial interests in the corporation as to make the raising of funds from outsiders unimportant. In such cases proxies are solicited for the necessary votes or for the "moral" effect.

[18] *Supra* p. 47.

[19] In the Interborough Rapid Transit Company unification matter above referred to, one Deposit Agreement (dated March 15, 1930) provided for the deposit with the same committee of capital stock and voting trust certificates therefor.

election of directors, to control the corporate business and affairs.''[20] On the other hand, a protective committee may achieve its purpose not only
through the board of directors but where necessary
against the wishes of the board, having in appropriate cases the aid of the judicial machinery.[20a]
This essential difference is functionally recognized.
The usual voting-trust agreement confines the powers of the trustees to the election of directors, the
collection of dividends and the distribution of the
dividends to the certificate holders. Protective committees are generally empowered to do all things
expedient in procuring the desired result.[21]

A characteristic difference in point of view between the voting-trust and the protective committee (and also the opposition proxy-committee) is
likewise important. The former is directed towards
general stability in management, the maintenance
of the *status quo*[22] for a number of years; the latter towards the overturn of the *status quo* (in part
at least) for the accomplishment of a special, spe-

[20] Manson v. Curtis, 223 N. Y. 313, 319, 119 N. E. 559, 561 (1918).

[20a] A protective committee has the status of its depositors and
may maintain suits to the same extent as the depositors. Trustees
System Co. v. Payne, 65 F. (2d) 103 (C. C. A. 3d, 1933); Bullard v.
City of Cisco, 62 F. (2d) 313 (C. C. A. 5th, 1932). For the relief
obtainable in the courts, see Chap. VI. A committee may be afforded
privileges not granted to a single security-holder, see *infra* p. 205,
note 136.

[21] It should perhaps be expressly noted that the word "control"
is not used in this book solely in its limited sense of command over
a majority of the voting stock, but also in the broader sense of
power to use the corporation for the realization of a desired end.

[22] In reorganizations, the voting trust device is used to assure con-
tinuance of the status brought about by the reorganization.

cific purpose. This difference is not frequently found as explicitly delineated as it was in the case of the Seaboard Air Line Railway. Early in 1904 the company was under the control of a group of bankers by virtue of a voting-trust theretofore created in connection with certain financing, but differences of opinion on financial matters soon arose and an opposition stockholders' protective committee was organized by another group of bankers.[23] The deposit agreement expressly authorized the committee to institute an action for the dissolution of the voting-trust.[24]

As an outgrowth of these fundamental differences it is generally true that voting-trusts aim to continue in being as long as legally possible, with substantially no power of withdrawal in the depositor, whereas protective committees endeavor to terminate their existence as soon as their objects can be achieved, or accomplishment becomes patently impossible, and allow considerably freer exercise of the right of withdrawal.[25]

[23] (1904) 79 COMMERCIAL & FINANCIAL CHRONICLE 152, 734.
[24] Cushing, Voting Trusts, (2d. Ed. 1927) 25. A similar situation existed in the Interborough unification matter above mentioned; but there the "protective committee" directed its efforts towards electing a voting trustee favorable to its views, rather than towards attacking the voting trust agreement *per se* (see New York Times, Aug. 26, 1930, at 3). The voting trust agreement, dated Oct. 1, 1922, provided that vacancies among the trustees be filled by vote of the certificate holders and that the trustees should elect as directors of the Company persons nominated by various financially interested groups, including the certificate holders.
[25] A few more particular differences between voting trusts and protective committees are reserved for note hereafter.

The Committee

The committee is self-constituted, willing itself into being. The present tendency is to invite, in addition to large holders of the security, men of experience and prestige so that their names will serve to create confidence in the committee.[26] Committee members need not have any personal interest in the security or the corporation,[27] and it would seem that they may even have independent interests.[28] But they may not make contracts for secret profits.[29] An officer of the corporate-trustee under a bond-indenture may serve on a committee for holders of bonds issued thereunder [30] but that circumstance may induce the court, in a foreclosure

[26] GERSTENBERG, FINANCIAL ORGANIZATION & MANAGEMENT (1924) 663; DEWING, FINANCIAL POLICY OF CORPORATIONS (1926) 937-8. For criticism of surreptitious and irresponsible banker-control over committees, see, Lowenthal, The Investor Pays (1933). In a recent matter (Associated Rayon Corporation) two banking houses acting in their firm names constituted the Committee (see New York Times, May 14, 1930, at 45, 46). The protective agreement, dated May 14, 1930, provided: "S. & Co. and L. Brothers shall act respectively as copartnerships and in case of any change in either firm such firm as from time to time constituted shall be deemed parties of the second part hereunder, as though originally named herein, and the survivors or continuing members of any such firm may execute any assignment or transfer necessary to vest in the successor firm all powers, rights, or title of the prior firm hereunder."

[27] Haines v. Kinderhook & Hudson Ry., 33 App. Div. 154, 53 N. Y. Supp. 368 (1898).

[28] Bank of Manhattan Trust Co. v. Ellda Corp., 147 Misc. 374, 265 N. Y. Supp. 115 (1933).

[29] Marshall v. Lovell, 19 F. (2d) 751 (C. C. A. 8th, 1927) *cert. den.* 276 U. S. 616, 48 S. Ct. 207, 72 L. Ed. 733.

[30] Palmer v. Bankers Trust Co., 12 F. (2d) 747 (C. C. A. 8th, 1926). As to the right of a foreign corporation to act as a committee, see Gifford v. Commonwealth Bond Corp., 237 App. Div. 871, 261 N. Y. Supp. 960 (1933).

suit brought by the trustee, to permit non-depositing bondholders to intervene.[31] While the practice is looked upon with varying degrees of favor, or disfavor, by different courts, even a receiver of the corporation may act as a member of a committee of its security-holders and will be required to resign only when a conflict between his two trusts is foreshadowed.[32] It would seem that an officer of the corporation, owing a trust duty to all its security-holders, should not place himself in the position of acting only for some of them.[33] There is however no impropriety in the directors unofficially nominating a committee when there is need for one.[34]

The committee informally brought together takes its legal status, *nunc pro tunc* as it were, from the "deposit agreement" which it prepares to give itself formal being.

The Deposit Agreement and the Powers, Duties and Liabilities of the Committee Thereunder

The committee's counsel[35] should not, in the words of Paul D. Cravath,[36] "attempt to evolve a

[31] Central Trust Co. v. Chicago, R. I. & P. R. R., 218 Fed. 336 (C. C. A. 2d, 1914).

[32] Fowler v. Jarvis-Conklin Mtge. Co., 63 Fed. 888 (C. C. S. D. N. Y. 1894).

[33] Jackson v. Ludeling, 88 U. S. 616 (1874).

[34] Abbott v. Waltham Watch Co., 260 Mass. 81, 91, 156 N. E. 897 (1927).

[35] As to counsel's conduct in soliciting deposits, see People v. Ashton, 347 Ill. 570, 180 N. E. 440 (1932).

[36] CRAVATH, The Reorganization of Corporations, in Some Legal Phases of Corporate Financing, Reorganization and Regulation (1917) 164.

deposit agreement out of his own consciousness''. So many agreements are now readily available that they should be freely used as models; [37] however, the availability of forms and the ease of the "scissors and paste" method must not lead to forgetfulness of the need to frame each agreement to meet its specific purpose. This must be sought after, not by narrow limitations, nor by undue reliance upon mere broad sweeping general clauses.

The parties to the agreement are the members of the committee, who execute the instrument, and the depositors, who become such under the provisions of the agreement, either by executing the agreement, or merely by depositing their securities and accepting certificates of deposit therefor.[38]

After the usual designation of the parties and the recital of the circumstances leading to the ex-

[37] A "bondholders' protective agreement" in a reorganization is analyzed and printed in full in TRACY, CORPORATE FORECLOSURES (1929) 15-19, 409-427. Dewing, in his FINANCIAL POLICY OF CORPORATIONS (1926), quotes at length the late Adrian H. Joline's summary of such agreements (pp. 939-940). Other types of deposit agreements are printed in FLETCHER, CORPORATION FORMS (2d ed., 1923) 746, 1503. Mr. Cravath's lecture, *supra* note 36, contains many helpful suggestions as to their preparation. Many of the cited cases contain lengthy quotations from, and detailed descriptions of, the agreements involved.

[38] The depositary may, but need not, be a party. If the committee is empowered to employ a depositary, it may do so, and the depositary need not be a party to the agreement in order to act. It is well, however, to procure the depositary's approval of the proposed deposit agreement, because it is vitally concerned with the provisions thereof, particularly with those dealing with its duties and immunities. It is customary to name the depositary in the agreement and give the committee power to change it.

ecution of the deposit agreement, the customary form proceeds more or less along the following outline:

(A) The committee is constituted as such.

(B) Provision is made for the deposit of the designated securities.

(C) The depositary is named and its powers and duties are set forth, as are the powers of the committee with respect to the depositary.

(D) The depositors agree not to take any independent action with respect to the deposited securities, and the rights of the committee in and to the deposited securities are defined.[39]

(E) Terms and conditions of deposit, such as time within which deposit must be made, the committee being given power to vary.[40]

---

[39] In the older forms the committee was generally described as having title to the deposited securities and all the rights of owners. In the newer forms the committee is given the same broad powers, but to be exercised by virtue of an irrevocable power of attorney from the depositors to the committee, the depositors reserving title until such time as the committee, at its option, elects to take title, which option is generally exercisable by the filing of a notice of election with the depositary. One advantage of this procedure is to enable the committee to file a larger number of claims in bankruptcy. Voting trustees are generally given the full powers of "absolute owners", subject only, in some cases, to special limitations.

[40] When it is doubtful whether the value of the deposited securities will be sufficient to create a fund for committee expenses, the payment of a sum may be made a condition of deposit. Although voting trustees generally reserve the power to charge certificate holders with expenses and to withhold such charges from dividends received, it is a common practice to place the burden of the expenses upon the

(F) Provisions with respect to the issuance, transfer, registration, etc., of certificates of deposit.

(G) Methods of giving notice to depositors.

(H) Specific powers to meet the particular situation.[41]

(I) Provisions with respect to dissent and withdrawal by depositors.[42]

(J) General powers to committee.[43] Among the customary ones are: *a* To add to their number, accept resignations and fill vacancies; *b* To act by a majority [44] and the members by proxy; *c* To employ depositary, counsel, engineers and other agents, and to pay them; *d* To fix their own compensation; [45]

corporation (see Cushing, *supra* note 24, pp. 46–49); but see Clark v. National Steel & Wire Co., 82 Conn. 178, 72 Atl. 930 (1909), where it was held that, the corporation not being a party to the voting trust agreement, it could not pay expenses incurred by the trustees thereunder.

[41] Express powers will not be extended by "construction", Industrial General Trust, Ltd. v. Tod, 170 N. Y. 233, 63 N. E. 285 (1902). It is proper to provide that any contemplated new corporation may be organized under the laws of a state to be selected by the committee, even if the laws of such state differ from those of the domicile of the old corporation or from that of the situs of the agreement, Cowell v. City Water Supply Co., 130 Iowa 671, 105 N. W. 1016 (1906).

[42] It is usual to require the payment of a *pro rata* share of the expenses as a condition for the exercise of the right of withdrawal.

[43] No general powers are implied, Industrial General Trust, Ltd. v. Tod, *supra* note 41.

[44] Haines v. Kinderhook & Hudson Ry. Co., *supra* note 27; Coppell v. Hollins, 91 Hun 570, 36 N. Y. Supp. 500 (1895), *aff'd.,* 159 N. Y. 551, 54 N. E. 1089 (1899).

[45] But the compensation which the committee vote to themselves is subject to judicial review, Livingston v. Falk, 217 App. Div. 360, 217 N. Y. Supp. 131 (1926).

e To use the deposited securities for expenses and for purposes of plan either by sale or pledge or otherwise; [46] *f* To adjust claims and institute suits; *g* To construe the agreement,[47] supply omissions, correct defects and (usually only with the consent of a specified percentage of the depositors) to change the agreement; [48] *h* To deal for their own individual benefit with securities of the class called for deposit, and to deal with the corporation.[49]

(K) Exculpatory clauses in favor of committeemen designed to limit liability of each for his own wilful misconduct only,[50] and in favor of depositary, particularly aiming to protect it in acting upon directions of the committee.

(L) Relieving the committee from responsi-

---

[46] The committee would have implied power to make necessary expenditures, Cowell v. City Water Supply Co., *supra* note 41.

[47] The committee's construction must be fair, not arbitrary, and made in good faith, Industrial & General Trust, Ltd. v. Tod, *supra* note 41; Industrial & General Trust, Ltd. v. Tod, 180 N. Y. 215, 73 N. E. 7 (1904).

[48] A provision to the effect that all depositors shall be bound by the action of a majority is valid, Olcott v. Powers, 60 Hun 583, 15 N. Y. Supp. 263 (1891).

[49] Such a clause waiving the usual contrary rule applicable to trustees is valid, Miller v. Dodge, 28 Misc. 640, 59 N. Y. Supp. 1070 (1899). The broad powers granted to the committee by the typical agreement have been severely criticised. See Lowenthal v. Georgia Coast & P. R. Co., 233 Fed. 1016, 1021 (D. C. S. D. Ga. 1916), *affd.*, 238 Fed. 795 (C. C. A. 5th 1917).

[50] No one member would be liable for the defaults of another, Riker v. Alsop, 27 Fed. 251 (C. C. S. D. N. Y. 1886), *revd.* (on other grounds), 155 U. S. 448, 15 Sup. Ct. 162 (1894). As to exculpatory clauses generally, *infra*, p. 82 *et seq.*

bility for failure of plan; in some agreements the committee expressly undertakes to endeavor in good faith to carry out purpose.[51]

(M) Denying power to committee to obligate depositors personally, but subjecting the deposited securities to all charges incurred by committee.

(N) Provisions as to expiration and termination.

(O) Procedure for accounting by committee.

(P) Disclaimer of any obligations to non-depositors.

The deposit agreement is of course a contract and its terms may not be disregarded.[52] In so far as its construction is concerned, the courts endeavor to apply two principles, leaning towards one or the other as the equities of the situation as seen by the particular court seem to demand. One of these rules of construction is that the deposit agreement will be construed most favorably to the depositors

[51] It would seem that such an obligation should be implied (Patterson v. Guardian Trust Co., 144 App. Div. 863, 866, 129 N. Y. S. 807 (1911)) but see Colonial Trust Co. v. Wallace, 183 Fed. 897 (C. C. S. D. N. Y. 1910).

[52] Cox v. Stokes, 156 N. Y. 491, 51 N. E. 316 (1898); Habirshaw Electric Cable Co. v. Habirshaw Electric Co., 296 Fed. 875 (C. C. A. 2d, 1924). Deposit agreements have not been subjected to the attacks on their validity which were so vigorously urged against voting trust agreements. This may be due to the fact that most deposit agreements which have reached the courts involved bonds, rather than voting stocks, where the legal problems are somewhat more difficult. It may also be due to the trend away from such attacks even where voting trust agreements are involved. See *supra* p. 50, note 83.

and strictly against the committee.[53] The other of
these principles is that the agreement will be construed liberally to enable the committee to achieve
the desired results.[54]

A good indication of how the courts have actually met this inconsistency—verbal inconsistency
at least—can be obtained from looking at a few
cases wherein questions as to the powers of reorganization committees were involved.

In *Mills* v. *Potter*,[55] the court expressly accepted
as sound the rule that the agreement "should be
construed strictly", but proceeded, in view of the
"peculiar" circumstances and the "situation of
the parties", to give the agreement a rather broad
and liberal meaning. The agreement involved was
a usual reorganization agreement under which the
committee was specifically authorized to purchase
the property upon foreclosure, raise money for
"the purposes of the agreement" and "supply
defects or omissions in the plan". The committee was required to allot "to the certificate
holders their proportionate interests in the securities of any new company which may be organized".
The plan and circulars issued by the committee
indicated that improvements to the property were

[53] Carter v. First Nat. Bank, 128 Md. 581, 98 Atl. 77 (1916); Industrial & General Trust, Ltd. v. Tod, 170 N. Y. 233, 180 N. Y. 215,
supra notes 41, 47; United Water Works v. Omaha Water Co., 164
N. Y. 41, 58 N. E. 58 (1900). This rule is justified on the double
ground that the depositors are *cestuis que trusts* and that the agreement is prepared by the committee.

[54] Venner v. Fitzgerald, 91 Fed. 335 (C. C. S. D. N. Y. 1899);
White v. Wood, 129 N. Y. 527, 29 N. E. 835 (1892).

[55] 189 Mass. 238, 75 N. E. 627 (1905).

necessary and that new money would be required for that purpose. The court held that the committee acted properly in continuing to hold the stock of the new corporation to which the property had been conveyed "for a reasonable time" and during that time causing the corporation to make contracts and raise moneys for improvements by means of a mortgage prior in lien to the securities distributable to the depositors.

A New Jersey court [56] showed the same spirit when it construed "matters of detail" to include not only formal matters "but also such alterations in the terms of the agreement itself (not changing the plan) as might be deemed necessary or advisable to effectuate the object". The reorganization agreement there provided for the issuance of bonds payable "in thirty years", and the court held it to have been within the province of a "committee of detail", appointed to carry out the plan, to grant the corporation the option to prepay the bonds before maturity.

In sharp contrast are the decisions rendered against the "Bondholders' Committee" in the American Water Works reorganization by the New York Court of Appeals [57] and by a federal court sitting in Massachusetts.[58] In these cases a clause of the agreement reading:

---

[56] Lehigh Coal & Navigation Co. v. Central R. R., 34 N. J. Eq. 88 (1881).

[57] United Water Works Co. v. Omaha Water Co., *supra* note 53.

[58] United Water Works Co. v. Stone, 127 Fed. 587 (C. C. D. Mass. 1904).

"The committee shall prior to the conveyance of any purchased property to a new company, submit to the certificate holders a detailed plan of reorganization, which shall be
binding upon all said holders, unless the holders of a majority in interest of the outstanding
certificates shall, within thirty days, file with
the trust company their written dissent from
said plan . . ."

was construed to give to the committee power only
to provide for "details", "minor particulars", and
not "matters of substance", the court having construed the deposit agreement as setting forth the
substance of the reorganization plan. Accordingly
a plan providing for recognition of junior security-
holders[59] was held outside the provisions of the
agreement, and the creation of a voting-trust of the
stock of the new corporation was held violative of
the requirement in the agreement that the "committee shall, after payment of the expenses of foreclosure and all expenses incurred by the committee,
and its compensation, allot to the certificate holders their proportionate interests in the new company".[60] Because of these variations depositors

[59] See also Farmers Loan & Trust Co. v. Centralia & C. R. R.,
96 Fed. 636 (C. C. A. 7th, 1899) where it was held that a bondholders' committee was not authorized to consent to the issuance of
receivers' certificates to be prior in lien to the deposited bonds. As to
the necessity for consent, see, Union Trust Co. v. Illinois Midland
Co., 117 U. S. 434, 6 S. Ct. 809, 29 L. Ed. 963 (1886).

[60] Warren v. Pim, 65 N. J. Eq. 36, 55 Atl. 66 (1903); Warren v.
Pim, 66 N. J. Eq. 353, 59 Atl. 773 (1904) (which contain an exhaustive discussion of the validity of voting trusts) involved ques-

were held not bound by the plan notwithstanding the fact that a majority had not dissented.

Another reorganization committee, which had very broad powers to deal with property acquired upon a foreclosure sale and which was specifically authorized to create such liens "as may be necessary in the discretion of the committee to carry out the plan . . . or to protect or develop the said property . . . or for any purpose the committee may deem wise or necessary", determining that exploration work was necessary, entered into an agreement with an "Exploration Company" under which it was to do the work and expend such sums "as in its uncontrolled discretion it deemed necessary" and for the repayment of which it was given a lien. Despite the conceded good faith of the committee and the Exploration Company,[61] it was held that the agreement was beyond the powers of the committee on the ground that it could not delegate the discretion vested in it to another.[62]

One of the unsettled problems is the effect to be given the exculpatory clauses of the agreement, which ordinarily in the most sweeping terms seek to relieve members of the committee from any liability except each for his own wilful default. The question is, of course, part of the general problem

tions as to the extent to which a committee may go in setting up a voting trust, even where its creation was specifically, but in general terms, authorized by the depositors.

[61] But it should be noted that the committee had failed to disclose to the depositors the agreement with the Exploration Company.

[62] Titus v. U. S. Smelting, R. & M. Exp. Co., 231 Fed. 205 (1916), aff'd., 240 Fed. 881 (C. C. A. 2d, 1917).

as to how far liability may be contracted away, and more specially by fiduciaries.[63]

It may be stated that no provision can shield the committee from liability if it acts in bad faith.[64] If the court finds bad faith, the committee may be held liable for the losses sustained without regard to whether the members of the committee profited personally and without the necessity of first setting aside the deposit agreement.[65] On the other hand, when the court finds that the committee acted in good faith, the exculpatory clauses will be given full effect.[66] In such cases there is no liability for errors of judgment or for being "overreached" when the agreement stipulates that there is no liability except for "wilful malfeasance or gross negligence".[67] The danger lies in the possibility that a court may conclude that a breach of the deposit agreement is proof of bad faith.

In *Industrial & General Trust, Ltd.* v. *Tod*,[68] the agreement conferred "almost unlimited powers" upon the committee, gave it power to construe the agreement and supply omissions, and the committee was expressly exempted from liability except for "wilful misconduct". The committee failed to publish a plan of reorganization until *after* the re-

[63] See (Note) Immunity Clauses in Corporate Trust Indentures, (1933) 33 Columbia L. Rev. 97; Posner, Liability of the Trustee Under the Corporate Indenture (1928) 42 Harvard L. Rev. 198, 239.

[64] Parker v. New England Oil Co., 13 F. (2d) 158 (D. Mass. 1926), *revd.*, 19 F. (2d) 903 (C. C. A. 1st, 1927).

[65] *Ibid.*

[66] Van Siclen v. Bartol, 95 Fed. 793 (C. C. E. D. Pa. 1899).

[67] *Ibid.*

[68] *Supra* note 47.

organization had been completed. The provisions of the agreement were construed to have *impliedly* required the publication of a plan *before* reorganization, so that the depositors might have a reasonable opportunity to dissent, and the committee was held liable to a depositor.[69]

It is not clear under what circumstances a court may remove a committee and appoint a receiver to act in its stead.[70] It would seem that the court should limit its interference to the removal of an improper committee, leaving it to the depositors to elect a new one.[71]

The Depositary and its Certificates of Deposit.

As we have seen, it is more usual not to require would-be depositors to sign the deposit agreement, but to provide for their adherence to the agreement by the deposit of securities and the acceptance of certificates of deposit therefor. These certificates are usually issued by a trust company chosen by the committee as its "depositary". The trustee under a bond-indenture may act as depositary for a committee of holders of bonds issued thereunder.[72] Certificates of deposit are, at common-law,

---

[69] The only indication of "bad faith" in the opinions is that the committee had assured the plaintiff that a plan would be formulated in advance. On the other hand, one of the dissenting justices pointed out that there was no charge of either fraud or wilful misconduct.

[70] See Harrigan v. Pounds, 239 App. Div. 1, 265 N. Y. S. 676 *revg.* 147 Misc. 666, 264 N. Y. S. 363 (1933).

[71] See Bank of Manhattan Trust Co. v. Ellda Corporation, *supra* note 28, at p. 379.

[72] Fidelity Trust Co. v. Washington-Oregon Corp., 217 Fed. 588

not negotiable instruments,[73] but every effort is
made to render them negotiable in fact and in law.
In form they are made transferable either by mere
delivery (bearer certificates) or by transfer on
books kept for that purpose by the depositary. It
is not infrequent to list certificates of deposit upon
stock exchanges, if the securities they represent
are so listed.[74] Legal negotiability is sought after
by appropriate provisions in the deposit agreement.[75] Negotiability may, of course, be conferred
by statute.[76]

In general the situation with regard to the issuance and transfer of certificates of deposit is
analogous to that with regard to corporate stock.[77]

(W. D. Wash. 1914); Palmer v. Bankers Trust Co., *supra* note 30;
Guaranty Trust Co. v. Chicago, M. & St. P. Ry., 15 F. (2d) 434
(N. D. Ill. 1926).

[73] Chicago, R. I. & P. R. R. v. Howard, 74 U. S. 392 (1868).

[74] The Federal Trade Commission takes the position that certificates of deposit must be registered under the Securities Act of 1933.
This view finds support in the definitions of Sec. 2 (4) and in the
Report of the House Committee on Interstate and Foreign Commerce (73d Congress, 1st Session, Report No. 85, pp. 11, 16). It
may, however, be seriously contended that the issuance of certificates
of deposit is not a "public" offering and therefore exempt, Sec. 4
(1). See opinion of A. H. Dean to that effect, in "Fortune", August,
1933, p. 97. Because of this requirement, protective committees are
now frequently asking only for proxies or powers-of-attorney and
not for the deposit of the securities, thus obviating the necessity
for issuing certificates. This method has its weaknesses, *supra* p. 68.
See Matter of Application of Chilson Re Public Industrials Corporation, *supra* note 16b.

[75] As to whether negotiability may be conferred by agreement, see
note (1924) 33 YALE L. J. 302, Beutel, Negotiability by Contract
(1933) 28 ILLINOIS L. REV. 205.

[76] See Article 8 (adopted 1926) of N. Y. PERSONAL PROPERTY
LAW dealing with "security receipts".

[77] Cassagne v. Marvin, 143 N. Y. 292, 38 N. E. 285 (1894). This

The requirement of the agreement that the security must be deposited with the depositary in exchange for its certificate of deposit may be waived by the committee, and it is waived, if the committee, by one of its members or officers, accepts a security tendered for deposit.[78]

Depositors.

The "depositors" are, by definition, those who are parties to the deposit agreement by virtue of holding certificates of deposit.[79]

Ordinarily—and it should be expressly so provided—one is a party to the agreement only to the extent of the securities deposited, but, in the absence of a provision to the contrary, a court may find that one who has signed a deposit agreement as the holder of a stated number of shares of stock is also bound as to after-acquired stocks and bonds.[80]

It is for the depositors that the committee is trustee [81] and it is to them that it owes fiduciary obligations.[82] It is not fruitful to attempt exact definition as to whether the relationship is one of

is also true of voting trust certificates, see Union Trust Co. v. Oliver, 214 N. Y. 517, 108 N. E. 809 (1915).

[78] Hitchock v. Midland R. R., 33 N. J. Eq. 86, *affd.*, 34 N. J. Eq. 278 (1880).

[79] The failure actually to receive a certificate of deposit will not deprive one of the right to participate, if in fact he has deposited with the committee, Hitchock v. Midland R. R., *supra note* 78.

[80] Tillotson v. Independent Breweries Co., 216 Mo. App. 412, 268 S. W. 425 (1925). But *cf.* Riker v. Alsop, *supra* note 50.

[81] United Waterworks, Ltd. v. Stone, *supra* note 58.

[82] Cassagne v. Marvin, *supra* note 77; Carter v. First National Bank, *supra* note 53.

agency, bailment, assignment, or trust. All these terms, and others, have been applied by the courts [83] but all are consistent with the notion of a fiduciary relationship.[84] One of the results is that a depositor may compel the committee to account.[85] The "agency" of the committee is not such that it may bind the depositors personally in favor of third persons, the committee alone being liable as principal on its contracts.[86] But where the obligations incurred are proper the committee may, in the absence of provisions in the agreement to the contrary, obtain reimbursement from the depositors on an implied agreement by the depositors to pay necessary expenses.[87] And, of course, the committee may bind the deposited securities.[88]

[83] *Agency*—Miller v. Dodge, *supra* note 49; Industrial & Gen. Trust, Ltd. v. Tod, *supra* note 47. *Contra:* Mines Management Co. v. Close, 186 App. Div. 23, 174 N. Y. Supp. 80 (1919). *Bailment*— Industrial & Gen. Trust, Ltd. v. Tod, *supra.* *Assignment*—Mines Management Co. v. Close, *supra.* *Trust*—Cowell v. City Water Supply Co., *supra* note 41; United Water Works Co. v. Omaha Water Co., *supra* note 53; American Trust Co. v. Holtsinger, 226 Mass. 30, 114 N. E. 956 (1917); Parker v. New England Oil Corp., 4 F. (2d) 392 (1924), *revd.,* 19 F. (2d) 903 (C. C. A. 1st, 1927). *Power of Attorney coupled with an interest*—Parker v. New England Oil Corp., *supra* note 64.

[84] Bergelt v. Roberts, 144 Misc. 832, 836, 258 N. Y. S. 905, *affd.,* 236 App. Div. 777, 258 N. Y. S. 1086 (1932).

[85] Mawhinney v. Bliss, 117 App. Div. 255, 102 N. Y. Supp. 279 (1907), *affd.,* 189 N. Y. 501, 81 N. E. 1169 (1907). The court found the allegations of the complaint to be inconsistent with "good faith" on the part of the committee, and refused to pass on the question whether a depositor might, before the committee is afforded a reasonable opportunity to perform, compel an accounting without alleging bad faith, negligence, or breach of trust.

[86] Mines Management Co. v. Close, *supra* note 83.

[87] Fidelity Ins. Co. v. Lenning, 106 Pa. 144 (1884).

[88] Central Trust Co. v. Carter, 78 Fed. 225 (C. C. A. 5th, 1896).

The aim of the courts is to keep all depositors on equality;[89] but the failure of some to perform their obligations[90] does not affect the other depositors,[91] nor serve to relieve the committee from its trusteeship.[92]

The deposit agreement may contain an agreement adopting in advance any plan which the committee may formulate.[93] It is more customary, however, to require the committee to promulgate a plan and give the depositors the right to dissent therefrom.[94] A provision to the effect that any promulgated plan shall be binding upon all depositors unless a majority dissent is valid.[95]

Depositors may withdraw deposited securities only pursuant to the terms of the deposit agreement,[96] but the abandonment by the committee of its functions,[97] or a breach of duty on the part of the committee,[98] may justify withdrawal. Thus it has been held[99] that the issuance of a new bond

[89] Fuller v. Venable, 118 Fed. 543 (C. C. A. 4th, 1902).

[90] Each depositor must of course comply with the terms of the agreement in order to be entitled to participation. Carpenter v. Catlin, 44 Barb. Ch. 75 (N. Y. 1865).

[91] Cushman v. Bonfield, 139 Ill. 219, 28 N. E. 937 (1891).

[92] Indiana, I. & I. R. R. v. Swannell, 157 Ill. 616, 41 N. E. 989 (1895).

[93] Ginty v. Ocean Shore R. R., 172 Cal. 31, 155 Pac. 77 (1916); Colonial Trust Co. v. Wallace, *supra* note 51.

[94] The dissent must be *in toto;* that is, one may not accept parts of the plan and reject other parts. Miller v. Dodge, *supra* note 49.

[95] Cowell v. City Water Supply Co., *supra* note 41.

[96] Habirshaw Electric Cable Co. v. Habirshaw Electric Co., *supra* note 52.

[97] Lucey Mfg. Corp. v. Morlan, 14 F. (2d) 920 (C. C. A. 9th, 1926).

[98] Industrial & Gen. Trust, Ltd. v. Tod, *supra* note 47.

[99] Miller v. Rutland & Washington R. R., 40 Vt. 399 (1867).

issue in an amount substantially larger than provided for in the agreement is sufficient to release depositors. In a case[100] where the deposit agreement was construed as imposing no obligation upon the committee, which had the right to terminate the agreement at its pleasure, it was held, in the absence of an express prohibition, that a depositor might withdraw at any time. A clause expressly permitting withdrawal within sixty days from the publication of a plan was there held not to deprive a depositor of the right to withdraw before the formulation of a plan.

In a proper case, a depositor may also have the right to rescind.[101]

Of course, a depositor may cease to be such, if the agreement so provides—and it usually does, not only by withdrawal, but also by the mere transfer to another of his certificate of deposit, but then the securities remain bound and the transferee becomes the depositor.

Non-Depositors and Third Persons.

The agreement need not be open to all the security-holders of a corporation, nor even to all of the same class.[102] While, ordinarily, the committee

---

[100] Colonial Trust Co. v. Wallace, *supra* note 51; *cf.* Habirshaw Electric Cable Co. v. Habirshaw Electric Co., *supra* note 52 at 880.

[101] Each depositor may exercise such right on his own behalf only and may not maintain a class-suit on behalf of all depositors for rescission. Harrigan v. Pounds, *supra* note 70.

[102] Fidelity Ins. & Safe Deposit Co. v. Roanoke Street Ry., 98 Fed. 475 (C. C. W. D. Va. 1899); Munson v. Magee, 22 App. Div. 333, 47 N. Y. Supp. 942 (1897), *affd.* 161 N. Y. 182, 55 N. E. 916 (1900); Moss v. Geddes, 28 Misc. 291, 59 N. Y. Supp. 867 (1899).

endeavors to procure the largest amount of deposited securities of the permitted class, there is no obligation upon the committee to call attention to its existence or to solicit deposits.[103] Although there may be circumstances under which the committee may become chargeable with fiduciary obligations to other interested parties,[104] it may be stated as a general rule that the committee owes no duty to non-depositors.[105] But it should be careful not to hold itself out as acting for all.[106] Provisions in the deposit agreement indicating that holders of other classes of securities may be permitted certain participation under the plan, may be only *ex gratia* and not impose any liability in their favor.[107]

A non-depositor may not compel the acceptance of his securities after the expiration of the time limited for deposit, even though the committee may

In reorganizations under judicial supervision, the court may possibly insist upon a reasonable right of participation for all of the same class; but as to that see Rodgers, Rights and Duties of the Committee in Bondholder Reorganization (1929) 42 HARVARD L. REV. 899; *infra* Chap. VII esp. p. 205, note 136. It is generally required, either by statute or decision, that voting-trust agreements be open to all stockholders.

[103] Moss v. Geddes, *supra* note 102. Voting trust statutes generally require that voting-trust agreements be public and open to inspection by all stockholders. See Gow v. Consolidated Coppermines Corp., 165 Atl. 136 (Del. 1933) for a discussion of the duty of a proxy-committee to disclose its purpose.

[104] See Parker v. New England Oil Co., 8 F. (2d) 392 (D. Mass. 1925), *revd.* 19 F. (2d) 903 (C. C. A. 1st, 1927).

[105] Bound v. South Carolina R. R., 78 Fed. 49 (C. C. A. 4th, 1897); Wilson v. Waltham Watch Co., 293 Fed. 811 (D. C. Mass. 1923); Harrigan v. Pounds, *supra* note 70.

[106] Walker v. Whelan, 4 Phila. 389 (Pa. 1861).

[107] Miller v. Dodge, *supra* note 49.

be accepting belated deposits from others.[108] On the other hand, the committee having accepted a deposit after the time limited therefor, a demand on the part of depositors that the late-comers be excluded will be regarded as lacking "the essential element of equity".[109] Even where participation may be compelled, it must be sought seasonably.[110]

Generally, the subject of "strangers' dealings" with the committee may be sufficiently summarized by saying, in addition to what has already been noted, that third-persons are held chargeable with notice as to the terms of the deposit agreement.[111] However, the terms of the agreement will probably be liberally construed in favor of innocent third-persons, particularly where the complaining depositor has received benefits or has been guilty of laches.[112]

Committee Communications.

Active committees make it a practice to issue from time to time statements as to their progress and prospects. Although this desire to make their proceedings public is a wholly laudable one, great

---

[108] Keane v. Moffly, 217 Pa. 240, 66 Atl. 319 (1907).

[109] Walker v. Montclair & Greenwood Lake Ry., 30 N. J. Eq. 525 (1879). This was a proceeding to set aside a foreclosure sale; but query whether the same result would be reached in a direct proceeding promptly brought to enforce the terms of the agreement. This note of course assumes that the deposit agreement, contrary to the usual practice, vests no discretion in the committee as to the time within which to accept deposits.

[110] Landis v. West Pa. R. R., 133 Pa. 579, 19 Atl. 556 (1890).

[111] Central Trust Co. v. Carter, 78 Fed. 225 (C. C. A. 5th, 1896).

[112] Lyman v. Kansas City & A. R. R., 101 Fed. 636 (C. C. W. D. Mo. 1900).

care must be exercised in the preparation of all committee communications to depositors, non-depositors, and to the depositary. The need for caution arises especially because, under the usual agreement, the committee is empowered to take various actions which become effective and binding upon the giving of certain specified notice. It is, therefore, important always to distinguish sharply between mere informative announcements and notices of formal action. These matters do not frequently reach the stage of litigation, but there is at least one reported case [113] that indicates the danger. In that case, a "Plan and Agreement of Reorganization" provided for the issuance of first mortgage bonds in an amount up to $100,000,000. The committee was empowered to modify the agreement, provided a copy of the proposed change be lodged with the depositary and advertised. The committee issued an announcement that "no material modification of the plan appears necessary except that the two classes of the junior bonds . . . may have to be offered a somewhat smaller allotment in the new first mortgage bonds . . . so as to enable the committee to limit the issue of new first mortgage 4 per cent bonds [which under the plan was fixed at $100,000,000] to $75,000,000 for reorganization purposes, . . ." The announcement concluded with the statement:

"While modifications in the other features of the plan appear not to be required under

[113] Barnard v. Fitzgerald, 23 Misc. 181, 50 N. Y. Supp. 309 (1898).

present conditions, the committee deems it prudent to postpone the formal declaration that the plans all become operative. . . ."

Thereafter the committee declared operative the "plan of reorganization with the modification heretofore published". Upon the reorganization the committee found it necessary to issue $90,000,-000 of new first mortgage bonds. The plaintiff sued to restrain the issuance of more than $75,000,000, claiming that the committee's announcement constituted a modification of the plan. The decision was in favor of the committee because no modification was filed with the depositary, the advertising of the notice was not in the manner specified for modifications, and no provision for dissent and withdrawal was made as required by the agreement in cases of modification. The court also held that the announcement "did not constitute a representation or warranty binding upon the committee".

Termination of Agreement and Accounting by Committee.

Most agreements provide for a definite date of termination,[114] coupled with some limited power to the committee to extend the date, and give to the committee unlimited power to terminate the agreement at any earlier date.[115]

[114] This may be required by certain stock exchanges, if the certificates of deposit are to be listed. The New York Stock Exchange requires that deposit agreements terminate within five years.

[115] The power to terminate the agreement does not render it void

It is customary to impose upon the committee the duty to account at the termination of the agreement and to provide the mechanics therefor. Where the organization or reorganization of a corporation is contemplated, the accounting may be rendered to the board of directors of the corporation. Where the entire corporation is not involved, the committee may file an accounting with the depositary under appropriate provisions of the agreement making such filed account conclusive upon all depositors who do not object thereto within a limited time. In case of objections the newer agreements provide for the arbitration of disputed items.

The committee may maintain an action in equity for the settlement of its accounts.[116] Although it may be preferable expressly to cover the matter in the deposit agreement, it would seem that, even in the absence of express provision therefor, the committee may, in such a suit, obviate the necessity of joining as defendants all depositors if it can bring itself within the equitable rules concerning representative suits. In general, these rules require a showing that it would be impossible or exceedingly inconvenient to sue all the depositors (because they are too numerous, are unknown, or are beyond

for want of mutuality. White v. McCullagh, 74 W. Va. 160, 81 S. E. 720 (1914). But see Colonial Trust Co. v. Wallace, *supra* note 51.

[116] Mills v. Potter, *supra* note 55; Coppell v. Hollins, *supra* note 44. For a case involving an accounting by voting trustees upon a sale of the deposited stock pursuant to a supplemental agreement authorizing such sale, see, Lewis v. Adriance, 100 Misc. 725, 166 N. Y. S. 774 (1916), *affd.* 179 App. Div. 958 (1917), *affd.* 226 N. Y. 663, 123 N. E. 876 (1919).

the jurisdiction) and that those sued sufficiently represent the interests of the absentees.[117]

[117] See, generally, 21 C. J. 284-297; 34 C. J. Sec. 1422. The International Committee of Bankers on Mexico brought such a suit (Lamont v. Travelers Ins. Co., New York Supreme Court, New York County, No. 34326-1932). The complaint was dismissed on other grounds (NEW YORK LAW JOURNAL, January 31, 1933, p. 611).

CHAPTER VI.

SUITS IN EQUITY BY MINORITY STOCKHOLDERS *

Generally what is good for the stockholders is good for their corporation, and conversely what is good for the corporation is good for its stockholders. But what is good, in business as in morals, is not always beyond debate. Differences of opinion as to the proper course of corporate conduct are therefore inevitable. Unanimity not infrequently is also prevented by the fact that each stockholder gives weight to factors that interest him alone and not necessarily solely in his capacity of stockholder in the particular corporation. Indeed, in view of the network of corporations that now pervades life a person is not infrequently in direct competition with corporations whose stock he owns. These conflicts of opinion and interest are in most cases settled within the corporation, but the resort to courts by dissatisfied minorities is an increasingly common practice.

I

EQUITABLE INTERVENTION

In approaching the problem of when and to what

* The substance of this chapter was published in the University of Pennsylvania Law Review for April, 1933 (Vol. 81, p. 692).

extent courts of equity will interfere in the internal affairs of a corporation, it seems expedient first to note the "general principles", so that we may thereafter better appreciate the different lines of thought available to a chancellor faced with the facts of a particular controversy.

The starting dictum is that "a court of equity has no visitorial powers over corporations, except such as may be expressly conferred on it by statute."[1] The first breach made in this absolute rule was that equity would at the instance of stockholders give redress against *ultra vires* acts.[2] The proposition that equity would interfere in cases of *ultra vires* acts had its converse that "so long as the corporation keeps within the limits of its charter" equity would not interfere.[3]

The simple test of *power* did not long suffice. The chancellor was soon faced with charges of abuse of power. He thereupon imposed upon

[1] Latimer v. Eddy, 46 Barb. 61, 67 (N. Y. 1864). We shall in the main confine ourselves to non-statutory powers of equity. Some attempt has been made to fix by statute the right of minority stockholders to resort to equity, *e.g.*, GA. CODE ANN. (Michie, 1926) § 2224.

[2] Leslie v. Lorillard, 110 N. Y. 519, 18 N. E. 363 (1888) ; Murrin v. Archbold Cons. Coal Co., 232 N. Y. 541, 134 N. E. 563 (1921) ; Manderson v. Commercial Bank, 28 Pa. St. 379 (1857) ; Langolf v. Seiberlitch, 2 Pars. Eq. Cas. 64 (Pa. 1851). For additional cases see 3 COOK, CORPORATIONS (8th ed. 1923) § 669. As a result of increasingly liberal general corporation statutes and the use of the broadest possible terminology in certificates of incorporation, the problem of *ultra vires* is now of slight importance. See (1932) 45 HARV. L. REV. 1393. The problems with which we will be concerned are those arising out of the exercise of powers which concededly exist.

[3] Fountain Ferry Turnpike Road Co. v. Jewell, 8 B. Mon. 140, 145 (Ky. 1848).

those who had the power the obligation not to act fraudulently or in bad faith,[3a] or treat the minority unfairly or inequitably.[3b] The opinion in *Ervin* v. *Oregon Railway & Navigation Company*[4] indicates the many threads that are intertwined in the present-day concept of the power of equity to intervene in intra-corporate controversies.

"Plainly, the defendants have assumed to exercise a power belonging to the majority, in order to secure personal profit for themselves, without regard to the interests of the minority. They repudiate the suggestion of fraud, and plant themselves upon their rights as a majority to control the corporate interests according to their discretion. They err if they suppose that a court of equity will tolerate a discretion which does not consult the interests of the minority. It cannot be denied that minority stockholders are bound hand and foot

[3a] Flynn v. Bklyn. City R. R. Co., 158 N. Y. 493, 53 N. E. 520 (1899); Hinds v. Fishkill & M. Gas Co., 96 App. Div. 14, 88 N. Y. Supp. 954 (1st Dept. 1904). There is no "definition" of "fraud" beyond "the immemorial test of fair and conscientious dealing," see Shonfeld v. Shonfeld, 260 N. Y. 477, 184 N. E. 60 (1933).

[3b] Southern Pacific Co. v. Bogert, 250 U. S. 483, 39 Sup. Ct. 533 (1919); Jones v. Missouri-Edison Elec. Co., 144 Fed. 763 (C. C. A. 8th, 1906); Godley v. Crandall & Godley Co., 212 N. Y. 121, 105 N. E. 818 (1914); Colby v. Equitable Trust Co., 124 App. Div. 262, 108 N. Y. Supp. 978 (1st Dept. 1908), *aff'd.*, 192 N. Y. 535, 84 N. E. 1111 (1908), majority sustained; Outwater v. Public Service Corp., 103 N. J. Eq. 461, 143 Atl. 729 (1928), *aff'd.*, 104 N. J. Eq. 490, 146 Atl. 916 (1929); Windhurst v. Central Leather Co., 101 N. J. Eq. 543, 138 Atl. 772 (1927), *aff'd.*, 107 N. J. Eq. 528, 153 Atl. 402 (1931), majority sustained.

[4] 27 Fed. 625 (C. C. S. D. N. Y. 1886).

to the majority in all matters of legitimate administration of the corporate affairs; and the courts are powerless to redress many forms of oppression practiced upon the minority under the guise of legal sanction, which fall short of actual fraud. This is a consequence of the implied contract of association by which it is agreed, in advance, that a majority shall bind the whole body as to all transactions within the scope of the corporate powers. . . . When a number of stockholders combine to constitute themselves a majority in order to control the corporation as they see fit, they become for all practical purposes the corporation itself, and assume the trust relation occupied by the corporation towards its stockholders. . . . The corporation itself holds its property as a trust fund for the stockholders who have a joint interest in all its property and effects, and the relation between it and its several members is, for all practical purposes, that of trustee and *cestui que trust*." [5]

We have here the three major concepts which a court of equity must now reconcile and apply to the facts before it: (1) the majority are supreme in the management of the purely business affairs of the corporation; (2) the majority may not commit frauds; and (3) the minority are the beneficiaries of a trust.

[5] *Id.* at 630-631.

Madsen v. *Burns Bros.*[6] affords a good illustration of the application of the first of these concepts. In 1930, Burns Bros. sustained a loss of almost $1,400,000 and the owners of a small minority of its stock thereupon petitioned for the appointment of a receiver to the end that the corporation cease doing business.[7] The court dismissed the complaint, saying:

"Whether the business of a corporation should be operated at a loss during a business depression, or close down at a smaller loss, is a purely business and economic problem to be determined by the directors, and not by the court."[8]

[6] 108 N. J. Eq. 275, 155 Atl. 28 (1931).

[7] The petition was filed under Section 65 of the New Jersey Corporation Act which authorizes any stockholders owning at least 10% of the capital stock of a corporation to petition the court of chancery, which is given the power to enjoin the transaction of business and appoint a receiver if it is satisfied that the corporation's "business has been and is being conducted at a great loss and greatly prejudicial to the interests of its creditors or stockholders, so that its business cannot be conducted with safety to the public and advantage to the stockholders." Although the proceedings were statutory the remarks of the chancellor are couched in general equity phraseology.

[8] *Supra* note 6, at 279. The case also involved the propriety of a debt-funding operation. The court held that this too was a "business and economic" problem upon which "the judgment of the majority of the board of directors must prevail in the absence of fraud, *ultra vires*, illegality, or a showing of *mala fides* or abuse of power tantamount to fraud." The court found that the corporation was not insolvent and that the loss was not due to mismanagement. But it has been said that "losses resulting from ignorant or even foolish mismanagement cannot be recovered". Smith v. Chase & Baker Piano Mfg. Co., 197 Fed. 466, 471 (E. D. Mich. 1912). "Mere errors of judgment are not sufficient as grounds for equity interference". Leslie v. Lorillard, *supra* note 2. For other cases where courts

In a leading case[9] the same view was expressed as follows:

"It is not, however, every question of mere administration or policy in which there is a difference of opinion among the shareholders that enables the minority to claim that the action of the majority is oppressive, and which justifies the minority in coming to a court of equity to obtain relief. Generally, the rule must be that in such cases the will of the majority shall govern. The court would not be justified in interfering even in doubtful cases, where the action of the majority might be susceptible of different constructions. . . . Otherwise the court might be called upon to balance probabilities of profitable results to arise from the carrying out of the one or the other of the different plans proposed by or on behalf of different shareholders in a corporation and to decree the adoption of that line of policy which seemed to it to promise the best results, or at least to enjoin the carrying out of the opposite policy. This is no business of

refused to interfere on the ground that the questions involved were purely of business policy see Theis v. Spokane Falls Gas Light Co., 49 Wash. 477, 95 Pac. 1074 (1908) (expansion of corporation); Ellerman v. Chicago Junction Rys. Co., 49 N. J. Eq. 217, 23 Atl. 287 (1891) (acquisition of competing business); Matter of Hinds, Noble & Eldridge, 172 App. Div. 140, 158 N. Y. Supp. 249 (1916), affd. 218 N. Y. 715, 113 N. E. 1058 (1916) (change of name); Carter v. Spring Perch Co., 113 Conn. 636, 155 Atl. 832 (1931) (change of place of business and change in quality and price of product).

[9] Gamble v. Queens County Water Co., 123 N. Y. 91, 25 N. E. 201 (1890).

any court to follow.'' [10]

The practical justification for this yielding to the majority is found in the need for efficiency and expedition. The corporation must function. Better an erroneous decision than an interminable stalemate. The theoretical justification is found in the terms of the contract stated to exist between the stockholders and the corporation as embodied in the charter, by-laws, statutes and common-law. [11] Justification for the intervention of equity to prevent fraud [12] is obvious. [13] In *Flynn* v. *Brooklyn City Railroad Company,* the New York Court of Appeals said:

"To these general rules [that 'courts have

---

[10] *Id.* at 99.

[11] See Jones v. Missouri-Edison Electric Co., *supra* note 3b. Colby v. Equitable Trust Co., *supra* note 3b, at 266; COOK, CORPORATIONS (8th ed. 1923) §§ 493, 669. The propriety of treating the mere purchase of a stock certificate as the equivalent of intelligent consent to all the terms of the "contract" is outside our scope. See *supra,* p. 7.

[12] Equity "has ever refused to define [fraud] lest the craft of man evade the definition." Shonfeld v. Shonfeld, *supra* note 3a, at 479.

[13] Most of the cases involving charges of fraud involve interested directors or holding companies. These are among the major problems in corporation law today, but the limitations of space prevent any special treatment of them in this book. See SPELLMAN, CORPORATE DIRECTORS (1931) c. ix; Mound, *Suits Alleging Mismanagement of Subsidiaries by Holding Companies or Parent Companies,* published as an appendix to BONBRIGHT AND MEANS, THE HOLDING COMPANY (1932); BERLE, STUDIES IN THE LAW OF CORPORATE FINANCE (1928) c. viii; Bowman, *The Validity of Contracts Between Corporations Having Common Directors* (1906) 4 MICH. L. REV. 577; James, *Interested Directors in Corporate Transactions* (1931) 6 IND. L. J. 413; Note (1933) 81 U. OF PA. L. REV. 598.

nothing to do with the internal management of business corporations'], however, there are some exceptions, and the most important is that founded on fraud. While courts cannot compel directors or stockholders proceeding by the vote of a majority, to act wisely, they can compel them to act honestly, or undo their work if they act otherwise. Where a majority of the directors, or stockholders, or both, acting in bad faith, carry into effect a scheme which, even if lawful upon its face, is intended to circumvent the minority stockholders and defraud them out of their legal rights, the courts interfere and remedy the wrong." [14]

The application of the doctrines of trusts to corporations has undergone many changes, and the end is not yet. If a trust relationship is found, the jurisdiction of equity follows almost inevitably and the "breach of trust of one who occupies a fiduci-

[14] 158 N. Y. 493, 507-8, 53 N. E. 520, 524 (1899). The complaint in this case was dismissed because it failed sufficiently to allege a prior demand on the corporation to sue. In an earlier case, Barr v. N. Y. L. E. & W. R. R. Co., 96 N. Y. 444 (1884), the same court sustained a complaint by a minority stockholder of a lessor corporation against its lessee, to enforce payment of rent under the lease, which alleged that the lessee controlled the lessor. See also Steinfeld v. Copper State Min. Co., 37 Ariz. 151, 163, 290 Pac. 155, 160 (1930), where it is suggested that the majority owe to the minority the duty not only to exercise good faith but also to exercise "care and diligence." There is a conflict in the decisions as to the degree of care to which directors are held. See 2 THOMPSON, CORPORATIONS (3d ed. 1927) c. 50; Briggs v. Spaulding, 141 U. S. 132, 11 Sup. Ct. 924 (1891); Kavanaugh v. Commonwealth Trust Co., 223 N. Y. 103, 119 N. E. 237 (1918); People v. Mancuso, 255 N. Y. 463, 175 N. E. 177 (1931).

ary relation while in the exercise of a lawful power is as fatal in equity to the resultant act or contract as the absence of the power."[15] That the corporation itself is a trustee for the stockholders is well settled.[16] Nor is there any doubt that directors are "trustees" for the corporation.[17] Although it is sometimes stated that they are trustees "for the stockholders",[18] if this be taken to mean the several stockholders individually, the statement is not entirely correct.[19] However, the problems to be presented in this chapter involve primarily the relationship between the majority and the minority. Is it one of trust? At one extreme is complete denial of the notion that stockholders are trustees for each other.[20] This view has been vigorously asserted.

[15] Jones v. Missouri-Edison Electric Co., *supra* note 3b, at 771.

[16] Hyams v. Old Dominion Co., 113 Me. 294, 306, 93 Atl. 747, 752 (1915). Generally, when the word "trustee" is used in corporate litigation, it is used merely as a convenient abbreviation for describing a somewhat uncertain type of fiduciary, and not in its strictly technical sense.

[17] See 3 FLETCHER, Cyclopedia of Corporation (Perm. Ed. 1932), § 838. Because directors are not technical trustees even for the corporation, Shaw v. Davis, 78 Md. 308, 318, 28 Atl. 619, 622 (1894), they are permitted to profit personally in certain situations. See Stanton v. Schenck, 140 Misc. 621, 251 N. Y. Supp. 221 (1931).

[18] Jackson v. Ludeling, 88 U. S. 616 (1874).

[19] See Wilgus, *Purchase of Shares of Corporation by a Director from a Shareholder* (1910) 8 MICH. L. REV. 267; Laylin, *The Duty of a Director Purchasing Shares of Stock* (1918) 27 YALE L. J. 731; Smith, *Purchase of Shares of Corporation by a Director from a Shareholder* (1921) 19 MICH. L. REV. 698; Walker, *The Duty of Disclosure by a Director Purchasing Stock from His Stockholder* (1923) 32 YALE L. J. 637; Note (1925) 10 CORN. L. Q. 509; Mariash, *Fiduciary Relationship Between Director and Stockholder*, N. Y. L. J., Feb. 20, 1933, at 1022.

[20] Windmuller v. Standard Distilling & D. Co., 114 Fed. 491 (C. C.

"Whenever any action of either directors or stockholders is relied on in a suit by a minority stockholder for the purpose of invoking the interposition of a court of equity, if the act complained of be neither *ultra vires,* fraudulent, nor illegal, the court will refuse its intervention because powerless to grant it, and will leave all such matters to be disposed of by the majority of the stockholders in such manner as their interests may dictate, and their action will be binding on all, whether approved of by the minority or not. . . . The fact that the same persons hold the majority of the stock in both companies does not of itself enlarge the court's jurisdiction, the act complained of furnishes the test of jurisdiction, and it must be *ultra vires,* fraudulent or illegal; nothing short of this will suffice. . . . They [stockholders] are not trustees or quasi trustees for each other. . . . And if the proposed lease be not *ultra vires* or unlawful or fraudulent, no court, at the instance of a minority stockholder, or at the instance of anyone else, has the power or the right to restrain the majority from dealing with the property as they may deem most advantageous to their own interests. Any other doctrine would put it in the power of a single stockholder, owning but one

N. J. 1902); Shaw v. Davis, *supra* note 17; Niles v. N. Y. C. & H. R. R. Co., 69 App. Div. 144, 74 N. Y. Supp. 617 (1902), *affd.* 176 N. Y. 119, 68 N. E. 142 (1903); Gamble v. Queens C. W. Co., *supra* note 9. *Cf.* Yerrall, *The Extent to Which a Stockholder, as Such, is a Fiduciary in Massachusetts* (1931) 16 MASS. L. Q. (4) 59.

share out of many hundreds, to transfer the entire management of a corporation to a court of equity and would effectually destroy the right of the owners of the property lawfully to control it themselves. It would make a court of equity practically the guardian, so to speak, of such a corporation and would substitute the Chancellor's belief as to what contracts a corporation ought, as a matter of expediency, or policy, or business venture to make, instead of allowing such questions to be settled by the persons beneficially interested in the property.'' [21]

At the other extreme is the suggestion that ''all powers granted to a corporation or to the management of a corporation, or to any group within the corporation . . . are necessarily and at all times exercisable only for the ratable benefit of all shareholders as their interest appears [and] that, in consequence, the use of the power is subject to equitable limitation when the power has been exercised to the detriment of such interest, however absolute the grant of power may be in terms, and however correct the technical exercise of it may have been.'' [22] These attempts to subordinate corpora-

[21] Shaw v. Davis, *supra* note 17, at 316, 318, 328, 28 Atl. at 621, 622, 625.

[22] Berle, *Corporate Powers as Powers in Trust* (1931) 44 HARV. L. REV. 1049. See also Berle, *Non-Voting Stock and "Bankers' Control"* (1926) 39 HARV. L. REV. 673. There is current an extra-corporate "trust" notion which holds that business corporations have "a social service as well as a profit-making function" and specifically have

tion law into a mere phase of the law of trusts have, of course, not gone unchallenged. One criticizes the trustee theory as being in derogation of the contract nature of corporate enterprises.[23] Another on the grounds of corporate efficiency and the lack of sufficient business knowledge and experience on the part of courts.[24] The courts have chosen a middle-course, holding that majority stockholders who do *in fact* control occupy a fiduciary relation to the minority,[25] but that such trust relationship does not arise from the mere power to elect directors by virtue of majority stock ownership.[26] The distinction has been well put in *Robotham* v. *Prudential Ins. Co.*:

fiduciary obligations to their employees, customers and to the general public. See Dodd, *For Whom are Corporate Managers Trustees?* (1932) 45 Harv. L. Rev. 1145. *Cf.* Berle, *For Whom Corporate Managers are Trustees* (1932) 45 Harv. L. Rev. 1365.

[23] Swaine, Book Review (1929) 38 Yale L. J. 1003.

[24] Kline, Book Review (1929) 42 Harv. L. Rev. 714. Mr. Kline also suggests that "any movement to increase the power of stockholders as such runs counter to the historical evolution of corporations." Modern stockholders want dividends—not control! See also *supra*, p. 46, note 70.

[25] Meeker v. Winthrop Iron Co., 17 Fed. 48, (C. C. W. D. Mich. 1883); Farmers' Loan & Trust Co. v. N. Y. & N. R. Co., 150 N. Y. 410, 430, 44 N. E. 1043, 1048 (1896); Jones v. Missouri-Edison Elec. Co., *supra* note 3b, at 771; Kidd v. New Hampshire Traction Co., 74 N. H. 160, 178, 66 Atl. 127, 136 (1907). If the fact of control be there, the technique or manner of its exercise is of no importance. Southern Pacific Co. v. Bogert, *supra* note 3b, at 492. A minority may occupy the position of trustee if it in fact controls (for instance, with the aid of proxies). Hyams v. Calumet & Hecla Mining Co., 221 Fed. 529, 541 (C. C. A. 6th, 1915).

[26] Wood, *The Status of Management Stockholders* (1928) 38 Yale L. J. 57. In Wheeler v. Abilene Natl. Bank Bldg. Co., 159 Fed. 391 (C. C. A. 8th, 1908), the court said, at 393-4: "The holder of the majority of the stock of a corporation has the power, by the election

"Authorities have been cited to support the proposition that an individual or a corporation holding a majority of the capital stock of another corporation sustains, by reason of such holding a fiduciary relation to the minority stockholders. But these authorities only hold, in effect, that the fiduciary relation arises when the majority stockholder assumes control of the corporation and dictates the action of the directors. The majority stockholder is not made a trustee for the minority stockholders in any sense by the mere fact that he holds a majority of the stock, or by the further fact that he uses the voting power of his stock to elect a board of directors for the corporation. The majority stockholder does not necessarily control the directors whom he appoints, and, in fact, he has no right to control them, and if they are controlled by him, they may be violating their duty, for which he also may be liable. . . . No liability of the majority stockholder to the minority stockholder for

of biddable directors and by the vote of his stock to do everything that the corporation can do. His power to control and direct places him in its shoes, and constitutes him the actual, if not the technical trustee for the holders of the minority of the stock." But in that case the majority of the stock was owned by one person who was also a director and president of the corporation. See also Tefft v. Schaeffer, 148 Wash. 602, 269 Pac. 1048 (1928) ; Harrison v. Thomas, 112 Fed. 22 (C. C. A. 5th, 1901) ; Hiscock v. Lacy, 9 Misc. 578, 590, 30 N. Y. Supp. 860, 868 (1894). The UNIFORM BUSINESS CORPORATION ACT, 9 U. L. A. (1932), approved by the American Bar Association in (1928) 53 A. B. A. R. 92, provides, in § 28 II, that holders of voting stock "stand in a fiduciary relation to the entire body of shareholders" if there be non-voting stock. See also *supra* p. 53, note 93.

the misdeeds of his common trustees—the directors—can arise from the mere fact that the majority stockholder had the power to appoint, or, in fact, did appoint, these trustees. Such liability, however, may arise if the majority stockholder has made the derelict trustees his agents and dictated their conduct and thus caused a breach of fiduciary duty." [27]

The courts have also imposed the obligations of trustees upon stockholders when acting under statutory power to make a corporate decision,[27a] and in favor of the holders of non-voting securities.[27b] Since courts of equity will concededly restrain fraudulent conduct on the part of those in control of a corporation, the question of whether or not they should be deemed trustees may seem at first impression inconsequential. The answer to the question has, however, serious practical consequences. Cases of so-called "actual fraud" are not frequent and when they do arise, they should not be difficult of solution. In close cases the decision may well depend upon whether the court approaches the facts from the point of view that the defendants are trustees for the plaintiffs. If it does, it will judge their conduct by "the punctilio

[27] 64 N. J. Eq. 673, 689-690, 53 Atl. 842, 848 (1903).

[27a] Kavanaugh v. Kavanaugh Knitting Co., 226 N. Y. 185, 123 N. E. 148 (1919) dissolution; *contra:* Windmuller v. Standard D. & D. Co., *supra* note 20. Jones v. Missouri-Edison Electric Co., *supra* note 3b, consolidation; Wheeler v. Abilene Natl. Bank Bldg. Co., *supra* note 26, sale of assets.

[27b] *Supra* p. 53, note 93.

of an honor the most sensitive" instead of merely by "the morals of the market place." [28] If the defendants be trustees the burden of justifying their conduct is upon them.[29]

Having made our obeisance to principles we can proceed with an examination of typical fact-situations which have confronted the courts in applying them.

Dividends,[30] *salaries, etc.*

Since the primary desire of stockholders is to

[28] "A trustee is held to something stricter than the morals of the market place. Not honesty alone, but the punctilio of an honor the most sensitive, is then the standard of behavior", Cardozo, C. J., in Meinhard v. Salmon, 249 N. Y. 458, 464, 164 N. E. 545, 546 (1928). It has been asserted that law does, and should, lag behind ethics. Swaine, *supra* note 23.

[29] Geddes v. Anaconda Mining Co., 254 U. S. 590, 41 Sup. Ct. 209 (1921); Ross v. Quinnesec Iron Mining Co., 227 Fed. 337 (C. C. A. 6th, 1915); Hyams v. Calumet & Hecla Mining Co., *supra* note 25, at 540; Harrison v. Thomas, *supra* note 26, at 29; Booth v. Land Filling & Imp. Co., 68 N. J. Eq. 536, 59 Atl. 767 (1905); Sage v. Culver, 147 N. Y. 241, 247, 41 N. E. 513, 514 (1895). *Cf.* Wentz v. Scott, 10 F. (2d) 426 (C. C. A. 6th, 1926).

[30] See Wormser, *May the Courts Compel the Declaration of a Corporate Dividend* (1918) 3 So. L. Q. 281, reprinted in *The Disregard of the Corporate Fiction and Allied Corporation Problems* (1929). For collection of cases, see 11 FLETCHER, *op. cit. supra* note 17, §§ 5325-5327. We shall here deal only with the rights of common stockholders. The holders of preferred stock are on a somewhat different footing, their rights being primarily governed by the contract embodied in the charter. See Wabash Ry. Co. v. Barclay, 280 U. S. 197, 50 Sup. Ct. 106 (1930); Cratty v. Peoria Law Lib. Ass'n, 219 Ill. 516, 76 N. E. 709 (1906); Scott v. Baltimore & Ohio R. R. Co., 93 Md. 475, 49 Atl. 327 (1901); N. Y. L. E. & W. R. R. v. Nickals, 119 U. S. 296, 7 Sup. Ct. 209 (1886); Boardman v. Lake Shore & M. So. Ry., 84 N. Y. 157 (1881); Storrow v. Texas Cons. Co. *etc.* Ass'n, 87 Fed. 612 (C. C. A. 5th, 1898); Hastings v. Inter-

receive dividends, it is readily understandable why the resort to the courts to obtain them is so frequent. At the same time it is in this field, which is essentially entirely one of business policy, that the power of the directors comes closest to being absolute.

The earliest cases took the view that the courts were powerless to interfere,[31] except, of course, in cases of fraud.[32] The unwillingness to interfere persists,[33] tempered by the view that equity should act where there is a clearly "improper" refusal to

national Paper Co., 187 App. Div. 404, 175 N. Y. Supp. 815 (1919); Pardee v. Harwood Elec. Co., 262 Pa. 68, 105 Atl. 48 (1918); Berle, *op. cit. supra* note 13, c. v. and vi; Berle, *supra* note 22, at 1060; Note (1932) 45 HARV. L. REV. 1374-1376. As to rights of policyholders in mutual life insurance companies, see Russell v. Washington Life Ins. Co., 62 Misc. 403, 115 N. Y. Supp. 950 (1909).

[31] State v. Bank, 6 La. 745 (1834); Williams v. Western Union Tel. Co., 93 N. Y. 162, 192 (1883); McNab v. McNab & Harlin Mfg. Co., 62 Hun 18, 16 N. Y. Supp. 448 (1891), *aff'd.* 133 N. Y. 687, 31 N. E. 627 (1892).

[32] Anderson v. W. J. Dyer & Bros., 94 Minn. 30, 101 N. W. 1061 (1904); Burden v. Burden, 159 N. Y. 287, 308, 54 N. E. 17, 23 (1899). Of course, in order to obtain dividends it must appear that there is an available surplus. See Liebman v. Auto Strop Co., 241 N. Y. 427, 150 N. E. 505 (1926) (involving the distribution of stock in another corporation as a dividend). But the mere showing of a large available surplus is not, *per se,* sufficient to move a court to intervene. Burden v. Burden, *supra;* Trimble v. Amer. Sugar Ref. Co., 61 N. J. Eq. 340, 48 Atl. 912 (1901). *Cf.* Griffing v. A. A. Griffing Iron Co., 61 N. J. Eq. 269, 48 Atl. 910 (1901). As a condition precedent to relief from the courts the complaining stockholder must also show that he has exhausted his remedies within the corporation. Wilson v. American Ice Co., 206 Fed. 736 (D. N. J. 1913).

[33] Marks v. American Brewing Co., 126 La. 666, 52 So. 983 (1910); Miller v. Crown Perfumery Co., 125 App. Div. 881, 110 N. Y. Supp. 806 (1908); Hlawati v. Maeder-Hlawati Co., 289 Pa. 233, 137 Atl. 235 (1927).

declare dividends.[34] One of the earliest cases
wherein a court compelled the declaration of a dividend is *Hiscock* v. *Lacy*.[38]

The corporation there involved was a national
bank whose capital was represented by 4,000 shares
of which the defendant owned a majority and the
plaintiff 1,243. For years the bank had paid regular
dividends of 8 to 10 per cent. In 1887 some differences arose between the plaintiff and the defendant and the plaintiff caused certain corporate action to be taken which was highly disagreeable to
the defendant. Chagrined, the defendant quietly
accumulated stock until in 1889 he owned a majority thereof and proceeded to elect a board of
directors of his own choosing, and to remove the
plaintiff entirely from the management of the
bank. The directors whom he elected were either
relatives, nominees, or the owners of an insignifi-
cant number of shares. In the aggregate the entire
board, exclusive of the defendant, did not own more
than 200 shares. They immediately adopted defendant's announced policy not to declare dividends.
The salaries of defendant's friends were increased,
so that the expenses of the bank were doubled.
There was no ready market for the stock and the
defendant was unwilling either to sell his stock or
buy more. Admittedly, the bank was able to pay
dividends. It had a surplus equal to 50 per cent. of
its capital, which was more than it had been during

[34] Stevens v. U. S. Steel Corp., 68 N. J. Eq. 373, 377, 59 Atl. 905,
907 (1905).
[38] *Supra* note 26.

the years when dividends were paid. Under these circumstances the court found that the refusal to declare dividends was "without reasonable cause and in bad faith for the purpose of punishing the minority interest" and that although the defendant was not guilty of "intentional fraud" the plaintiff was entitled to redress. A dividend of not less than 12 per cent. was ordered.[39]

Probably the most famous dividend case is that which involved the Ford Motor Company, before Henry Ford bought out the minority.[40]

The Ford Motor Company was organized in 1903 with an initial capital of $100,000, representing $49,000 in cash and $51,000 in property. Stock was issued to Henry Ford, the Dodge brothers, James Couzens and several others. By 1908, without further investment by the stockholders, its capital stock was increased to $2,000,000. In addition to regular monthly dividends of 5 per cent., the company paid special dividends which for the years 1911-1915 aggregated $41,000,000. Despite these dividends, the corporate surplus in 1916 was almost $112,000,000, of which almost $54,000,000 was in

[39] For similar cases see Crichton v. Webb Press Co., 113 La. 167, 30 So. 926 (1904); Channon v. H. Channon Co., 218 Ill. App. 397 (1920) (motive for non-dividend policy in family quarrel. Dividend ordered.). Cf. City Bank Farmers Trust Co. v. Hewitt Realty Co., 257 N. Y. 62, 177 N. E. 309 (1931), where the court refused to order a dividend, finding justifiable business reasons for non-declaration notwithstanding family quarrel.

[40] Dodge v. Ford Motor Co., 204 Mich. 459, 170 N. W. 668 (1919). Of course, this case is hardly "typical" but, since the courts have generally declined to intervene except in special circumstances, it seems preferable to consider in detail cases where the court did act rather than the many where it did not.

cash. For the year ending July 31, 1916 the profits were almost $60,000,000. At this time Henry Ford owned 58 per cent. of the capital stock of the company and controlled its policies. He announced that since all the stockholders had received back in dividends more than they had invested, no further special dividends would be paid but that all earnings, above the regular dividend of 5 per cent. per month, would be put back into the business for the purpose of extending the business and employing more men at better wages. He also adhered to the policy of reducing the sales price of the cars so that from an original price of $900, the sales price in August 1916 was $360. In furtherance of Henry Ford's expansion program, the company undertook the purchase of iron mines and ships, the building of steel foundries and the now well-known River Rouge plant. No special dividend having been paid since October 1915, the plaintiffs, owning about 10 per cent. of the capital stock, protested and receiving no satisfaction, brought suit to enjoin the expansion program and to compel the distribution of 75 per cent. of the cash surplus to stockholders. Mr. Ford's testimony confirmed the view that he was being motivated in his policies by "certain sentiments, philanthropic and altruistic, creditable to Mr. Ford" or, as the plaintiffs charged, he proposed to run the corporation as a "semi-eleemosynary institution and not as a business institution". The trial court enjoined the expansion program and decreed the declaration of a dividend equal to 50 per cent. of the cash surplus. On appeal the injunction as to the expansion program was reversed because "the experience of the Ford Motor Company is evidence of capable management" and "judges are not business experts" but the decree as to dividends was affirmed. In justification, the court said:

"The difference between an incidental humanitarian expenditure of corporate funds for the benefit of the employees, like the building of a hospital for their use and the employment of agencies for the betterment of their condition, and a general purpose and plan to benefit mankind at the expense of others, is obvious. . . . A business corporation is organized and carried on primarily for the profit of the stockholders. . . . There is committed to the discretion of directors, a discretion to be exercised in good faith, the infinite details of business, including the wages which shall be paid to employees, the number of hours they shall work, the conditions under which labor shall be carried on, and the prices for which products shall be offered to the public. . . . It is not within the lawful powers of a board of directors to shape and conduct the affairs of a corporation for the merely incidental benefit of shareholders and for the primary purpose of benefiting others." [41]

[41] 204 Mich. at 506-507, 170 N. W. at 684. See Dodd, *supra* note 22; Note (1919) 3 A. L. R. 443. As to the right to sell products below cost see Matter of Pierson, 44 App. Div. 215, 60 N. Y. Supp. 671 (1899) ; Trimble v. American Sugar Ref. Co., *supra* note 32.

It is most unusual to find corporate managers diverting funds to social purposes rather than pay dividends, but it is not infrequent that corporate funds are paid out as "salaries" rather than to minority stockholders as dividends.[41a] Most of the cases involving salary questions turn on the self-interest of the directors who voted them [42] but some go further.

Salaries paid to officers must bear some reasonable relation to the value of their services.[43] But courts will not review salaries voted by the board unless they are so clearly excessive as to amount to a fraud upon the corporation.[43a]

In *Godley* v. *Crandall & Godley Co.*,[44] it appeared that a closely owned corporation was paying to its directors and certain other employee-stockholders 9 per cent. on their capital stock in addition to dividends of 6 per cent. received by all stockholders. At the suit of a minority stockholder recovery of this 9 per cent. was had notwithstanding the fact that it had been denominated by the directors as "additional salaries" and its payment

[41a] Obvious forms of discrimination in dividends among stockholders of the same class are of course prohibited, see, (Annotation 1928) 55 A. L. R. 8, 65. See, Payne, *supra* p. 5, note 16.

[42] See SPELLMAN, *op. cit. supra* note 13; Annotation (1923) 27 A. L. R. 300. In Tefft v. Schaeffer, *supra* note 26, an unsuccessful attempt was made to apply the rule against a director voting salary to himself to a director voting salary to a majority stockholder when he, the director, owned only one share. *Cf. Harrison* v. *Thomas, supra* note 26, Hiscock v. Lacy, *supra* note 26.

[43] Rogers v. Hill, 289 U. S. 582, 53 S. Ct. 731 — L. Ed. — (1933).

[43a] Bates Street Shirt Co. v. Waite, 130 Me. 352, 156 Atl. 293 (1931).

[44] *Supra* note 3b.

ratified by the defendants in their capacity of majority stockholders.[45]

In *Heublin* v. *Wight*,[46] the court undertook to pass in detail upon salaries paid. It recognized the validity of the general principle that courts would not review salary action taken by the majority however "unwise or mistaken" they considered it but held it inapplicable to a case where the majority stockholders were the very ones to receive the salaries in question.[46a] The court considered, among other things, the annual profits of the corporation, the contributions of capital made by the stockholders and the returns received by them thereon, the work done by the defendants and by other employees, the salaries of other employees and prior salaries of the defendants. The court fixed a salary for each of the defendants and on appeal[47] the decree was affirmed. In response to

[45] See Scott v. Lorillard Co., 108 N. J. Eq. 153, 154 Atl. 515 (1931), *affd.* 109 N. J. Eq. 417, 157 Atl. 388 (1931).

[46] 227 Fed. 667 (D. Md. 1915). See also Backus v. Finkelstein, 23 F. (2d) 531, 536-7 (D. Minn. 1924). In the further course of that litigation it was held that the defendants had forfeited all right to compensation by acts in breach of trust. 23 F. (2d) 360-361 (D. Minn. 1927). *Cf.* Jacobson v. Brooklyn Trust Co., 184 N. Y. 152, 161-2, 76 N. E. 1075, 1078 (1906), where the court refused to give consideration to the prosperity of the corporation. See also Kreitner v. Burgweger, 174 App. Div. 48, 160 N. Y. S. 256 (1916) to the effect that officers may not increase their own salaries merely because of increasing prosperity.

[46a] See also, Lillard v. Oil, Paint & Drug Co., 70 N. J. Eq. 197, 56 Atl. 254, 58 Atl. 188 (1905); Carr v. Kimball, 153 App. Div. 825, 139 N. Y. Supp. 253, *affd.* 215 N. Y. 634, 109 N. E. 1068 (1915); Schall v. Althaus, 208 App. Div. 103, 203 N. Y. Supp. 36 (1924).

[47] 238 Fed. 321 (C. C. A. 4th, 1916).

appellants' contention that even if the salaries were excessive the court could only order their return and not fix future salaries by "perpetual injunction", the court "assumed that the decree is based on and has application only to existing conditions [and that] if those conditions should undergo material change, so that large earnings were realized under efficient and capable management, the payment of proper and reasonable salaries though greater than the amounts fixed by the decree would not be prohibited by the injunction now in force".

New stock issues, sale of unissued stock, etc.

The most general equitable limitation upon the power of directors to issue new stock is found in the doctrine of pre-emptive rights.[48] The exceptions which have been grafted on the doctrine and the radical differences between the corporations of today with their complicated financial and voting set-ups and the corporations of 1807 when the doctrine was first enunciated [49] have induced a trend away from arbitrary rules towards the view that the rights of stockholders should be measured by considerations of fairness in each case rather than by dogma.[50] In view of this tendency and the prev-

---

[48] See Morawetz, *Preemptive Right of Shareholders* (1928) 42 HARV. L. REV. 186; Frey, *Shareholders' Preemptive Rights* (1929) 38 YALE L. J. 563; Drinker, *The Preemptive Right of Shareholders to Subscribe to New Shares* (1930) 43 HARV. L. REV. 586; Berle, *supra* note 22, at 1050-1060.

[49] Gray v. Portland Bank, 3 Mass. 363 (1807).

[50] See Hammer v. Werner, 239 App. Div. 38, 265 N. Y. S. 172 (1933).

alent practice of stipulating against pre-emptive rights in certificates of incorporation, we shall here confine our discussion to a few cases that passed on the facts involved from the point of view of equity rather than the rules of pre-emptive rights.

In *Luther* v. *C. J. Luther Co.*,[51] the board of directors voted to sell thirty-nine shares of unissued original stock to the individual defendants, who at the time controlled the board, in spite of the fact that a majority of the outstanding stock was owned by the plaintiffs. The result of the sale was to vest a majority of the authorized stock in the defendants. The board determined, in the opinion of the trial court "honestly", that control of the corporation in the plaintiffs would be dangerous to the corporation and against its best business interests. The appellate court treated the stock as "mere property over which the powers of the directors are the same as over any other assets of the corporation" and therefore not subject to pre-emptive rights, but held nevertheless that the sale, its purpose being to take control from one faction and give it to another, was in breach of the duty of the directors not "to dispose of or manage property of the corporation to the end and for the purpose of giving to one part of their *cestuis que trustent* a benefit and advantage over, or at the expense of, another part". The stock was ordered

---

[51] 118 Wis. 112, 94 N. W. 69 (1903). See also Elliott v. Baker, 194 Mass. 518, 80 N. E. 450 (1907). The court there suggests that when there is a contest for control the directors should take advantage of the fact to get higher prices for unissued stock.

returned to the corporation against repayment of the sale price.

In a recent New York case [52] the court was guided by the same principles but reached an opposite result because of the presence of other factors. The corporation had seventy-six unissued shares and its board voted fifty thereof to one Graham at par in payment of a debt due him and the remaining twenty-six shares to one Ageno, a director, for cash, which it used to pay another debt. No opportunity was given to any other stockholder to subscribe. Graham thereafter transferred his shares to Ageno's sister, who was also a director. As a result, Ageno's faction had control of the corporation. The plaintiffs, minority stockholders, sued to compel return of the stock and to restrain the voting thereof. The trial court found that the issue was in good faith to satisfy debts rather than to shift control. In support of this conclusion it was noted that at the time of their issuance there was no active contest for control, that the stock was sold for full value, and that the twenty-six shares issued to Ageno did not carry control. On appeal the Court of Appeals stated that even when no preemptive right exists "directors may not authorize the issue of unissued stock to themselves for the primary purpose of converting them from minority to majority stockholders",[53] but affirmed the

[52] Dunlay v. Avenue M. Garage & R. Co., 253 N. Y. 274, 170 N. E. 917 (1930). *Cf.* Essex v. Essex, 141 Mich. 200, 104 N. W. 622 (1905).

[53] For an application of this dicta see Hammer v. Werner, *supra* note 50.

lower court's dismissal of the complaint on the ground that, on the findings of the trial court, there was no "breach of trust" and that minority stockholders may not in the absence thereof interfere in questions of business management.

The directors of the International Silver Company, who owned preferred stock but no common stock, proposed to issue common stock at $50 a share to both preferred and common stockholders on the same basis. Because there were more shares of preferred than common then outstanding, most of the new stock would go to the holders of preferred stock. By the certificate of incorporation of the company, the preferred stock was entitled on dissolution only to par and the common stock was entitled to the remainder. At the time of the proposed issuance the company had a large surplus. On the application of common stockholders, the court held the result would be unjust to the common stockholders and granted a preliminary injunction restraining the issue.[54]

The subsequent history of this stock issue is of interest. After the granting of the preliminary injunction against the directors' original plan, it having been contended by plaintiffs that the common stock was worth very much more than $50 a share, the directors proposed to sell the stock to the highest bidder. A preliminary injunction to restrain this was denied.[55] The court took the view

[54] Borg v. International Silver Co., 2 F. (2d) 910 (S. D. N. Y. 1924).
[55] Borg v. International Silver Co., 11 F. (2d) 143 (S. D. N. Y. 1925), *affd.* 11 F. (2d) 147 (C. C. A. 2d, 1925).

that the method proposed was proper to realize full value for the shares (indicating, however, that the directors would not be permitted to turn to their own advantage information not available to other bidders) and that therefore it ought not to interfere with the board's discretion as to method or even on the question whether there was any need for selling the stock merely because the board's motives might be suspect.

Even under the broadest powers in the directors as to the consideration for which they may issue stock, a court of equity will intervene when the consideration fixed is unfair to existing stockholders.[56] Thus, there may not be unfair discrimination between different classes of stockholders as to the prices at which they may purchase the same kind of stock unless such difference in price is justified by business reasons.[57]

"While an arbitrary sale of the same issue of stock at different prices to different persons [even non-stockholders] would not be sanctioned, such differential sales will be sustained

[56] Bodell v. General Gas & Elec. Corp., 15 Del. Ch. 119, 132 Atl. 442 (1926), *affd.* 15 Del. Ch. 420, 140 Atl. 264 (1927); Atlantic Refining Co. v. Hodgman, 13 F. (2d) 781 (C. C. A. 3d, 1926), *revg.* 300 Fed. 590 (D. Del. 1924).

[57] Bodell v. General Gas & Elec. Corp., *supra* note 56. The court refused to interfere with the action of the board, finding that the financial justification offered by the directors for selling stock to different classes of existing stockholders at different prices was not "unwarranted and unfair", and that the directors acted "for what they believed to be the advantage of the corporation and all its stockholders."

if based on business and commercial facts, which in the exercise of fair business judgment, lead directors to follow such a course."[58]

The result of the foregoing cases seems to be that, in addition to the limitations imposed by the doctrine of pre-emptive right, directors may not exercise their power to issue new stock or sell treasury stock

(a) for the purpose of shifting control of the corporation; but courts will not intervene where the change of control is merely an incidental result of the issue which was made in good faith for business reasons;
(b) except at fair prices;
(c) so as to modify unfairly the existing relative rights of different classes of stockholders in the corporate property;
(d) at different prices to different persons unless justified by business reasons.

Purchase of stock; its own and that of other corporations.

The first problem in connection with the right of a corporation to purchase its own stock is one of *power,* but with that we are not here concerned.[59] Assuming the existence of the power, what are the limitations upon its exercise?[60] The cases involv-

[58] Atlantic Ref. Co. v. Hodgman, *supra* note 56, at 788. Here too the action of the board was not disturbed.

[59] See Wormser, *The Power of a Corporation to Acquire Its Own Stock* (1915) 24 YALE L. J. 177. Cases are collected in 5 THOMPSON, CORPORATIONS (3d ed. 1927) §§ 4081-2.

[60] See Levy, *Purchase by a Corporation of Its Own Stock* (1930)

ing solvent corporations and therefore excluding questions of creditors' rights and of the right to purchase except out of surplus are few.[61] Where fraud appears, the purchase will be enjoined.[62] On the other hand, where the action is taken in good faith to aid the corporation, the purchase will be sustained.[63] Assuming the absence of fraud, there is no need to permit all stockholders to sell merely because the privilege is given to one.[64] But funds

15 MINN. L. R. 1, for discussion of this question from standpoint of creditors as well as of dissenting stockholders. Mr. Levy concludes that the legitimate objects of re-purchase can be achieved in other ways, that the power is subject to abuse, that the resort to equity is an inadequate remedy, and that the power should be denied by statute. The writer does not concur in this conclusion. The New York Stock Exchange requires that investment trusts do not purchase their own common stocks except "under exceptional and special circumstances". The object is the prevention of trading in the companies own stock. "The employment of corporate funds to speculate in the stock of the company to which the funds belong is not a practice to be encouraged." Coleman v. Columbia Oil Co., 51 Pa. 74 (1865). But special circumstances may justify this, see Hammer v. Werner, *supra* note 50; Berle, *Liability for Stock Market Manipulation* (1931) 31 Columbia L. R. 264, 277–8.

[61] For discussions of the rights of stockholders among themselves when the purchase is not out of surplus, see Graselli Chemical Co. v. Aetna Explosives Co., 258 Fed. 66 (S. D. N. Y. 1918); Barrett v. Webster Lumber Co., 275 Mass. 302, 175 N. E. 765 (1931). Purchases except out of surplus are in some jurisdictions prohibited by statute. See N. Y. PENAL LAW (1909) § 664. For rights of creditors, see *infra* pp. 177–178.

[62] Lowe v. Pioneer Threshing Co., 70 Fed. 646 (C. C. D. Minn. 1895). This is so even if the action be taken under the guise of capital reduction proceedings. Theis v. Durr, 125 Wis. 651, 104 N. W. 985 (1905).

[63] Ruffner v. Sophie Mae Candy Corp., 35 Ga. App. 114, 132 S. E. 396 (1926); Copper Belle Mining Co. v. Costello, 11 Ariz. 334, 95 Pac. 94 (1908); Gilchrist v. Highfield, 140 Wis. 476, 123 N. W. 102 (1909).

[64] Wisconsin Lumber Co. v. Telephone Co., 127 Iowa 350, 101

properly ascribable to one class of stock. *e. g.*, accrued dividends, may not be used to retire stock of another class.[65]

The terminology of the opinions in cases involving the purchase of stock of other corporations is such that any attempt to segregate rigidly the problem of power from that of the abuse thereof is difficult. The courts seem to say that when the object or purpose of the purchase is proper the corporation has the power to make it but that when the end is improper the purchase is *ultra vires*. It would perhaps be simpler, and certainly more consistent with present day charters and practice, to recognize freely that corporations have the *power* to purchase stock in other corporations, but that its exercise will be restrained if abused to the injury of one entitled to complain. A traditional standard for judging the propriety of a stock purchase was

N. W. 742 (1904). See also Barrett v. W. A. Webster Co., *supra* note 61. Indeed this is implicit in all the cases (except those based on unanimous consent) sustaining purchases by corporations of their own stock. *Cf.* Berger v. United States Steel Corp., 63 N. J. Eq. 809, 53 Atl. 68 (1902). See also General Investment Co. v. American Hide & Leather Co., 98 N. J. Eq. 326, 129 Atl. 244 (1925), to the effect that under the New Jersey statute a corporation buying stock for *retirement* must purchase ratably from all stockholders. Shares of stock are not retired by mere purchase. 5 THOMPSON, CORPORATIONS (3d ed. 1927) § 4084. Capital reductions must in the absence of a contrary statute be effected ratably among all stockholders. See Note (1926) 44 A. L. R. 35. A mere purchase of its own stock by a corporation is not a capital reduction, *In re* Atlantic Printing Co., 60 F. (2d) 553 (D. C. Mass. 1932). But a corporation's capital may not be distributed among its stockholders except by way of a capital reduction pursuant to statute, Stevens v. Olus Mfg. Co., 72 Misc. 508, 130 N. Y. S. 22, *aff'd.* 146 App. Div. 951 (1911).

[65] General Inv. Co. v. American Hide & Leather Co., *supra* note 64.

whether or not it would aid the authorized business of the corporation, but with the present-day use of multi-power clauses in charters and the interdependence of business its sufficiency is rapidly passing.[66] An older case which discussed the subject in terms of *ultra vires* but which actually applied equitable criteria to a stock purchase is *Robotham* v. *Prudential Insurance Company.*[67] The insurance company was authorized to purchase stock in other corporations for "investment". The directors sought to purchase a majority of the stock of a trust company under an arrangement whereby the trust company would simultaneously acquire stock control of the insurance company. The result would be that the board of the insurance company, by virtue of their power to vote the trust company's stock, would become self-perpetuating. The court found that the "control" feature rather than the "investment" element was uppermost in the minds of the directors and, at the suit of a minority stockholder of the insurance company, enjoined the purchase.[68] While the court referred to the high price being paid for the stock and its low yield, it is reasonable to assume that if the "control" scheme were absent the court would have refused to interfere with the action of the board in the exercise of its business judgment. This is exactly what a court

[66] For collection of cases on power of corporations to purchase and hold stock, see 5 THOMPSON, CORPORATIONS (3d ed. 1927) §§ 4063-4077.

[67] *Supra* note 27.

[68] To like effect, Anglo-American Land M. & N. Co. v. Lombard, 132 Fed. 721 (C. C. A. 8th, 1904).

of the same state did in the case of one corporation purchasing the stock of a competing company.[69]

Amendment of by-laws.

A court will, of course, refuse to interfere with the adoption by the majority of a by-law dealing with ordinary administrative or business matters.[70] On the other hand, where it is clear that action under the proposed by-law would necessarily be improper a court may enjoin its adoption. Thus stockholders were enjoined from voting upon an amendment to the by-laws of the corporation so as to provide for extra dividends to stockholders who were also employees, notwithstanding the assertion that the proposed plan was merely one fixing extra compensation to employees.[71]

An early leading case laid down the principle that "vested rights" may not be taken from minority stockholders without their consent by by-law amendments.[72] In that case the capitalization of the corporation was fixed by the by-laws which provided for their amendment by the majority of the stockholders. Originally there was only one

---

[69] Ellerman v. Chicago Junction Rys. *etc.* Co., *supra* note 8. But it was later charged by another minority stockholder that the Ellerman suit was collusive. The charge was not sustained. Willoughby v. Chicago Junction Ry. Co., 50 N. J. Eq. 656, 669-676, 25 Atl. 277, 282-284 (1892).

[70] Burden v. Burden, *supra* note 32 (by-law giving extensive powers to general manager).

[71] Scott v. P. Lorillard Co., *supra* note 45. *Cf.* Rogers v. Hill, *supra* note 43.

[72] Kent v. Quicksilver Mining Co., 78 N. Y. 159 (1879).

class of stock and the court held [73] that a second class, preferred as to dividends, could not be created, even though offered to all stockholders upon the same terms, without unanimous consent.[74]

Amendment of Charters.[75]

We shall here not consider involuntary amendments imposed upon the corporation by the legislature[76] but only those voluntarily adopted by the majority[77] and shall assume that the power of amendment has been expressly reserved.[78] Under such circumstances the only limitation which seems to have as yet received judicial sanction is that "vested rights" may not be destroyed.[79] A claim to

[73] By way of *dicta;* the decision was against the plaintiffs because of their laches, acquiescence, *etc.*

[74] The ruling was overcome by legislation permitting the creation of preferred stock by a two-thirds vote of stockholders. See Dresser v. Donner Steel Co., 247 N. Y. 553, 556-7, 161 N. E. 179, 180 (1928). The subject is now considered in connection with the amendment of charters rather than of by-laws, *infra.*

[75] See Dodd, *Dissenting Stockholders and Amendments to Corporate Charters* (1927) 75 U. OF PA. L. REV. 585, 723; Cades, *Constitutional and Equitable Limitation on the Power of the Majority to Amend Charters* (1928) 77 U. OF PA. L. REV. 256.

[76] *Supra* pp. 13–15.

[77] Throughout this book we use the word "majority" to signify the percentage sufficient under the governing law to adopt a course of conduct, it may be 51%, 67% or 75%.

[78] Nor shall we treat the right of a dissenting minority to compel the corporation to buy their stock at appraised values under statutes. See Levy, *Rights of Dissenting Shareholders to Appraisal and Payment* (1930) 15 CORN. L. Q. 420; Robinson, *Dissenting Shareholders: Their Rights to Dividends and the Valuation of Their Shares* (1932) 32 COL. L. REV. 60; *infra* note 88.

[79] *Re* the rule against "fundamental" amendments except by unanimous consent, see *supra* p. 14.

accumulated dividends is such a "vested right" that may not be wiped out by charter amendment.[80] But a change in future dividend rights has been held valid.[81] Thus in *Davis* v. *Louisville Gas & Electric Co.*[82] the court refused to interfere with the adoption of an amendment altering the dividend rights of the Class B stock and depriving it of other "material rights", and justified its position by accepting the view of the majority, *acting in "good faith"*, that the best interests of the corporation required added benefits for the Class A stock.

[80] Morris v. American Public Utilities Co., 14 Del. Ch. 136, 122 Atl. 696 (1923); Lonsdale Securities Corp. v. International Mercantile Marine Co., 101 N. J. Eq. 554, 139 Atl. 50 (1927). See also Colgate v. U. S. Leather Co., 73 N. J. Eq. 72, 67 Atl. 657 (1907), *revd.* 75 N. J. Eq. 229, 72 Atl. 126 (1909). *Cf.* Windhurst v. Central Leather Co., *supra* note 3b. *Quaere*, whether the benefit of a sinking fund requirement is such a vested right. In Yoakum v. Providence Biltmore Hotel Co., 34 F. (2d) 533 (D. R. I. 1929), an amendment depriving a preferred stock of its sinking fund rights was held invalid, but it is not clear that the same result would have been reached if the court had held applicable a subsequently adopted statutory provision couched in broader terms.

[81] Davis v. Louisville Gas & Electric Co., 16 Del. Ch. 157, 142 Atl. 654 (1928); Peters v. U. S. Mortgage Co., 13 Del. Ch. 11, 114 Atl. 598 (1921). *Cf.* Allen v. White, 103 Neb. 256, 171 N. W. 52 (1919). Nor is an amendment changing cumulative to straight voting invalid. Maddock v. Vorclone Corp., 147 Atl. 255 (Del. Ch. 1929). And a change from par value to no par value stock is also valid. Randle v. Winona Coal Co., 206 Ala. 254, 89 So. 790 (1921).

[82] *Supra* note 81. The decision has been criticized. See Cades, *supra* note 75; Putnam, *State Interference, Under the Reservation Clause, With Contracts Between the Stockholders of Corporation* (1929) 7 N. Y. U. L. Q. 487.

Sale,[83] *Consolidation,*[84] *Reorganization*[85] *and Dissolution.*[86]

While the various matters indicated by this subheading may be separate and distinct from each other, in practice most corporate transactions of the kind which will be here considered involve more than one. Much has already been written on this subject.[87] Much of the discussion is, however, concerned with the existence of adequate power in the majority and its compliance with statutory and charter provisions. We here, as throughout this chapter, assume the most sweeping statutory and charter provisions and technical compliance with all their terms. The question of the minority's right to redress in equity is also tied up with its

[83] Meaning a voluntary sale of all or substantially all the assets of the corporation. The *power* to sell without unanimous consent will be assumed. See Warren, *Voluntary Transfers of Corporate Undertakings* (1917) 30 HARV. L. REV. 335. See also Annotation 79 A. L. R. 624 (1932).

[84] Including "merger".

[85] See Chapter VII.

[86] See Fain, *Limitations of the Statutory Power of Majority Stockholders to Dissolve a Corporation* (1912) 25 HARV. L. REV. 677. The right of the minority to compel dissolution will be considered hereafter in connection with the question of the form of relief which may be obtained in equity.

[87] In addition to the articles cited *supra* notes 78, 86, see Lattin, *Equitable Limitations on Statutory or Charter Powers Given to Majority Stockholders* (1932) 30 MICH. L. REV. 645; Lattin, *The Minority Stockholder and Intracorporate Conflict* (1932) 17 IOWA L. BULL. 313; Hills, *Consolidation of Corporations by Sale of Assets and Distribution of Shares* (1931) 19 CALIF. L. REV. 349; Berle, *supra* note 22, at 1069-1072. There is a somewhat unique procedure in Pennsylvania. See Lauman v. Lebanon Valley R. R. Co., 30 Pa. 42 (1858), and the cases which have followed it, and, as to preferred stock, Petry v. Harwood Electric Co., 280 Pa. 142, 124 Atl. 302 (1924).

rights under statutory provisions affording a right to compel the corporation to buy its stock at appraised value,[88] but since those rights, except in a very few states by virtue of express provision in their statutes, are not deemed exclusive,[89] and since the statutory right is not yet universal, it seems desirable to examine a few typical cases in equity not influenced thereby. Even if appraisal statutes come to preëmpt the field, these cases should be helpful in formulating general concepts as to equitable limitations upon majorities.

The majority having the power to sell all the corporate assets, the courts will not review the "expediency" of such a sale but will intervene only to prevent or redress fraud.[90] A sale at less than fair value is fraudulent.[91]

---

[88] See Wiener, *Payment of Dissenting Stockholders* (1927) 27 COL. L. REV. 547; Lattin, *Remedies of Dissenting Stockholders Under Appraisal Statutes* (1931) 45 HARV. L. REV. 233; *Capital Reclassification as an Alteration of Preferential Rights Under Appraisal Statutes* (1933) 42 YALE L. J. 952; articles cited *supra* note 78. For developments during 1931 see Note (1932) 45 HARV. L. REV. 1396-1403.

[89] See Goodison v. North American Securities Co., 40 Ohio App. 85, 178 N. E. 29 (1931). *Cf.* Willson v. Waltham Watch Co., 293 Fed. 811 (D. C. Mass. 1923).

[90] J. H. Lane Co. v. Maple Cotton Mills, 226 Fed. 692 (C. C. A. 4th, 1915), on rehearing sale set aside because the directors were the purchasers, 232 Fed. 421 (C. C. A. 4th, 1916).

[91] Hinds v. Fishkill & Matteawan Gas Co., 96 App. Div. 14, 88 N. Y. Supp. 954 (1904). See Wheeler v. Abilene Nat. Bk. Bldg. Co., *supra* note 26. Relief was granted in Geddes v. Anaconda Mining Co., *supra* note 29; Nave-McCord Mercantile Co. v. Ranney, 29 F. (2d) 383 (C. C. A. 8th, 1928). Relief was denied in Allaun v. Consolidated Oil Co., 147 Atl. 257 (Del. Ch. 1929); Allied Chemical & Dye Corp. v. Steel & Tube Co., 14 Del. Ch. 1, 64, 120 Atl. 486, 122 Atl. 142 (1923); Wall v. Anaconda Copper Mining

The *Steel & Tube* case[92] is most instructive because of the detailed review of the testimony contained in the opinions. The plaintiffs, owning about
20 per cent. of the common stock of Steel & Tube
Co., sued to enjoin a proposed sale of all its assets
to Youngstown Sheet & Tube Co. for about $73,-
000,000. Control of the corporation was vested in
a syndicate which owned about 60 per cent. of the
common stock and some preferred stock. Promi-
nent in the syndicate was a banking firm which
had previously distributed an issue of its preferred
stock at $98 a share. Under the terms of the pro-
posed sale the preferred stock would be redeemed
at $110 a share. The plaintiffs charged that the
syndicate had a selfish interest in putting through
the sale in that it was their desire to liquidate their
common stock holdings quickly and that the retirement of the preferred at $110 would greatly en-
hance the bankers' good will. The court did not
consider this interest sufficient to vitiate their approval of the sale, but nevertheless granted a preliminary injunction on a showing that the book
value of the assets was over $94,000,000. There-

Co., 216 Fed. 242 (D. Mont. 1914), *affd. sub nom.* Wall v. Parrot
S. & C. Co., 244 U. S. 407, 37 Sup. Ct. 609 (1917). The result is
frequently influenced by the court's determination as to where the
burden of proof lies. While there is some conflict in the decisions, it
is safe to assume that when the sale is to the majority itself or to
those affiliated with it, the burden of justification will be on the
defendants, Geddes v. Anaconda Mining Co., *supra,* but that whenever the board is independent, and without a personal interest in the
transaction, there is a presumption of fairness which the plaintiffs
must overcome. Allied Chemical & Dye Corp. v. Steel & Tube Co.,
supra; Allaun v. Consolidated Oil Co., *supra.*

[92] *Supra* note 91.

upon a hearing was had as to the adequacy of the price and on all the evidence the court dissolved the injunction because it was not satisfied that the discrepancy between the value of the assets and the sales price was so great "that it is to be attributed not to a difference of opinion upon a highly debatable question but rather to bad faith".

Merger terms too must be "fair".

The Equitable Life Assurance Society owned about 67 per cent. of the stock of the Equitable Trust Company and 49 per cent. of that of the Mercantile Trust Company, and proposed a merger of the two. Under the proposed terms, the new stock would be issued in the ratio of one for one of the old Mercantile stock and one for two of the old Equitable stock or $435 in cash per share. It appeared that the book value of Mercantile was $452 a share and that of the Equitable $440. The court nevertheless refused to intervene at the suit of a minority stockholder of the Equitable and justified the difference in treatment of the two stocks by comparing the business situation of the two trust companies, the Mercantile earning 51 per cent. on each share and the Equitable only 25 per cent. It also heeded pessimistic forecasts as to the future prospects of the Equitable.[93]

---

[93] Colby v. Equitable Trust Co., *supra* note 3b. Some of the facts appear in Morse v. Equitable Life Assurance Society, 124 App. Div. 235, 108 N. Y. Supp. 986 (1908). The court was unmistakably influenced by the fact that only 1% of the Equitable stock was opposing the merger.

A preferred stockholder of Central Leather Company attacked the merger between that company and U. S. Leather Company on the ground that it was inequitable. For each share of preferred stock entitled to accumulated dividends of $43 and 7 per cent. annual dividends ahead of the common, there was to be given $5 in cash, one-half share of a new preferred stock entitled to dividends at the rate of $3.50 per annum, and three-fourths share of a Class A stock having priority over the common stock in dividends to the extent of $3 per annum. The court held the terms not inequitable in view of the financial conditions of the two companies.[94]

In *Outwater v. Public Service Corp.*,[95] the court did enjoin a proposed merger. The plaintiffs were minority stockholders in operating utilities whose properties were leased to a corporation which (through a subsidiary) owned the majority stock of the corporations. The leases were for 999 years at net rentals which assured dividends to the stockholders. The purpose of the proposed merger was to change the leaseholds into fees. The stockholders of each of the corporations were to receive for their common stock a 6 per cent. cumulative preferred non-voting stock on a basis that would afford

[94] Windhurst v. Central Leather Co., *supra* note 3b. *Cf.* Colgate v. U. S. Leather Co. and cases cited *supra* note 80. In MacFarlane v. North American Cement Corp., 157 Atl. 396 (Del. Ch. 1928), a preferred stockholder unsuccessfully challenged a merger on the ground that the common stock was receiving an undue proportion of the consideration being received for the entire corporation.

[95] 103 N. J. Eq. 461, 143 Atl. 729 (1928), *affd.* 104 N. J. Eq. 490, 146 Atl. 916 (1929).

them a slightly better yield than their common stock under the leases. The preferred stock was to be redeemable after three years. There was no "actual intent to defraud the minority". The court accepted as "an abstract proposition" that a court of equity has no right "to interfere in the internal affairs of the merging companies in the absence of fraud, actual or constructive", but was induced to grant the injunction primarily because of the redemption feature. This, in the view of the court, resulted in a compulsory sale of their common stock by the minority for the equivalent of a three year promissory note and was violative of the principle that "continued membership, until dissolution, is an inherent property right in corporate existence".

In another case [96] a consolidation was held "unfair" and therefore a "legal fraud". The consolidation was between the Missouri-Edison Company and the Union Electric Company, both of which were controlled by the same interests. The attack on the consolidation was by a preferred stockholder of Missouri-Edison. The finding that the terms of consolidation were not fair to the plaintiff was the result of an analysis of the figures which disclosed that whereas the Union company contributed only 6/32nds of the combined assets, it received securities representing four-fifths thereof, and that although the Edison preferred stock was entitled to a prior claim on one-half of the com-

[96] Jones v. Missouri-Edison Electric Co., supra note 3b.

bined assets, it received only 5/32nds.[97]

The need for equality implicit in the Missouri-Edison case was some years later made explicit by the United States Supreme Court in *Southern Pacific Co.* v. *Bogert*.[98] It there appeared that the Southern Pacific sought to incorporate into its own system the Houston & Texas Central Railway, control of which it owned through a subsidiary, upon terms which would permit it to acquire the new stock to be issued for the property at $26 a share, whereas others, including the minority stockholders, would be required to pay over $71 a share for the same stock. The court said:

> "If through that control a sale of the corporation's property is made and the property acquired by the majority, the minority may not be excluded from a fair participation in the fruits of the sale. . . . The essential of the liability to account sought to be enforced in this suit lies not in fraud or mismanagement, but in the fact that, having become a fiduciary through taking control of the old Houston Company, the Southern Pacific has secured fruits which it has not shared with the minority. The wrong lay not in acquiring the stock, but in refusing to make a pro rata distribution on equal terms among the old Hous-

[97] See also Paterson v. Shattuck Arizona Copper Co., 186 Minn. 611, 244 N. W. 281 (1932) where the court condemned a consolidation between two mining companies upon terms which gave to one of the companies which had no liquid assets 9/16ths of the stock.

[98] *Supra* note 3b.

ton Company shareholders."[99]

The right to continue in the corporation suggested in the *Outwater* case may be sufficient to prevent dissolution by the majority. The statutory power to dissolve given to the majority may not be used to "freeze out" the minority. Thus, in *Godley v. Crandall & Godley Co.,*[100] an action for an accounting was sustained, the court finding that the action of the majority in discontinuing the business and liquidating it was in bad faith to enable a new corporation which they organized to acquire it. The "fiduciary" theory which underlies the limitation upon the majority's right to dissolve in "bad faith" was expressed by the New York Court of Appeals as follows:

"The directors, in reaching their belief [as to whether the dissolution is 'advisable'] cannot consider or give weight to their personal wishes, comfort or advantage. Whether or not the dissolution is wise or expedient for themselves as apart from the corporation or any or all of the other stockholders they can neither question nor determine. Their action must be based upon the belief that the interests and

---

[99] 250 U. S. at 492, 39 Sup. Ct. at 537.

[100] *Supra* note 3b. See also Paine v. Saulsbury, 200 Mich. 58, 166 N. W. 1036 (1918), where the court refused a judicial dissolution at the request of the majority because the corporation was prosperous and the primary object of the dissolution was to get rid of the minority. *Cf.* Slattery v. Greater New Orleans Realty & Dev. Co., 128 La. 871, 55 So. 558 (1911).

welfare of the corporation and the stockholders generally will be promoted by the dissolution. The belief may be erroneous or ill-founded, but it must be formed in good faith. . . . The relation of the directors to the stockholders is essentially that of trustee and *cestui que trust*. . . . Undoubtedly no trust relation ordinarily exists between the stockholders themselves or between the stockholders and the corporation, because the stockholders, ordinarily, are strangers to the management and control of the corporation business and affairs. . . . The section 221 [General Corporation Law] imposes upon the stockholders the ultimate determination of the important question whether or not the corporation shall be dissolved forthwith. The stockholders are bound to determine and control this particular part of the corporation's affairs, in regard to which they occupy a relation of trust as between themselves and the corporation, and are burdened and restricted by fiduciary obligations. When a number of stockholders constitute themselves, or are by law constituted, the managers of corporate affairs or interests they stand in much the same attitude towards the other or minority stockholders that the directors sustain, generally, towards all the stockholders, and the law requires of them the utmost good faith. . . . In taking corporate action under the statute, the stockholders are acting for the corporation and for each other and they cannot use their corporate power in bad faith or for their individual advantage or purpose."[101]

A contrary conclusion had been reached some seventeen years earlier by a federal court sitting in New Jersey.[102] In that case the defendant corporation owned a majority of the common stock of another corporation and had guaranteed the dividends on its preferred stock. The court refused to enjoin the dissolution of said corporation, at the suit of a preferred stockholder who claimed that the purpose of the dissolution was to avoid the guaranty, holding that stockholders are in no sense trustees for each other and are not to be barred from voting because of a personal interest in the matter.

In a still earlier case [103] the court also held that it may not inquire into the "motives" which actuate the majority in its desire to dissolve the corporation, but held it liable to the minority for the fair value of the assets, the majority itself having

[101] Kavanaugh v. Kavanaugh Knitting Co., *supra* note 27a, at pp. 192, 194.

[102] Windmuller v. Standard Distilling & Distributing Co., *supra* note 20. *Cf.* Allen v. Distilling Co., 87 N. J. Eq. 531, 100 Atl. 620 (1917), *affd. sub nom.* U. S. Industrial Alcohol Co. v. Distilling Co. 89 N. J. Eq. 177, 104 Atl. 216 (1918). See also *In re* Pneumatic Tube Steam Splicer Co. 60 F. (2d) 524 (D. Md. 1932), sustaining right of directors, who also are majority stockholders, to file voluntary petition in bankruptcy.

[103] Ervin v. Oregon Ry. & Nav. Co., 20 Fed. 577 (C. C. S. D. N. Y. 1884), appeal dismissed 136 U. S. 645, 10 Sup. Ct. 1072 (1889).

acquired them.[104]

II

PRACTICE AND PROCEDURE

Those who challenge the adequacy of the judicial relief available to minority stockholders do so primarily on the grounds of delay, expense, and "pitfalls".[105] Occasionally it is urged that judges are incompetent to deal with business problems.

Minority stockholders' suits are not the exclusive exemplars of the law's delays and hence it is not a special problem.[106] Nor is judicial incompetence manifested only in corporate litigation. If the contention is that not even competent judges are able to deal with "business" problems, it is pointless. Courts must, as they are continuously doing, deal with business problems and the fact that corporate

---

[104] The property was acquired for $2,300,000 but the court fixed its value at $5,500,000, refusing to accept a mere liquidating value, but seeking instead its value as a going concern at the time of dissolution. *Cf.* Green v. Blunett, 110 S. W. 108 (Texas, 1908) ; and Watkins v. National Bank, 51 Kan. 254, 32 Pac. 914 (1893), where the courts refused to hold the defendants liable for "good will".

[105] "It is all very well to say that the minority stockholder has his redress if his company is being managed in an adverse interest. He hasn't. . . . Litigating against one of these powerful systems is an expensive business. The pitfalls and delays are endless. It is a luxury reserved for the large holders and then only when they have plenty of money and infinite patience." Samuel Untermyer, *Some Needed Legislative Reforms in Corporate Management*, an address, New York County Lawyers' Assn., Jan. 5, 1911. Professor Wormser is satisfied "that our courts have shown an intelligent realization of the implied obligations of corporate entities and their managers". BOOK REVIEW (1933) 19 A. B. A. J. 113.

[106] Indeed, in many cases, as we shall hereafter see, preliminary and summary relief is obtainable *pendente lite*.

machinery may be involved does not alter the situation.[107] The element of expense is undeniably serious for the small stockholder acting alone but, generally, he need not act alone and may readily join with other stockholders in the same position.[108] The advantage which the management has in its ready access to all information, in its business contacts, and in the availability of the corporate treasury cannot be gainsaid.[109]

The "pitfalls" presumably are to be found in the rules of practice and procedure,[110] but before considering them it seems desirable to express a caution. A stockholder's suit is but a single step in what has been aptly described as a "campaign". It begins with the first efforts to obtain information from the corporation[111] and very frequently ends, not with victory or defeat in the courtroom, but in a negotiated compromise. It is for this reason that the law reports do not give a full and complete picture of the struggle between majorities and minorities.

---

[107] "* * * leaders of the Bar have for many years found the Federal Judiciary notably competent in the handling of the legal aspects of reorganization, * * *". Rosenberg, Corporate Reorganization and the Federal Court (1924) vi.

[108] See Chap. V.

[109] To some extent these advantages are balanced by the relative ease with which a minority stockholder with a plausible cause of action may force the maintenance of the *status quo pendente lite* when the management may desire immediate action.

[110] We assume familiarity with equity pleading and practice and shall discuss only a few special problems.

[111] See Chap. IV.

The nature of the suit.

Suits brought by individual stockholders are more or less indiscriminately referred to as representative, or as derivative, or merely as stockholders' suits. It would seem that they can be classified into three categories. There is the purely personal cause of action for the violation of a private right. In this category are suits to compel the transfer of stock,[112] to enforce recognition of pre-emptive rights,[113] or to recover damages for breach of a contract in favor of the stockholder.[114] The remaining two categories involve the enforcement of corporate rights. One group consists of those cases where the suit is against a third person to recover a benefit for the corporation which it has itself refused to seek.[115] In these "derivative" suits the corporation is a nominal defendant, sued because of its unwillingness to act as plaintiff, but the direct beneficiary of a victory by the plaintiff.[116] The last group consists of those strictly intra-corporate suits where the plaintiff brings a "representative"

---

[112] *E.g.*, Knox v. Terpezone Co., 215 N. Y. 259, 109 N. E. 250 (1915).

[113] *E.g.*, Stokes v. Continental Trust Co., 186 N. Y. 285, 78 N. E. 1090 (1906) ; Hammer v. Werner, *supra* note 50.

[114] *E.g.*, Refusal to convert convertible stock: Marony v. Wheeling & Lake Erie Ry. Co., 33 F. (2d) 916 (S. D. N. Y. 1929) ; Cheatham v. Wheeling & Lake Erie Ry. Co., 37 F. (2d) 593 (S. D. N. Y. 1930).

[115] *E.g.*, Barr v. N. Y. L. E. & W. R. R. Co., *supra* note 14. See Glenn, *The Stockholder's Suit* (1924) 33 YALE L. J. 580.

[116] At times the forces that caused the corporation to decline to sue may cause it actively, either openly or surreptitiously, to espouse the cause of the defendants. This is invariably true when the "third-party" defendants are the controlling directors.

suit on his own behalf and on behalf of all other stockholders similarly situated.

This attempt at cataloging is suggested merely as a convenient device for handling most situations and is not intended to indicate that all stockholders' suits can be arbitrarily placed in one group or another exclusively. In litigation there is inevitable overlapping. A single stockholder's personal suit may determine a whole course of corporate conduct. So too the issues involved in a strictly intra-corporate conflict over policy may be presented to the courts in the form of a suit for an accounting against officers or directors and thus take on the procedural ear-marks of a case of the second group. Nor is it always possible to determine with exactness whether the right being asserted is a corporate or a personal right. A series of New York cases that have been the subject of much discussion[117] may be used to delineate the problem that sometimes exists.

In *Niles* v. *New York Central and Hudson River Railroad Company*,[118] the plaintiff, a stockholder of the New York & Northern Railroad Company, sued to recover damages sustained by him as the result of an alleged conspiracy on the part of the defendants to procure the property of the New York & Northern for the New York Central &

[117] Note (1915) 28 HARV. L. REV. 409; (1916) 25 YALE L. J. 154; (1923) 23 COL. L. REV. 498; (1929) 42 HARV. L. REV. 705; Comment (1929) 38 YALE L. J. 965.

[118] 176 N. Y. 119, 68 N. E. 142 (1903). See also Major v. American Malt & Grain Co., 110 Misc. 132, 181 N. Y. Supp. 152 (1920). *Cf.* Nave-McCord Mercantile Co. v. Ranney, *supra* note 91.

Hudson River. A demurrer to the complaint was sustained. The Court of Appeals took the position that the injury resulting from the wrongs of the defendants was to the corporation and that the depreciation in the value of plaintiff's stock was an incidental result of the injury sustained by the corporation. The court was influenced in denying direct relief to the plaintiff by the fact that corporate creditors had prior rights and that the recognition of plaintiff's cause would have given a similar cause of action to every stockholder. This decision was followed without much difficulty until *General Rubber Co.* v. *Benedict.*[119] The General Rubber Company (of New Jersey) owned practically all of the capital stock of the General Rubber Company of Brazil. Benedict was a director of the plaintiff but not of the subsidiary company. The complaint charged that Benedict in violation of the obligations which he owed the plaintiff as one of its directors concealed from it the fact that an employee of the subsidiary company was misapplying that company's funds. The plaintiff asked damages for the amount by which the value of its shares of the subsidiary company was lessened as a result of the defalcations. The Appellate Division sustained the complaint by a 3-2 decision. On a further appeal to the Court of Appeals the complaint was again sustained; this time by a 4-2 decision. The minority argued that the direct injury was to the subsidiary corporation and that the

[119] 215 N. Y. 18, 109 N. E. 96 (1915), *affg.* 164 App. Div. 332, 149 N. Y. Supp. 880 (1914).

plaintiff as a stockholder had no right to sue for its indirect damage. The majority apparently distinguished the earlier cases by emphasizing that the obligation of the defendant to the plaintiff was by virtue of his position as director but that any liability of his to the subsidiary corporation would exist, if at all, on an entirely different basis. In support of this distinction some reliance was placed upon *Ritchie* v. *McMullen*.[120] In that case, one Ritchie, who had pledged corporate stocks and bonds with certain persons as collateral for a loan, alleged that they conspired to render his property valueless and in furtherance of that conspiracy mismanaged the corporation whose securities he had pledged. The court, per Taft, J., held the principle that a stockholder cannot obtain direct relief for injuries to the corporation inapplicable to the situation there presented because the wrongdoers owed Ritchie the direct duties of pledgees. These decisions induced the Supreme Court of Pennsylvania to sustain a complaint whereby an inventor sought to recover damages for alleged improper conduct on the part of the defendants with respect to a corporation to which the inventions had been assigned.[121]

On the authority of the *General Rubber Company* case, the New York Court of Appeals some years later sustained a claim against an administrator and his surety for loss sustained as a result of his peculations from a corporation in which the

---

[120] 79 Fed. 522 (C. C. A. 6th, 1897).
[121] Vierling v. Baxter, 293 Pa. 52, 141 Atl. 728 (1928).

estate owned stock and in which he acted as officer and director, notwithstanding the fact that the corporation had itself recovered a judgment against him for the same misappropriation.[122] The decision was not rendered without a powerful dissent which contended that decisions such as in the *General Rubber* and *Ritchie* cases can be regarded as sound only when the duty owing to the plaintiff is entirely different from that owing to the corporation and when the plaintiff's loss is not merely an indirect result of the injury to the corporation.[123]

If the wrong sought to be redressed be found to be a corporate injury certain consequences follow. The complaining stockholder may not sue for his own benefit but must sue for the benefit of the corporation.[124] It is not sufficient to sue merely on behalf of such stockholders as may join,[125] for the right is that of the corporation and not merely the joint right of the complaining stockholders.[126] The judgment accordingly must be in favor of the corporation and not in favor of the plaintiffs.[127] Under exceptional circumstances the plaintiffs may re-

[122] Matter of Auditore, 249 N. Y. 335, 164 N. E. 242 (1928).

[123] See Green v. Victor Talking Machine Co., 24 F. (2d) 378 (C. C. A. 2d, 1928), *certiorari* denied 278 U. S. 602, 49 Sup. Ct. 9 (1928).

[124] Davis v. Peabody, 170 Mass. 397, 49 N. E. 750 (1898).

[125] Zinn v. Baxter, 65 Ohio St. 341, 62 N. E. 327 (1901).

[126] Endicott v. Marvel, 81 N. J. Eq. 378, 388, 87 Atl. 230, 234 (1913), *aff'd.* 83 N. J. Eq. 632, 92 Atl. 373 (1914).

[127] Pollitz v. Wabash R. R. Co., 167 App. Div. 669, 152 N. Y. Supp. 803 (1915) ; Miller v. Crown Perfumery Co., *supra* note 33 ; Landis v. Sea Isle City Hotel Co., 53 N. J. Eq. 654, 33 Atl. 964 (1895) ; Zinn v. Baxter, *supra* note 125 and cases there cited.

ceive directly their proportionate interest in any recovery which would ordinarily go to the corporation.[128] Asserting as he does a right not his own, the common-law side of the court will not hear the minority stockholder.[129] But his right to sue in equity in a proper case was recognized long ago.[130] It is generally stated that as a condition precedent to the maintenance of such a suit it must appear that redress cannot be obtained within the

[128] Dill v. Johnston, 72 Okla. 149, 179 Pac. 608 (1919) (corporation out of business, defendant had converted all corporate assets to his own possession). *Cf.* Thompson v. Stanley, 20 N. Y. Supp. 317 (1892). In Baillie v. Columbia Gold Mining Co., 86 Ore. 1, 19, 166 Pac. 965, 970 (1917), the court said "We have found a few cases in which stockholders have sued on behalf of themselves and all others similarly situated for the redress of wrongs done the corporation, in which the court has in effect directed a dividend, by requiring the unfaithful majority to pay the minority its aliquot share of moneys taken from the corporate treasury: (citing cases). The doctrine of these cases is applicable only where the court can say that the powers of the directors will be abused to the injury of the complaining stockholders and that the circumstances clearly call for the declaration of a dividend."

[129] Smith v. Hurd, 12 Metc. 371 (Mass. 1847); Converse v. United Shoe Machinery Co., 185 Mass. 422, 70 N. E. 444 (1904); Smith v. Poor, 40 Me. 415 (1855); Allen v. Curtis, 26 Conn. 455 (1857); Craig v. Gregg, 83 Pa. 19 (1876); Howe v. Barney, 45 Fed. 668 (C. C. D. Ohio 1891); United Copper Securities Co. v. Amalgamated Copper Co., 244 U. S. 261, 37 Sup. Ct. 509 (1917); Hubbard v. Kensington Bank, 228 App. Div. 790, 240 N. Y. Supp. 45 (1930), *aff'd.* 254 N. Y. 587, 173 N. E. 878 (1930). In a proper case a suit commenced on the law side may be transferred to the equity side. Jacobs v. First National Bank, 35 F. (2d) 227 (W. D. La. 1929), *aff'd.* 48 F. (2d) 17 (C. C. A. 5th, 1931).

[130] Robinson v. Smith, 3 Paige 222 (N. Y. 1832); Dodge v. Woolsey, 18 How. 331 (U. S. 1855); Hawes v. Oakland, 104 U. S. 450 (1882); Miner v. Belle Isle Ice Co., 93 Mich. 97, 53 N. W. 218 (1892); Gibbs v. Morgan, 9 Idaho 100, 72 Pac. 733 (1903).

corporation,[131] but in so far as intra-corporate controversies are concerned this requirement is not substantial. Proof of a prior demand is not insisted upon where the alleged wrongdoers are in control of the corporation or it is obvious that prior demand upon the corporation would have been futile.[132]

Who may sue.

The suit may be maintained only by one who is a stockholder at the time of the prosecution of the suit.[133] This does not necessarily mean a stock-

---

[131] See Note (1931) 15 MINN. L. REV. 453. For the federal courts the requirements are embodied in Equity Rule 27, 28 U. S. C. A. (1928). See comments on said rule in BALLANTINE, CORPORATIONS (1930) 624-625; 4 COOK, CORPORATIONS (8th ed. 1923) § 740. *Quaere,* whether even in the federal courts the rule applies to actions brought by a stockholder to prevent the doing of an illegal act. See Dickinson v. Consolidated Traction Co., 114 Fed. 232, 242-3 (C. C. D. N. J. 1902), *affd.* 119 Fed. 871 (C. C. A. 3d, 1903), *certiorari* denied 191 U. S. 567, 24 Sup. Ct. 840 (1903); General Inv. Co. v. Lake Shore & M. S. Ry. Co., 250 Fed. 160, 174 (C. C. A. 6th, 1918).

[132] The cases are legion. See 4 COOK, CORPORATIONS (8th ed. 1923) § 741. Federal Equity Rule 27 does not apply to suits against the corporation's own formal proceedings. Binney v. Cumberland Ely Copper Co., 183 Fed. 650 (C. C. D. Me. 1910). If the corporation is no longer actively engaged in business, prior demand is not necessary. Crumlich's Adm'r v. Shen. Val. R. R. Co., 28 W. Va. 623 (1886); Dill v. Johnston, *supra* note 128; Thompson v. Stanley, *supra* note 128; Tennessee M. P. & M. Co. v. Ayers, 43 S. W. 744 (Tenn. 1897). But if the corporation continues in being the demand is necessary, although the corporation is legally dissolved. Taylor v. Holmes, 127 U. S. 489, 8 Sup. Ct. 1192 (1888). If there are no officers or directors the demand should be made upon the stockholders or liquidating trustees. Watts v. Vanderbilt, 45 F. (2d) 968 (C. C. A. 2d, 1930). See Note (1931) 40 YALE L. J. 1081.

[133] Edelstein v. Frank, 208 App. Div. 790 (N. Y. 1924). But see Porter v. Healy, 244 Pa. 427, 91 Atl. 428 (1914).

holder of record; actual ownership is sufficient.[134]
A de facto stockholder in a de facto corporation
may maintain a suit,[135] but a subscriber to stock not
issued may not.[136] The owner of an equitable interest in the stock may maintain the suit even though
the legal title is in another.[137]

When there is more than one plaintiff, the ownership of any one is sufficient for the prosecution of
the action.[138] If the complaining stockholder die,
the suit, if it be to enforce a corporate right, does
not fail, but may be continued by any other stockholder.[139]

One who was a stockholder at the time of the

---

[134] O'Connor v. International Silver Co., 68 N. J. Eq. 67, 59 Atl.
321 (1904), affd. 68 N. J. Eq. 680, 62 Atl. 408 (1905); Parrott v.
Byers, 40 Colo. 614 (1871); Security Trust Co. v. Pritchard, 190
N. Y. Supp. 871 (1921), mod. & affd. 201 App. Div. 142, 194 N. Y.
Supp. 486 (1922); Ervin v. Oregon Ry. & Nav. Co., 62 How. Pr. 490
(N. Y. 1882); Mitchell v. Aulander Realty Co., 169 N. C. 516, 86
S. E. 358 (1915). Contra: Brown v. Duluth M. & N. Ry. Co., 53 Fed.
889 (C. C. D. Minn. 1893); Hodges v. U. S. Steel Corp., 64 N. J. Eq.
90, 53 Atl. 601 (1902), revd. on other grounds, 64 N. J. Eq. 807, 54
Atl. 1 (1903).

[135] McMillan v. Lamb, 166 N. Y. Supp. 656 (1917).

[136] Busey v. Hooper, 35 Md. 15 (1871).

[137] Butler v. Butler Bros., 242 N. W. 701, 702, 704 (Minn. 1932);
Baum v. Sporborg, 146 App. Div. 537, 131 N. Y. Supp. 267 (1911);
McGeary v. Brown, 23 S. D. 573, 122 N. W. 605 (1909); U. S. etc.
v. O'Grady, 75 N. J. Eq. 301, 71 Atl. 1040 (1909); Chandler v. Bellanca Aircraft Corp., 162 Atl. 63 (Del. Ch. 1932). Both the pledgor,
Fisher v. Patton, 34 S. W. 1096 (Mo. 1896), and the pledgee, First
National Bank v. Stribling, 86 Pac. 512 (Okla. 1905), have sufficient
interest in the stock to sue. Contra: Whitaker v. Whitaker Iron Co.,
238 Fed. 980 (N. D. W. Va. 1916) (legatee under will). As to status
of a naked trustee see Greenough v. Alabama G. S. R. Co., 64 Fed. 22
(C. C. N. D. Ala. 1894).

[138] Holmes v. Camp, 176 App. Div. 771, 162 N. Y. Supp. 1014
(1917).

[139] Spring v. Webb, 227 Fed. 481 (D. Vt. 1915).

wrongs complained of may not maintain the suit after he has parted with his stock.[140] On the question whether the plaintiff must also have been a stockholder at the time of the consummation of the wrongs complained of, there is a division of authority. The federal courts, anxious to prevent collusive resort to them in preference to the local courts, insist upon this and the requirement is embodied in a rule.[141] Although this rule is only one of practice and in no sense binding upon the state courts it has nevertheless influenced some of them to adopt the requirement as a matter of principle.[142] The prevailing state court view is probably to the contrary.[143]

[140] Hanna v. Lyon, 179 N. Y. 107, 71 N. E. 778 (1904) ; Zinn v. Baxter, *supra* note 125; Dissette v. Lawrence Pub. Co., 9 Ohio C. C. (N. S.) 118 (1907) ; Rafferty v. Donnelly, 197 Pa. 423, 47 Atl. 202 (1900). One who was wrongfully induced to part with his stock to the defendants may maintain the suit and therein be restored to his original status. Price v. Union Land Co., 187 Fed. 886 (C. C. A. 8th, 1911).

[141] Equity Rule 27. The rule applies to an action commenced in a state court and removed to the federal court because of diversity of citizenship. Venner v. Great Northern Ry. Co., 153 Fed. 408 (S. D. N. Y. 1907), *affd.* 209 U. S. 24, 24 Sup. Ct. 28 (1908) ; Hitchings v. Cobalt Central Mines Co., 189 Fed. 241 (C. C. S. D. N. Y. 1910). But not where the removal is on the ground that a federal question is involved. Hand v. Kansas City So. Ry. Co., 55 F. (2d) 712 (S. D. N. Y. 1931). See *supra* note 131.

[142] Boldenwick v. Bullis, 40 Colo. 253, 90 Pac. 634 (1907) ; Home Fire Ins. Co. v. Barber, 67 Neb. 644, 93 N. W. 1024 (1903) ; Rankin v. Southwestern Brewery & Ice Co., 12 N. M. 54, 73 Pac. 614 (1903) ; Alexander v. Searcy, 81 Ga. 536, 8 S. E. 630 (1888) stock purchased while litigation pending, decision also strongly influenced by other factors such as laches.

[143] Montgomery Light & Power Co. v. Lahey, 121 Ala. 131, 25 So. 1006 (1898) ; Just v. Idaho Canal & Imp. Co., 16 Idaho 639, 102 Pac. 381 (1909) ; City of Chicago v. Cameron, 22 Ill. App. 91 (1886),

While it is frequently stated that the extent of plaintiff's stockholding in the corporation is immaterial,[144] it seems that this is only true where the defendants are guilty of illegality or fraud [145] and the plaintiff's right is an absolute one. If the plaintiff's financial interest in the corporation is small, that factor unmistakably influences the court,[146]

affd. 120 Ill. 447, 11 N. E. 899 (1887); Forrester v. Boston & Montana Cons. Copper Co., 21 Mont. 544, 55 Pac. 229 (1898); Winsor v. Bailey, 55 N. H. 218 (1875); Pollitz v. Gould, 202 N. Y. 11, 94 N. E. 1088 (1911); Santen v. United States Shoe Co., 25 Ohio N. P. (N. S.) 363 (1924); Rafferty v. Donnelly, *supra* note 140. Where the action is based on a state statute the federal court will apply the rule governing in that state. Hand v. Kansas City So. Ry. Co., *supra* note 141.

[144] Meyerhoff v. Banker's Securities, Inc., 105 N. J. Eq. 76, 147 Atl. 105 (1929); Gordon v. Brucker, 208 Ill. App. 188 (1917); Carver v. So. Iron & Steel Co., 78 N. J. Eq. 81, 78 Atl. 240 (1910); Stewart v. Erie & Western Tr. Co., 17 Minn. 372 (1871); Gifford v. N. J. R. R. Co., 10 N. J. Eq. 171 (1854). *Cf.* Tanner v. Lindell Ry. Co., 180 Mo. 1, 79 S. W. 155 (1904), as to *form* of relief. The principles here set forth relate also to the *number* of dissenters. For the purpose of federal jurisdiction, it is sufficient if the value of the corporation's right exceeds $3,000; the value of the plaintiff's undivided interest therein is immaterial. Hutchinson Box Board & Paper Co. v. Van Horn, 299 Fed. 424 (C. C. A. 4th, 1924). *Cf.* Cohn v. Cities Service Co., 45 F. (2d) 687 (C. C. A. 2d, 1930), where plaintiffs were asserting individual or "class" rights but not a corporate right. See Blume, *Jurisdictional Amount in Representative Suits* (1931) 15 MINN. L. REV. 501, 510.

[145] Even in fraud cases that factor is "a negative circumstance entitled to some consideration". Homer v. Crown Cork & Seal Co., 155 Md. 66, 141 Atl. 425 (1928).

[146] Windhurst v. Central Leather Co., *supra* note 94; Collins v. Martin, 248 S. W. 941 (Mo. 1922); Presidio Mining Co. v. Overton, 261 Fed. 933 (C. C. A. 9th, 1919); General Invest. Co. v. Bethlehem Steel Corp., 87 N. J. Eq. 235, 100 Atl. 347 (1917); Colby v. Equitable Trust Co., *supra* note 3b; Callaway v. Powhatan Imp. Co., 95 Md. 177, 52 Atl. 916 (1902); Rumney v. Detroit & M. Cattle Co., 116 Mich. 640, 74 N. W. 1043 (1898); Paterson v. Shattuck Arizona Copper Co., *supra* note 97. Albers v. Merchants' Exchange, 45 Mo.

especially in the consideration of discretionary matters.[147]

It is suggested that in all cases, except where the plaintiff has an unqualified legal right, if he represents a very small financial interest, the court limit its interference with the majority to assuring to all stockholders of the same class equality of treatment, but, if the opposition represents a substantial interest (especially if the stock does not have a ready market), the court should review the fairness and wisdom of the action proposed by the majority, allowing the majority, if it be honest and "disinterested", a presumption in favor of its action.

Discussion of the time when the plaintiff acquired his stock and the extent of his financial interest in the corporation is frequently coupled with the more inclusive question of his motives in litigating.[148] Although there are cases holding that a minority stockholder's suit may not be maintained where the plaintiff is acting not on his own behalf or on behalf of the corporation but rather at the behest of an adverse interest,[149] the general rule is

App. 206 (1891); Carson v. Allegany Window Glass Co., 189 Fed. 791 (C. C. D. Del. 1911).

[147] General Inv. Co. v. Lake Shore & M. S. Ry. Co., *supra* note 131; Johnson v. United Railways, 227 Mo. 423, 127 S. W. 63 (1910); Ryan v. Williams, 100 Fed. 172 (C. C. E. D. Va. 1900); Becker v. Hoke, 80 Fed. 973 (C. C. A. 7th, 1897); Greenough v. Alabama G. S. R. Co., *supra* note 137; Aldrich v. Union Bag & Paper Co., 81 N. J. Eq. 244, 87 Atl. 65 (1913). In the last cited case a receiver *pendente lite* was denied even though the directors had no financial interest in the corporation.

[148] For a collection of cases, Note (1930) 67 A. L. R. 1470.

[149] Forrest v. Manchester, Sheff. & L. Ry. Co., 4 DeG. F. & J. 126

that the plaintiff's motive in prosecuting the suit, or in acquiring the stock, is immaterial.[150] The rules applicable to "motive" ought, perhaps, to be more precisely formulated. Under the present state of the law, the following are submitted:

1. Where the majority, the directors, or the officers, are guilty of illegal acts, *i.e.*, of acts which the corporation itself cannot authorize or ratify, the motive of the complaining stockholder is immaterial.

2. Where the minority stockholder is insisting upon the fulfillment of a contract right, whether

(Eng. 1861); Beshoar v. Chappelle, 6 Colo. App. 323, 40 Pac. 244 (1895); Waterbury v. Merchants Union Exp. Co., 50 Barb. 157 (N. Y. 1867); Belmont v. Erie Ry. Co., 52 Barb. 637 (N. Y. 1869). *Cf.* Southwestern Portland Cement Co. v. Latta & Happer, 193 S. W. 1115 (Tex. Civ. App. 1917). See also Sparhawk v. Union Passenger Ry. Co., 54 Pa. 401, 452 (1867).

[150] Johnson v. King-Richardson Co., 36 F. (2d) 675 (C. C. A. 1st, 1930); Central R. R. Co. v. Collins, 40 Ga. 582 (1869); Macon Gas Co. v. Richter, 143 Ga. 397, 85 S. E. 112 (1913); Hodge v. U. S. Steel Corp., 64 N. J. Eq. 111, 53 Atl. 553 (1902); Bull v. International Power Co., 84 N. J. Eq. 6, 92 Atl. 796 (1914), *affd.* 85 N. J. Eq. 206, 96 Atl. 364 (1915); Ramsey v. Gould, 57 Barb. 398 (N. Y. 1870); Colman v. Eastern Counties Ry. Co., 10 Beav. 1 (Eng. 1846); Seaton v. Grant, L. R. 2 Ch. App. 459 (1867). This principle does not prevent inquiry to ascertain whether the plaintiff is the real party in interest. MacGinniss v. Boston & Montana C. C. & S. M. Co., 29 Mont. 428, 75 Pac. 89 (1904). Plaintiff's motive may influence the form of relief accorded him. Kingman v. Rome, W. & O. R. R. Co., 30 Hun 73 (N. Y. 1883); Lewisohn Bros. v. Anaconda Copper M. Co., 26 Misc. 613, 56 N. Y. Supp. 807 (1899); and may be considered on questions of credibility, Continental Securities Co. v. Belmont, 83 Misc. 340, 144 N. Y. Supp. 801 (1913), *affd.* 168 App. Div. 483, 154 N. Y. Supp. 54 (1915), *affd.* 222 N. Y. 673, 119 N. E. 1036 (1918). We are not here concerned with the special rules applicable to proceedings to obtain access to corporate books and records. See Chap. IV.

embodied in the charter, certificate of incorporation, or otherwise, his motive is immaterial. Illustrative of this class are cases of preferred stockholders seeking the payment of dividends.

3. Where the suit involves the propriety of the
exercise of a power vested in the majority, the directors, or the officers, the motive of the complaining minority stockholder is material (but not controlling), provided the inquiry is directed towards
aiding the court to determine, under *all* the circumstances, the effect of the litigation upon the
corporation and all interested therein, and not to
the ascertainment of whether the plaintiff is a
"good" or "bad" man. It is submitted that the
ultimate welfare of the corporation and of those
dependent upon it is a legitimate subject of inquiry
and that courts should make the inquiry openly
and not under the guise of determining whether
the plaintiff is "the real party in interest." [150a]

Bars.[151]

Even if there be a valid corporate right of action
the assertion of it by a particular stockholder may
be barred by his own prior conduct. Logically this
position is in apparent disregard of the basic
nature of the derivative suit, namely, that it is
brought to redress a corporate wrong and not for

[150a] See Tachna v. Pressed Steel Car Co., 112 N. J. Eq. 411, 164
Atl. 413 (1933).

[151] The author uses the word "bars" rather than "defenses" to
distinguish between matters which go only to the right of the particular plaintiff to complain (bars) and matters which go to defeat
the claim itself (defenses).

the individual benefit of the stockholder who happens to be plaintiff. From this notion it ought perhaps, in strict logic, to follow that the suit can only be barred by action on the part of the corporation, but such is not the law. Courts of equity have refused to permit the assertion of corporate rights by a stockholder who was personally estopped,[152] who had knowingly accepted benefits under the transaction sought to be attacked,[153] who had ratified or acquiesced in the transaction,[154] or who had otherwise waived his right to complain,[155] or was guilty of laches.[156]

[152] Pollitz v. Wabash R. R. Co., 207 N. Y. 113, 100 N. E. 721 (1921); Post v. Beacon Vacuum Pump & E. Co., 84 Fed. 371 (C. C. A. 1st, 1898); Klein v. Independent Brewing Assn., 231 Ill. 594, 83 N. E. 434 (1908). See also Harris v. Pearsall, 116 Misc. 366, 190 N. Y. Supp. 61 (1921).

[153] Wormser v. Metropolitan Street Ry. Co., 184 N. Y. 83, 76 N. E. 1036 (1906). See also Harris v. Pearsall, *supra* note 152.

[154] Pollitz v. Wabash R. R. Co., *supra* note 152; Burden v. Burden, *supra* note 32; Venner v. N. Y. C. & H. R. R. Co., 177 App. Div. 296, 164 N. Y. Supp. 626 (1917), *affd.* 226 N. Y. 583, 123 N. E. 893 (1919); Johnson v. King-Richardson Co., *supra* note 150; Pigeon River Ry. Co. v. Champion Fibre Co., 280 Fed. 557 (C. C. A. 4th, 1922); Watt's Appeal, 78 Pa. 370 (1875). *Contra:* Fitzgerald v. Fitzgerald & Mallory Const. Co., 41 Neb. 374, 58 N. W. 858 (1894); Roth v. Robertson, 64 Misc. 343, 118 N. Y. Supp. 351 (1909) as to acts *mala prohibita* or *mala in se.* See also Harris v. Pearsall, *supra* note 152. When a trustee seeks to bar his *cestui* by "ratification", it must appear that he made full disclosure, not only of the facts, but also of the *cestui's* legal rights. See Garrett v. Reid-Cashion Land & Cattle Co., 34 Ariz. 245, 270 Pac. 1044 (1928).

[155] Johnson v. King-Richardson Co., *supra* note 150.

[156] Kessler v. Ensley Co., 123 Fed. 546 (C. C. N. D. Ala. 1903); Venner v. N. Y. C. & H. R. R. Co., *supra* note 154; Stephany v. Marsden, 75 N. J. Eq. 90, 71 Atl. 598 (1908), *affd.* 76 N. J. Eq. 611, 75 Atl. 899 (1900); Ashhurst's Appeal, 60 Pa. 290 (1869). As to what constitutes laches see Cahall v. Burbage, 119 Atl. 574 (Del. Ch. 1922). At times the application of the doctrine of laches is made to

Freedom from these bars need not be pleaded by the plaintiff.[157] They constitute affirmative defenses which must be pleaded by the defendants unless they sufficiently appear upon the face of the complaint,[158] although a court may, on its own motion, take cognizance thereof.[159] Of course, their existence bars only the particular plaintiff against whom they operate and does not affect other stockholders even if they be co-plaintiffs.[160]

As the suit may be barred by the personal disabilities of the plaintiff notwithstanding its representative character so the individual plaintiff may, until others intervene,[161] deal with it as if it were

depend upon whether the relief sought is a matter of right or of discretion. See Pollitz v. Wabash R. R. Co., *supra* note 152; American Seating Co v. Bullard, 290 Fed. 896 (C. C. A. 6th, 1923).

[157] Horn Silver Mining Co. v. Ryan, 42 Minn. 196, 44 N. W. 56 (1889); Continental Securities Co. v. Belmont, 206 N. Y. 7, 13, 99 N. E. 138, 140 (1912).

[158] Sabre v. United Traction & Elec. Co., 156 Fed. 79 (C. C. D. R. I. 1907). The burden of proof is likewise upon the defendants. Mason v. Carrothers, 105 Me. 392, 408, 74 Atl. 1030, 1037 (1909).

[159] Hall v. Nash, 33 Colo. 500, 81 Pac. 249 (1905). See also Calivado Col. Co. v. Hays, 119 Fed. 202 (C. C. W. D. Pa. 1902).

[160] Endicott v. Marvel, *supra* note 126.

[161] Except when denied because of undue delay, McArdell v. Olcott, 62 App. Div. 127, 70 N. Y. Supp. 930 (1901); Streuber's Appeal, 229 Pa. 184, 78 Atl. 106 (1910), the right of intervention is freely granted. Southern Pacific Co. v. Bogart, *supra* note 3b. Indeed, no formal order is necessary. Coltrane v. Templeton, 106 Fed. 370 (C. C. A. 4th, 1901). *Cf.* Hay v. Brookfield, 160 App. Div. 277, 145 N. Y. Supp. 543 (1914), denying leave to a majority stockholder to intervene as a party defendant. See also Continental & Comm. T. & S. Bank v. Allis-Chalmers Co., 200 Fed. 600 (D. C. E. D. Wis. 1912) denying intervention to a stockholder of defendant in a foreclosure suit. Where the plaintiff is acting for the controlling interests, other stockholders will be permitted to intervene. Thayer v. Kinder, 45 Ind. App. 111, 90 N. E. 323 (1909). For a case of intervention by a

his own, at least until decree entered, and may discontinue it.[162]

In accordance with the idea that the purchaser of stock acquires all the rights of the vendor, including the right to attack prior transactions, and no more, it is held that when a prior owner of the stock has participated in or consented to the alleged improprieties, no subsequent owner of that stock may attack them.[163] Under present marketing

holder of non-voting preferred stock, see Hamlin v. Toledo, *etc.* R. R. Co., 78 Fed. 664 (C. C. A. 6th, 1897). The status of the intervenor may cure defects in jurisdiction, Grant v. Greene Cons. Copper Co., 169 App. Div. 206, 154 N. Y. Supp. 596 (1915), *affd.* 223 N. Y. 655, 119 N. E. 1053 (1915), but will not destroy or change jurisdiction as originally fixed. Wichita R. R. & T. Co. v. Public Utilities Commission, 260 U. S. 48, 43 Sup. Ct. 51 (1922); Thouron v. East Tenn. V. & G. Ry. Co., 38 Fed. 673 (C. C. E. D. Tenn. 1889). So too, if the intervenor is a stockholder, it may save the action even though the original plaintiff is not. Hanna v. Lyon, *supra* note 140. After intervention the original plaintiff may not abandon or discontinue the suit, and upon his failure to prosecute it the intervenor may. Manning v. Mercantile Trust Co., 37 Misc. 215, 75 N. Y. Supp. 168 (1902); Culver Lumber Co. v. Culver, 81 Ark. 102, 99 S. W. 391 (1906); McAlpin v. Universal Tobacco Co., 57 Atl. 418 (N. J. 1904). Intervenors may be allowed compensation for their attorneys. Goodman v. Von Cotzhausen, 171 Wis. 351, 177 N. W. 618 (1920). Intervention in the Federal Court is also governed by Equity Rule 37.

[162] Brinckerhoff v. Bostwick, 99 N. Y. 185, 1 N. E. 663 (1885); Bernheimer v. Wallace, 186 Ky. 459, 217 S. W. 916 (1920). The last cited case contains a discussion of the court's duty to protect unrepresented stockholders. The phrase "as if it were his own" is too broad because it entirely overlooks the essential fiduciary character of the plaintiff. See National Power & Paper Co. v. Rossman, 122 Minn. 355, 142 N. W. 818 (1913); Whitten v. Dabney, 171 Cal. 621, 154 Pac. 312 (1915). For the effect of his acts upon others, see *infra* p. 166.

[163] Babcock v. Farwell, 245 Ill. 14, 91 N. E. 683 (1910); Home Fire Ins. Co. v. Barber, *supra* note 142. This is an affirmative defense to be pleaded by the defendants. Continental Securities Co. v. Belmont, *supra* note 157. *Contra:* Trimble v. Amer. Sugar Ref. Co., *supra* note 32.

conditions this principle has an element of unfairness in it, if we accept the view that a stockholder
should be permitted to sue for prior wrongs, because it is most rare for a purchaser to have any
direct contact with his transferor, or any knowledge of his actions as stockholder. Indeed, the purchaser generally neither knows nor cares whose
stock he is purchasing.[164]

Necessary Defendants.
The corporation is a necessary party to the suit [165]

[164] In cases against promoters (reference to which we are avoiding
in this book) an attempt is frequently made to escape from the consequences of this rule by treating the initial issuance to the promoters, in those cases where they immediately return or make available
to the corporation stock for public sale, as a mere subterfuge. Cali-
fornia-Calaveras Min. Co. v. Walls, 170 Cal. 285, 149 Pac. 595
(1915); Mason v. Carrothers, *supra* note 158; Fred. Macey Co. v.
Macey, 143 Mich. 138, 106 N. W. 722 (1906); American Forging Co.
v. Wiley, 206 Mich. 664, 173 N. W. 515 (1919); Santen v. U. S. Shoe
Co., *supra* note 143; Anderson v. Johnson, 45 R. I. 17, 119 Atl. 642
(1923); Pittsburgh Mining Co. v. Spooner, 74 Wis. 307, 42 N. W.
259 (1889); Pietsch v. Milbrath, 123 Wis. 647, 101 N. W. 388 (1904).
See Berle, *Bankers' and Promoters' Stock Profits* (1929) 42 HARV.
L. REV. 748, 756-759.

[165] City of Davenport v. Dows, 18 Wall. 626 (U. S. 1874); Porter
v. Sabin, 149 U. S. 473, 13 Sup. Ct. 1008 (1892) receiver of insolvent
corporation should be joined; Lawrence v. Southern Pacific Co.,
180 Fed. 822 (C. C. E. D. N. Y. 1910) appeal dismissed *sub nom.*
Bogart v. So. Pac. R. R. Co., 228 U. S. 137, 33 Sup. Ct. 497 (1913);
Hyams v. Old Dominion Co., 204 Fed. 681 (D. Me. 1913), *aff'd.* 209
Fed. 808 (C. C. A. 1st, 1913); McNeely v. E. I. DuPont de Nemours
Powder Co., 263 Fed. 252 (D. Del. 1920); Busch v. Mary A. Riddle
Co., 283 Fed. 443 (D. Del. 1922); Beach v. Cooper, 72 Cal. 99, 13
Pac. 161 (1887); Von Arnim v. American Tube Works, 188 Mass.
515, 74 N. E. 680 (1905); McMillan v. Miller, 177 Mich. 511, 143
N. W. 631 (1913); Robinson v. Smith, *supra* note 130; Brady v.
Meenan, 204 App. Div. 390, 198 N. Y. Supp. 177 (1923). *Cf.* Toledo
Traction, Light & Power Co. v. Smith, 205 Fed. 643 (N. D. Ohio

but neither all the directors nor even all the alleged wrongdoers are indispensable parties.[166]

Venue.

Homage is still paid to the general rule that "courts will not take jurisdiction of the internal affairs of a foreign corporation, or, in the exercise of visitorial powers, interfere with, supervise, administer, or direct the management of such a corporation",[167] and when convenient, in deference to this principle, it is best to sue in the state of domicile.[168] The principle cannot, however, be deemed an absolute bar to the maintenance of such suits

1913). With respect to dissolved corporations see (1931) 40 YALE L. J. 1081; Hamm v. Christian Herald Corporation, 236 App. Div. 639, 260 N. Y. Supp. 743 (1932).

[166] Eldred v. American Palace-Car Co., 99 Fed. 168 (C. C. D. N. J. 1900); Wickersham v. Crittenden, 93 Cal. 17, 28 Pac. 788 (1892); Von Arnim v. American Tube Works, *supra* note 165; Baker v. Baker, 122 Misc. 757, 204 N. Y. Supp. 11 (1924), *affd.* 212 App. Div. 850 (1924). *Cf.* Harden v. Eastern States Pub. Service Co., 14 Del. Ch. 156, 122 Atl. 705 (1923) corporation sole defendant. As to the propriety of their joinder see Berwind v. Van Horne, 104 Fed. 581 (C. C. S. D. N. Y. 1900); Schell v. Alston Mfg. Co., 149 Fed. 439 (C. C. N. D. Ill. 1906); Gray v. Fuller, 17 App. Div. 29, 44 N. Y. Supp. 883 (1897); McCrea v. McClenahan, 114 App. Div. 70, 99 N. Y. Supp. 689 (1906) as to stockholders.

[167] The cases are annotated in Note (1922) 18 A. L. R. 1383 and discussed in Note (1929) 29 COL. L. REV. 968. See Rogers v. Guaranty Trust Co., 288 U. S. 123, 53 S. Ct. 295, 77 L. Ed. 441 (1933).

[168] As to the jurisdiction of the federal court in such state see Doctor v. Harrington, 196 U. S. 579, 25 Sup. Ct. 355 (1905); Mills v. City of Chicago, 143 Fed. 430 (C. C. N. D. Ill. 1906), *affd.* 204 U. S. 321, 27 Sup. Ct. 286 (1907); Dodge v. Woolsey, *supra* note 130; Consumers' Gas Trust Co. v. Quinby, 137 Fed. 882 (C. C. A. 7th, 1905); New Albany Waterworks v. Louisville Banking Co., 122 Fed. 776 (C. C. A. 7th, 1903); Barnes v. Kornegay, 62 Fed. 671 (C. C. W. D. N. C. 1894).

elsewhere. In the first place, there is no uniformity in the decisions as to what constitute "internal affairs". Secondly, a distinction is frequently drawn between "controlling" management and "redressing" mismanagement. Finally, and of prime importance, the rule has come to be recognized as not one of jurisdictional power but only as one of policy and discretion. The result is that "foreign" courts do exercise their jurisdiction in a "proper" case. Broadly speaking, more and more weight is being given to the actual facts of the corporation's business activities as distinguished from its merely formal domicile.[169] A court which acquires jurisdiction of the necessary defendants may decline to act, even if satisfied that a grievance exists, in cases where "considerations of convenience, efficiency and justice point to the courts of the state of the domicile as appropriate tribunals for the determination of the particular case".[170]

Even if jurisdiction is entertained in a foreign state, the law of the forum will not necessarily govern; on certain questions the law of the domicile of the corporation will control,[171] and on others the

[169] See Harr v. Pioneer Mechanical Corp., 65 F. (2d) 332 (C. C. A. 2d. 1933) *cert. den.* —U. S. — (Oct. 1933), and dissent of Mr. Justice Stone in Rogers v. Guaranty Trust Co., *supra* note 167.

[170] Rogers v. Guaranty Trust Co., *supra* note 167; Note (1931) 44 HARV. L. REV. 437-439.

[171] Voorhees v. Mason, 243 Ill. 256, 91 N. E. 1056 (1910); Orton v. Edson Red. Mach. Co., 5 Ohio C. C. (N. S.) 540, *affd.* 75 Ohio St. 580, 80 N. E. 1126 (1905). See also Rogers v. Guaranty Trust Co., *supra* note 167 where the refusal of a "foreign" court to exercise jurisdiction because the case involved questions of law of the state of domicile was sustained. *Cf.* Hamm v. Christian Herald Corp., *supra* note 165; Harr v. Pioneer Mechanical Corp., *supra* note 169.

law of the place of performance of the acts involved.[172]

Form of Relief.[173]

A cause of action being established, it may be assumed that the court will "find the means of enforcing its decree" and that its powers will prove "as extensive as the exigencies of the case".[174] There is the whole array of equitable decrees to choose from and each case will be given "such remedy as its circumstances may require".[175] In making its decree the court is not circumscribed by any arbitrary designations of the precise form of relief; "it may vary, qualify, restrain, and modify the remedy it applies so as to do equity".[176]

When the action is strictly derivative the plaintiff can be granted only such relief as could be granted the corporation if it were plaintiff.[177] And

See Forum Non Conveniens and the "Internal Affairs" of a Foreign Corporation (1933) 33 COLUMBIA L. REV. 492.

[172] Old Dominion Copper M. & S. Co. v. Bigelow, 203 Mass. 159, 173-174, 89 N. E. 193, 200 (1909).

[173] We shall not attempt to be exhaustive; reference is made to the standard texts on equity pleading and practice. All the cases noted in this chapter illustrate the forms of relief available. In the next succeeding notes we shall merely refer to a few more illustrative cases.

[174] Wickersham v. Crittenden, *supra* note 166.

[175] Hyams v. Calumet & Hecla Min. Co., *supra* note 25, at 544.

[176] Jones v. Missouri-Edison Electric Co., *supra* note 3b, at 781. But a court will not work-up a case out of the facts to give the plaintiff relief which he does not ask. Tanner v. Lindell Ry. Co., *supra* note 144. We have already noted how the form of relief may be affected by the plaintiff's bad faith, *supra* note 150, or by his laches, *supra* note 156.

[177] Collins v. Penn-Wyoming Copper Co., 203 Fed. 726 (D. Wyo. 1912); Viley v. Wall, 159 La. 627, 105 So. 794 (1925).

conversely, in such a suit the plaintiff cannot be compelled to accept less than the corporation would be entitled to receive.[178]

The most commonly sought forms of redress are injunctions against threatened acts [179] and an accounting for past wrongs.[180] Occasionally redress against past acts is to be had by way of rescission [181] and future correct conduct is enforced by a decree of specific performance.[182]

The forms of relief most peculiar to corporate litigation, and the most drastic available, are the

---

[178] *E. g.*, money damages for his individual loss. Morris v. Elyton Land Co., 125 Ala. 263, 28 So. 51 (1899). *Cf.* Binney *v.* Cumberland Ely Copper Co., *supra* note 132, and Pennsylvania decisions cited *supra* note 87.

[179] Smith v. Chase Baker Piano Mfg. Co., *supra* note 8; Davidson v. American Blower Co., 243 Fed. 167 (C. C. A. 2d, 1917); Cuppy v. Ward, 187 App. Div. 625, 176 N. Y. Supp. 233 (1919), *aff'd.* 227 N. Y. 603, 125 N. E. 915 (1919); Schwab v. Potter Co., 194 N. Y. 409, 87 N. E. 670 (1909), *affg.* 120 App. Div. 36, 113 N. Y. Supp. 439 (1909).

[180] Sage v. Culver, *supra* note 29; Brock v. Poor, 216 N. Y. 387, 111 N. E. 229 (1915); Major v. American Malt & Grain Co., *supra* note 118: Fredendall v. Schrader, 45 Cal. App. 719, 188 Pac. 580 (1920); Barr v. N. Y. L. E. & W. R. R. Co., *supra* note 14.

[181] Carson v. Allegany Window Glass Co., *supra* note 146; Binney v. Cumberland Ely Copper Co., *supra* note 132; Metcalf v. American School Furn. Co., 122 Fed. 115 (C. C. W. D. N. Y. 1903); Morris v. Elyton Land Co., *supra* note 178; Macgill v. Macgill, 135 Md. 384, 109 Atl. 72 (1919); Kidd v. N. H. Traction Co., 72 N. H. 273, 56 Atl. 465 (1903). The right to rescission is frequently affected by the intervening rights of innocent persons, and rescission is frequently accompanied by an accounting against the wrongdoers. Such accounting is at times given in lieu of rescission. *Cf.* Johnson v. United Rys. *supra* note 147.

[182] Presidio Mining Co. v. Overton, 270 Fed. 388 (C. C. A. 9th, 1921), *certiorari* denied 256 U. S. 694, 41 Sup. Ct. 535 (1921) compelling a director to convey property to the corporation.

appointment of a receiver and its compulsory dissolution.

The power of a court of equity, independent of statute, to appoint a receiver of a solvent, going concern on the petition of a stockholder can no longer be doubted.[183] But it is still regarded as an extreme remedy to be granted only when clearly necessary [184] and when other forms of equitable relief, such as injunction, are insufficient.[185] The

[183] Burwrite Coal Briquette Co. v. Riggs, 274 U. S. 208, 47 Sup. Ct. 576 (1927); Columbia N. S. D. Co. v. Washed Bar S. D. Co., 136 Fed. 710 (C. C. E. D. Pa. 1905); Piza v. Butler, 90 Hun 254, 35 N. Y. Supp. 721 (1895); Hallenborg v. Greene, 66 App. Div. 590, 73 N. Y. Supp. 403 (1901); Schipper Bros. C. M. Co. v. Economy Domestic C. Co., 277 Pa. 356, 121 Atl. 193 (1923); Culver Lumber & Mfg. Co. v. Culver, *supra* note 161, on application of majority stockholder; 43 A. L. R. 246. *Cf.* Decker v. Gardner, 124 N. Y. 334, 26 N. E. 814 (1891); Davidson v. John Good Cordage Co., 63 App. Div. 366, 71 N. Y. Supp. 565 (1901); *In Re* Atlas Iron Const. Co., 38 N. Y. Supp. 172 (1895).

[184] Shera v. Carbon Steel Co., 245 Fed. 589 (D. W. Va. 1917); Collins v. Williamson, 229 Fed. 59 (C. C. A. 6th, 1915); Thoroughgood v. Georgetown Water Co., 9 Del. Ch. 84, 77 Atl. 720 (1910); Welcke v. Trageser, 131 App. Div. 731, 116 N. Y. Supp. 166 (1909); Thalmann v. Hoffman House, 27 Misc. 140, 58 N. Y. Supp. 227 (1899). For a time the courts displayed great liberality as to what constitutes a proper case for the appointment of a receiver. For a discussion of judicial trends as to this power see Gibbs v. Morgan, *supra* note 130; Brent v. B. E. Brister Sawmill Co., 103 Miss. 876, 60 So. 1018 (1913); Goodman v. Von Cotzhausen, *supra* note 161; Bowen v. Bowen-Romer Flour Mills Corp., 114 Kan. 95, 217 Pac. 301 (1923); Berkshire Pet. Co. v. Moore, 268 S. W. 484 (Tex. Civ. App. 1924). But see Tachna v. Pressed Steel Car Co., *supra* note 150a, calling a halt in a creditor's suit.

[185] Lowe v. Pioneer Threshing Co., *supra* note 62; New Albany Water Works v. Louisville Banking Co., *supra* note 168; United Electric Sec. Co. v. Louisiana Elec. Co., 68 Fed. 673 (C. C. E. D. La. 1895); Moore v. Associated P. & R. Corp., 14 Del. Ch. 97, 121 Atl. 655 (1923); Smallwood v. Smith, 197 App. Div. 533, 189 N. Y. Supp. 427 (1921).

164   CORPORATE CONTROL

appointment of a receiver may not be the sole or primary purpose of the suit, it must be merely provisional to some other ultimate relief.[186] When necessary, a receiver will be appointed if the directors are guilty of fraud and mismanagement.[187] But the charge of "mismanagement" must be based upon something more than differences of opinion as to business policies or methods.[188] Not even past misconduct will necessarily require the appointment of a receiver; the misconduct of the directors must be of such a character as to satisfy the court of their unfitness and of the probability of further loss or injuries to the corporation and stockholders.[189] Serious dissension in the corporation may also move a court to appoint a receiver.[190]

We have already noted that a court of equity

[186] Wilson v. Waltham Watch Co., *supra* note 89; Myers v. Occidental Oil Corp., 288 Fed. 997 (D. Del. 1923); Zuber v. Micmac Gold M. Co., 180 Fed. 625 (C. C. D. Me. 1910); Edwards v. Bay State Gas Co., 91 Fed. 942 (C. C. D. Del. 1898).

[187] Aiken v. Colorado River I. Co., 72 Fed. 591 (C. C. S. D. Colo. 1896); Hallenborg v. Greene, *supra* note 183; Jacobus v. Diamond Soda Water Mfg. Co., 94 App. Div. 366, 88 N. Y. Supp. 302 (1904).

[188] Hunt v. American Grocery Co., 80 Fed. 70 (C. C. D. N. J. 1897); Carson v. Allegany Window Glass Co., *supra* note 146; Thomas v. East End Opera House Co., 30 Pitts. L. J. (N. S.) 230 (1899).

[189] Carson v. Allegany Window Glass Co., *supra* note 146.

[190] Ellis v. Penn Beef Co., 9 Del. Ch. 213, 80 Atl. 666 (1911); Powers v. Blue Grass Bldg. Co., 86 Fed. 705 (C. C. D. Ky. 1898); Schipper Bros. Coal M. Co. v. Economy Domestic Coal Co., *supra* note 183. In most cases where a receiver is appointed on the ground of dissension there is "a more or less equal division between the contending factions". Note (1926) 43 A. L. R. 260; Hlawati v. Maeder-Hlawati Co., *supra* note 33. See N. Y. GEN. CORP. LAW, Sec. 103. *Cf.* Schuster v. Largman, 308 Pa. 520, 162 Atl. 305 (1932).

may at the suit of minority stockholders prevent the dissolution of the corporation.[191] Will it ever compel a dissolution? Although there is considerable language in the books to the effect that, exclusive of statute, a court of equity has no power to compel a dissolution of a corporation,[192] it has been held that under proper circumstances equity may direct dissolution.[192a] If we distinguish between the compulsory surrender of its corporate franchise and the winding up of its business as a going concern,[193] it seems that, at least with respect to the latter, the court certainly has the power.[194] Recognizing the gravity of its use, courts use their power to compel dissolution or liquidation sparingly and

[191] *Supra* p. 137.

[192] Republican Mountain S. Mines v. Brown, 58 Fed. 644 (C. C. A. 8th, 1893); Sidway v. Missouri Land & L. S. Co., 101 Fed. 481 (C. C. S. D. Mo. 1900); Taylor v. Decatur Mineral Land Co., 112 Fed. 449 (C. C. N. D. Ala. 1901), *aff'd.* 115 Fed. 1022 (C. C. A. 5th, 1902); Pearce v. Sutherland, 164 Fed. 609 (C. C. A. 9th, 1908); Myers v. Occidental Oil Corp., *supra* note 186; Benedict v. Columbus Const. Co., 49 N. J. Eq. 23, 23 Atl. 485 (1891); Denike v. N. Y. R. L. & C. Co., 80 N. Y. 599 (1880); Hlawati v. Maeder-Hlawati Co., *supra* note 33. *Cf.* Schipper Bros. C. M. Co. v. Economy D. C., *supra* note 183.

[192a] Kroger v. Jaburg, 231 App. Div. 641, 248 N. Y. S. 387 (1931).

[193] Sellman v. German Union Fire Ins. Co., 184 Fed. 977 (C. C. D. Del. 1909). See Note (1931) 44 HARV. L. REV. 437, 440.

[194] Miner v. Belle Isle Ice Co., *supra* note 130 (close corporation, dissension, fraud, mismanagement); Goodman v. Von Cotzhausen, *supra* note 161 (same situation and emphasis upon lack of good business qualities in controlling stockholders); Arents v. Blackwell's D. T. Co., 101 Fed. 338 (E. D. N. C. 1900) *aff'd.* 109 Fed. 1058 (C. C. A. 4th, 1901) (at the suit of majority). In Riley v. Callahan Mining Co., 28 Idaho 525, 155 Pac. 665 (1916), the same result was substantially obtained by compelling the corporation which had ceased to mine but had become a mere holding company to distribute its stock holdings. See also Note (1931) 44 HARV. L. REV. 437.

only when absolutely necessary for the adequate protection of the minority.[195]

Effect of Decree in One Suit on Other Stockholders.[196]

Where the suit is not merely a personal one [197] but is one on behalf of the corporation, a judgment obtained on the merits in one stockholder's suit binds all stockholders.[198] This result does not follow if the first judgment was obtained by fraud or collusion,[199] or, it would seem, if it were entered merely

[195] Presidio Mining Co. v. Overton, *supra* note 182; Brictson Mfg. Co. v. Close, 280 Fed. 297 (C. C. A. 8th, 1922); Sellman v. German Union Fire Ins. Co., *supra* note 193; Bixler v. Summerfield, 210 Ill. 66, 70 N. E. 1059 (1904).

[196] The mere pendency of one derivative suit may prevent the prosecution of another by another stockholder, Dresdner v. Goldman Sachs Trading Co., 148 Misc. 541, 265 N. Y. S. 913 (1933).

[197] Harris v. Pearsall, *supra* note 152; Colgan v. Fink, 167 App. Div. 718, 153 N. Y. Supp. 239 (1915). In Jackson v. Gardiner, 200 Fed. 113 (C. C. A. 1st, 1912), the importance of it appearing that the prior suit was on behalf of all who might join therein was stressed. *Cf.* Roberts v. Kennedy, 13 Del. Ch. 133, 116 Atl. 253 (1922). For "class" suits, see 21 C. J. 284-297, 34 C. J. 1002, § 1422.

[198] Dana v. Morgan, 232 Fed. 85 (C. C. A. 2d, 1916); Willoughby v. Chicago Junction Rys. Co., *supra* note 69; Goodbody v. Delaney, 80 N. J. Eq. 417, 83 Atl. 988 (1912); Grant v. Greene Cons. Copper Co., *supra* note 161; Hearst v. Putnam Mining Co., 28 Utah 184, 77 Pac. 753 (1904); Corey v. Independent Ice Co., 106 Me. 485, 76 Atl. 930 (1910); Hochman v. Mortgage Finance Corp., 289 Pa. 260, 137 Atl. 252 (1927). *Cf.* Southern Pacific Co. v. Bogert, *supra* note 3b. The same principle, of course, applies where the corporation itself acted in the first suit. Alexander v. Donohoe, 143 N. Y. 203, 38 N. E. 263 (1894). But minority stockholders may possibly be able to enjoin the prosecution of a suit by the corporation while it is under the control of directors interested in or associated with the defendants, Wile v. Burns Bros., 239 App. Div. 59, 265 N. Y. S. 461 (1933), or they may be able to intervene therein, Thayer v. Kinder, *supra* note 161.

[199] Willoughby v. Chicago Junction Rys. Co., *supra* note 69; Beers

on consent of the parties thereto without an actual *bona fide* litigation having been presented to the court for adjudication.[200]

Costs and Allowances.

For the purpose of receiving and paying costs the plaintiff is regarded as an individual plaintiff.[201] A successful plaintiff who sues on behalf of his corporation is entitled to an allowance for his expenditures, including counsel fees, out of the corporate funds,[202] but not against the individual de-

---

v. Denver & R. G. W. R. Co., 286 Fed. 886 (C. C. A. 8th, 1923); Levy v. Equitable Trust Co., 271 Fed. 49 (C. C. A. 8th, 1921); Gund v. Bullard, 73 Nebr. 547, 103 N. W. 309 (1905) applying the exception where in the first suit an issue was not fully or fairly presented.

[200] Metropolitan Elevated R. R. Co. v. Manhattan Elevated R. R. Co., 11 Daly 373 (N. Y. 1884); Cutter v. Arlington Casket Co., 255 Mass. 52, 151 N. E. 167 (1926); Spaulding v. North Milwaukee T. S. Co., 106 Wis. 481, 81 N. W. 1064 (1900). *Contra:* Zeitinger v. Hargardine-McKittriep Dry Goods Co., 309 Mo. 433, 274 S. W. 789 (1925); Kaufman v. Annuity Realty Co., 301 Mo. 638, 256 S. W. 792 (1923); Ralph v. Annuity Realty Co., 325 Mo. 410, 28 S. W. (2d) 662 (1930). By analogy: Jenkins v. Robertson, L. R. 1 Scotch & Div. App. Cas. 117 (1867); Kelley v. Town of Milan, 127 U. S. 139, 8 Sup. Ct. 1101 (1888); Union Bank v. Commissioners, 119 N. C. 214, 25 S. E. 966 (1896). See also *supra* note 162.

[201] Edwards v. Bay State Gas Co., *supra* note 186. An intervenor is not liable for costs accrued before his intervention. Whitten v. Dabney, *supra* note 162.

[202] Meeker v. Winthrop Iron Co., *supra* note 25; Beaudette v. Graham, 267 Mass. 7, 165 N. E. 671 (1929); Guay v. Holland System Hull Co., 244 Mass. 240, 138 N. E. 557 (1923); cases cited 13 FLETCHER, *Cyclopedia of Corporations* (Perm. Ed., 1932) § 6045. But his agreement with counsel as to amount is not necessarily binding upon the corporation or the court. Hutchinson Box Board & Paper Co., v. Van Horn, *supra* note 144; Saut v. Perronville Shingle Co., 179 Mich. 42, 146 N. W. 212 (1914). The same rules apply to an intervenor. Goodman v. Von Cotzhausen, *supra* note 161. See Hartman v. Oatman Gold M. & M. Co., 22 Ariz. 476, 198 Pac. 717 (1921), for an independent suit by a stockholder

fendants except pursuant to statute.[203] The plaintiff is not entitled to such an allowance where he has recovered only a personal judgment.[204] Generally an allowance is made only when there is an actual recovery by the corporation or a fund is brought into court for distribution.[205]

against corporation to recover expenditures. For cases involving the right of directors to employ counsel in minority stockholder's suits see Corey v. Independent Ice Co., *supra* note 198; McConnell v. Combination M. & M. Co., 31 Mont. 563, 79 Pac. 248 (1905); Godley v. Crandall & Godley Co., *supra* note 3b; Kannenberg v. Evangelical Creed Cong., 146 Wis. 610, 131 N. W. 353 (1911).

[203] Kilby v. Movius L. & L. Co., 55 N. D. 830, 215 N. W. 284 (1927).

[204] Boothe v. Summit Coal M. Co., 72 Wash. 679, 131 Pac. 252 (1913); Joyce v. Congdon, 114 Wash. 239, 195 Pac. 29 (1921).

[205] Alexander v. Atlantic & W. P. R. R. Co., 113 Ga. 193, 38 S. E. 772 (1901) (attorneys' fees not allowed in action resulting in injunction against *ultra vires* acts); Burley Tobacco Co. v. Vest, 165 Ky. 762, 178 S. W. 1102 (1915) (allowances denied where plaintiff established invalidity of an election of directors). *Cf.* Forrester & MacGinniss v. Boston & M. C. C. & S. M. Co., 29 Mont. 397, 76 Pac. 211 (1904). It would seem that a court might properly be allowed to consider non-tangible benefits resulting to the corporation even if not immediately serving to increase its physical assets.

CHAPTER VII.

CREDITOR CONTROL; OPERATING RECEIVERSHIPS; REORGANIZATIONS*

Creditor Rights.

In this section we shall examine the legal [1] rights, if any there be, of creditors who hold unmatured obligations [2] to control the management of the debtor corporation while it continues a solvent, going concern.[3] This limitation largely excludes from our purview the two subjects which have been the chief topics discussed in the law of corporate-creditors: the "trust fund" doctrine,[4] and the right of creditors to enforce stockholders' liability.[5] The first is

---

* The substance of this chapter is published in the Cornell Law Quarterly for December, 1933 (Vol. 19, p.   ).

[1] A factual control is of course exercised by the need to keep available sources of new credit.

[2] Primarily bondholders. The holders of past due obligations have well-defined legal rights. See Glenn, The Rights and Remedies of Creditors Respecting their Debtor's Property (1915). The exercise of these rights tends to force liquidation, a subject outside the scope of this book.

[3] In seeking the "principles" we may be forced to use dicta in cases which arose after the corporation had become insolvent.

[4] We shall of course be unable to avoid the underlying notion of this doctrine to the effect that creditors have a prior claim to the assets.

[5] In so far as "fraudulent conveyances" are concerned the rules are essentially the same as for individuals, 8 Thompson, Corps. (3d Ed. 1927) Sec. 6235.

169

excluded because it properly becomes applicable only when a corporation is insolvent [6] and probably is not even applicable to an insolvent corporation which continues as a going concern.[7] The second is excluded because the right may be exercised only after a judgment has been obtained [8] and the property of the corporation exhausted.[9] Generally, an unsecured creditor has no claim on his debtor's property in the absence of a judgment; the debt itself conferring no title to or equity in his property.[10] This rule is applicable to corporate as well as to individual debtors.[11]

---

[6] *McDonald* v. *Williams,* 174 U. S. 397, 19 S. Ct. 743, 43 L. Ed. 1022 (1899); *Sweet* v. *Lang,* 14 F. (2d) 762 (C. C. A. 8th, 1926); *Fear* v. *Bartlett,* 81 Md. 435, 32 Atl. 322, 33 L. R. A. 721 (1895). In this connection insolvency means merely the inability to pay debts in the ordinary course of the business, *Joseph* v. *Raff,* 82 App. Div. 47, 81 N. Y. S. 546, *affd.* 176 N. Y. 611, 68 N. E. 1118 (1903).

[7] 8 Thompson, Corps. (3d Ed. 1927) Secs. 6130, 6131, 6139. Under certain circumstances the doctrine is applied when the corporation has ceased to do business by reason of a sale of all its assets even though not insolvent. See *Hurd* v. *N. Y. & C. Steam Laundry Co.,* 167 N. Y. 89, 60 N. E. 327 (1901).

[8] *Fourth Natl. Bank* v. *Franklyn,* 120 U. S. 747, 7 S. Ct. 757, 30 L. Ed. 825 (1887); *Cutright* v. *Stanford,* 81 Ill. 240 (1876); *Handy* v. *Draper,* 89 N. Y. 334 (1882). *Cf. Wyman* v. *Wallace,* 201 U. S. 230, 12 S. Ct. 495, 50 L. Ed. 738 (1906); *Walton* v. *Coe,* 110 N. Y. 109, 17 N. E. 676 (1888); *Parker* v. *Adams,* 38 Misc. 325, 77 N. Y. S. 861 (1902). Performance of this condition precedent may be dispensed with when impossible of performance. See review of authorities in *United Glass Co.* v. *Vary,* 152 N. Y. 121, 46 N. E. 312 (1897).

[9] *Strelaw* v. *American Color Co.,* 162 Mich. 709, 127 N. W. 716 (1910); *Wetherbee* v. *Baker,* 35 N. J. Eq. 501 (1882); *Appeal of Means,* 85 Pa. 75 (1877). Under special circumstances this requirement may be dispensed with, *Shellington* v. *Howland,* 53 N. Y. 371 (1873).

[10] Glenn, *supra* note 2 at pp. 2–6.

[11] *Graham Button Co.* v. *Spillman,* 50 N. J. Eq. 120, 24 Atl. 571 (1892).

The sweeping dictum that creditors "have no right of control over corporate management and no interest in or to the assets of a solvent corporation" [12] is only partially true. It is true to the extent that creditors ordinarily have no voting rights [13] and hence have no right to participate in the election of directors or to contest the validity of corporate elections.[14] Nor may creditors attack an *ultra vires* transaction "unless it also resulted in depleting the assets of the corporation in fraud of creditors".[15]

The foregoing factors together with the fact that "at common law no individual liability was imposed upon the members or stockholders of a corporation" [16] made the growth of safeguards for the protection of corporate creditors inevitable. To

[12] *Sweet* v. *Lang, supra* note 6, at p. 766.

[13] Under certain statutes bondholders may not be given voting rights. See *Durkee* v. *People,* 155 Ill. 354, 40 N. E. 626 (1895) ; *Pollitz* v. *Wabash RR. Co.,* 167 App. Div. 669, 152 N. Y. S. 803 (1915). See also *Holt* v. *California Development Co.,* 161 Fed. 3 (C. C. A. 9th, 1908). *Cf. State* v. *McDaniel,* 22 Ohio 354 (1872) ; *Ecker* v. *Kentucky Ref. Co.,* 144 Ky. 264, 138 S. W. 264 (1911).

[14] 2 Thompson, Corps. (3d Ed. 1927) Sec. 1033.

[15] *Brent* v. *Simpson,* 238 Fed. 285, 291 (C. C. A. 5th, 1916) *cert. den.* 243 U. S. 639, 37 S. Ct. 743, 61 L. Ed. 942 ; *Force* v. *Age-Herald Co.,* 136 Ala. 271, 33 So. 866 (1902). *Cf. In re Hool Realty Co.,* 2 F. (2d) 334 (C. C. A. 7th, 1924), *cert. den.* 266 U. S. 633, 45 S. Ct. 225, 69 L. Ed. 479 ; *Washington Mill Co.* v. *Sprague Lumber Co.,* 19 Wash. 165, 52 Pac. 1067 (1898). There is a conflict of authority as to whether creditors may question the validity of corporate acts by directors and officers without requisite stockholders' consent. See *Royal Indemnity Co.* v. *American Bond & Mortgage Co.,* 289 U. S. 165, 53 S. Ct. 551, 77 L. Ed. 688 (1933) ; *Leffert* v. *Jackman,* 227 N. Y. 310, 125 N. E. 446 (1919).

[16] *Hoffman* v. *Worden Co.,* 2 F. Supp. 353, 354 (D. C. N. D. Cal. 1933) ; Warren, Safeguarding the Creditors of Corporations, 36 Harvard L. Rev. 509, 518–522 (1923).

have left them completely to the mercy of the stockholders would have been intolerable.

The primary sources of creditors' rights are certain statutory provisions now well-nigh universal.[17] In general, these have three major objectives: (1) to require that stock be issued only for adequate consideration;[18] (2) to maintain the stated capital by limiting the declaration of dividends[19] and by prohibiting the reduction of capital to an extent which would render the corporation insolvent;[20] and (3) to make certain financial information available by requiring the filing of periodic reports in a public office.[21]

[17] Limitations of space prevent reference to all the statutes and analysis of their differences. We shall therefore cite only the proposed Uniform Business Corporations Act, 9 U. L. A., approved American Bar Association 1928 (53 A. B. A. R. 92). We shall also take the liberty of treating expressions of courts under specific statutes as expressions of general principles. Due to the substantial uniformity in the American statutory schemes no serious error should result. For a study of the Massachusetts statutes, see Warren, *supra* note 16, at pp. 523–544.

[18] U. B. C. A. Secs. 15, 16, requiring payment "with cash, other property, tangible or intangible, or with necessary services actually rendered". See Dodd, Stock Watering (1930).

[19] U. B. C. A. Secs. 24, 25, prohibiting payment of dividends "except from the surplus of its assets over the aggregate of its liabilities" including its capital.

[20] U. B. C. A. Sec. 41, requiring that any proposed reduction shall "not reduce the fair value of the assets of the corporation to an amount less than the total amount of its debts and liabilities plus the amount of its capital stock as so reduced". Some jurisdictions expressly prohibit the purchase by a corporation of its own shares except out of surplus. See N. Y. Penal Law, Sec. 664.

[21] U. B. C. A. Secs. 18, 36, requiring report upon organization as to consideration received for shares and annual reports "as to its financial condition". The requirement of Sec. 18 that a report be filed as to the consideration received for its stock is far from universal, but see Delaware Gen. Corp. Law, § 23.

It is from these statutes that most cases take their "policy".[22] In addition, of course, creditors frequently bargain for and receive certain special rights by contract.[23] These creditor rights, statutory and contractual, are interpreted by the courts in the light of the relationship which they deem exists between the corporation (that is, its stockholders as represented by the management, the directors) and its creditors. The concept of what that relationship should be also gives rise to certain rights and obligations exclusive of statute and contract.

Directors of a solvent corporation are not "trustees"[24] for its creditors;[25] the relation between

[22] Because they are deemed to express a "public policy", acts in violation of them are more than mere ultravires acts. See *West Penn Chem. & Mfg. Co.* v. *Prentice*, 236 Fed. 891, 895 (C. C. A. 3d 1916). Prof. Warren is of the opinion that courts should not attempt to establish safeguards for corporate creditors but should leave the matter to legislation, *supra* note 16 at p. 547. "If it be said that in the field of business some of the realities of yesterday are the illusions of today; that the troublous times through which we are passing demonstrate the need for greater protection of creditors of corporations, that is a problem of financial and economic policy which is peculiarly within the province of the legislature. The legislative machinery possesses greater flexibility than the judicial process can or should have in such matters", Shientag, J. in *Quintal* v. *Adler*, 146 Misc. 300, 262 N. Y. S. 126 (1933).

[23] This field is as wide as all contract law—we shall advert only to a few typical cases.

[24] The word "trustee" has come to be used in corporate matters not in its strict technical sense but to describe a somewhat ambiguous fiduciary.

[25] *Bird* v. *Magowan*, 43 Atl. 278 (N. J. 1898); *Landis* v. *Sea Isle City Hotel Co.*, 31 Atl. 755, *affd.* 53 N. J. Eq. 654 (1895); *Force* v. *Age-Herald Co.*, *supra* note 15; *O'Conner M. & M. Co.* v. *Coosa F. Co.*, 95 Ala. 614, 10 So. 290 (1891). *Contra: Delano* v. *Case*, 121 Ill. 247, 12 N. E. 676 (1887); *Thomas* v. *Sweet*, 37 Kan. 183, 14 Pac. 545 (1889); *Hibernia Bank* v. *Succession of Caucienne*, 140 La. 969, 74

them "is that of contract and not of trust".²⁶ On this premise it is held that directors are not liable to creditors for negligence ²⁷ or for mismanagement.²⁸ The underlying thought is that creditors have a recognizable grievance only when the directors "fraudulently" divert assets of the corporation with a resulting destruction or lessening of

So. 267, L. R. A. 1917 D 402 (1917); *Pender* v. *Speight,* 159 N. C. 612, 75 S. E. 851 (1912). In *Sawyer* v. *Hoag,* 17 Wall. 610 (U. S. 1873), Mr. Justice Miller said (p. 623) : "* * * when the interest of the public, or of strangers dealing with this corporation is to be affected by any transaction between the stockholders who own the corporation and the corporation itself, such transaction should be subject to a rigid scrutiny, and if found to be infected with anything unfair to such third person, calculated to injure him, or designed intentionally and inequitably to screen the stockholder from loss at the expense of the general creditor, it should be disregarded or annulled so far as it may inequitably affect him".

²⁶ *Briggs* v. *Spaulding,* 141 U. S. 132, 147, 11 S. Ct. 924, 35 L. Ed. 662 (1891). Directors do become "trustees" for the creditors on insolvency or liquidation. See *Giles D. M. Co.* v. *Klauder-Weldon D. M. Co.,* 233 N. Y. 470, 476, 135 N. E. 854 (1922) ; *Olney* v. *Conanicut Land Co.,* 16 R. I. 597, 18 Atl. 181, 5 L. R. A. 361 (1889) ; *Darcy* v. *Bklyn. & N. Y. Ferry Co.,* 196 N. Y. 99, 89 N. E. 461 (1909).

²⁷ *Deaderick* v. *Bank,* 100 Tenn. 457, 45 S. W. 786 (1897) ; *Allen* v. *Cochran,* 160 La. 425, 107 So. 292 (1926) ; *U. S. Fidelity & Guaranty Co.* v. *Savings Bank,* 154 Iowa 588, 134 N. W. 857, 45 L. R. A. (N. S.) 421 (1912). *Cf.* Ellett v. Newland, 171 La. 1019, 132 So. 761 (1931). A trustee in bankruptcy has the right to sue for negligence and if he refuses creditors may do so, *Rural Credit Subscribers' Assn.* v. *Jett,* 205 Ky. 604, 266 S. W. 240 (1924).

²⁸ *Natl. Exchange Bank* v. *Peters,* 44 Fed. 13 (C. C. E. D. Va. 1890) app. dis. 144 U. S. 570, 25 S. Ct. 767, 36 L. Ed. 545 ; *Lyman* v. *Bonney,* 118 Mass. 222 (1875) ; *Wilson* v. *Stevens,* 129 Ala. 630, 29 So. 678 (1900) ; *Frost Mfg. Co.* v. *Foster,* 76 Iowa 535 (1889). Contra: *Anthony* v. *Jeffress,* 172 N. C. 378, 90 S. E. 414 (1916). Except by statute, see *Levy* v. *Paramount Publix Corp.,* 149 Misc. 129, 266 N. Y. S. 271 (1933). A trustee in bankruptcy succeeds to the right of the *corporation* to sue for mismanagement, *McEwen* v. *Kelly,* 140 Ga. 720, 79 S. E. 777 (1913).

the security behind their debt.[29]

The most frequent methods of diversion of corporate assets away from creditors are: [29a] (1) the payment of unlawful dividends; (2) the improper reduction of capital; and (3) the purchase by the corporation of its own stock out of capital. Much has already been written on the subject of unlawful dividends [30] and it must suffice here merely to note that it was the obligation not to pay out dividends improperly that gave rise to the notion that the capital of a corporation constituted a "trust fund" for the benefit of its creditors [31] and that the limitations upon dividend payments may

[29] This principle may be quite sufficient if it includes the recognition of the right to preventive relief to prevent such diversion as well as compensatory relief after the event. Although negligence and incompetence do result in endangering the security, it must be remembered that "fraud" is not defined (see Shonfeld v. Shonfeld, 260 N. Y. 477, 479, 184 N. E. 60 [1933]) and that the courts could in a "hard" case decribe "gross" negligence or mismanagement as "fraud in law". Furthermore, the first victims of loss caused by negligence or mismanagement on the part of the directors (if they are honest) are the stockholders and they are in a position to correct the situation.

[29a] The payment of excessive salaries of course also reacts to the detriment of creditors. In proper cases they may be recovered by legal representatives of the corporation and its creditors in the event of insolvency, see, Ellis v. Ward, 137 Ill. 509, 25 N. E. 530 (1890); McKey v. Swenson, 232 Mich. 505, 205 N. W. 583 (1925). But probably not, if made without fraud at a time when the corporation was solvent, see, Buell v. Lanski, 232 Ill. App. 500 (1924). See also, supra, pp. 116-118.

[30] Weiner, Theory of Anglo-American Dividend Law, 28 Columbia Law Rev. 1046 (1928), 29 Columbia Law Rev. 461 (1929), 30 Columbia Law Rev. 330, 954 (1930); Krauss, Maintenance of a Corporation's Capital, 9 Tenn. L. Rev. 215 (1931); (Note) Statutory Responsibility of Directors for Payment of Dividends out of Capital, 35 Yale L. J. 870 (1926); (Note) Actions against Stockholders to Recover Illegal Dividends, 33 Columbia Law Rev. 481 (1933).

[31] Wood v. Dummer, 3 Mason 308, 30 Fed. Cas. No. 17944 (C. C. Me. 1824).

not be circumvented by the use of subterfuge.[32]

Small v. *Sullivan* [33] is interesting. The complaint in an action brought by bondholders against directors, after the mortgage which secured the bonds had been foreclosed and the corporation liquidated in bankruptcy, to recover for the defendants' fraudulent conversion of assets to their own use was sustained. The complaint alleged that the defendants consolidated the debtor corporation, having net assets of $52,000,000 but an impaired capital position, with another corporation having assets of only $550, for the sole purpose of recapitalizing on a new basis which would make $2,000,000 available as surplus for distribution as dividends to themselves as stockholders, and that this purpose had been fully carried out. The statutory provisions for consolidation were fully complied with but the court held that this did not constitute a defense.[34]

There is a dearth of cases wherein creditors attack formal capital reductions, and this may indicate either that the statutes drawn for their protection [35] have proven effective,[36] or that capital

---

[32] *Small* v. *Sullivan,* 245 N. Y. 343, 157 N. E. 261 (1927) ; *Penn. Iron Works Co.* v. *Mackenzie,* 190 Mass. 61, 76 N. E. 228 (1906).

[33] *Supra* note 32. It is to be noted that subsequent statutory changes would have, if then in force, allowed a direct achievement of the result sought to be obtained, see dissenting opinion of Lehman, J. at p. 360.

[34] The mortgage stipulated that the bondholders had "no recourse" against the directors but the court held that this afforded no defense to a claim based on their subsequent fraud.

[35] *Supra,* note 20.

[36] See *Dominquez Land Co.* v. *Daugherty,* 196 Cal. 453, 468, 238 Pac. 697, 703 (1925) sustaining constitutionality of legislation vesting in a Corporations Commissioner the power to permit a distribu-

reductions are not frequently resorted to as a means of injuring creditors. There may be no distribution of "capital" among stockholders except by way of capital reduction [37] and there can be no capital reduction except pursuant to some express statutory authorization therefor.[38] However, a mere purchase by a corporation of its own stock does not constitute a reduction of capital [39] and therefore most of the litigation in this field has involved stock purchases which ordinarily require no formal public action.[40] Stock purchases may be made only out of "surplus" [41] and therefore neither notes nor agreements for purchase, even though

tion to stockholders of a surplus created by a capital reduction. See also *State ex rel. Radio Corp.* v. *Benson,* 128 Atl. 107 (Del. 1924) for the distinction between a statutory reduction in the number of shares and a reduction of capital.

[37] *Stevens* v. *Olus Mfg. Co.,* 72 Misc. 508, 130 N. Y. S. 22 *affd.* 146 App. Div. 951 (1911). A creditor may proceed directly against a stockholder who has improperly received a part of the corporate assets (*Trotter* v. *Lisman,* 209 N. Y. 174, 102 N. E. 575 (1913)) for the full amount thereof regardless of existing equities as between the stockholders, *Bartlett* v. *Drew,* 57 N. Y. 587 (1874); *Clapp* v. *Peterson,* 104 Ill. 26 (1882).

[38] *Sutherland* v. *Olcott,* 95 N. Y. 93 (1884); *Seignouret* v. *Home Ins. Co.,* 24 Fed. 332 (C. C. E. D. La. 1885). On the general subject of reductions of capital stock, see 44 A. L. R. 11 (1926).

[39] *In Re Atlantic Printing Co.,* 60 F. (2d) 553 (D. C. Mass. 1932). Shares of stock are not retired by mere purchase, 5 Thompson, Corps. (3 Ed. 1927) Sec. 4084.

[40] See, Wormser, The Power of a Corporation to Acquire Its Own Stock, 24 Yale L. J. 177 (1915); Levy, Purchase by a Corporation of its Own Stock, 15 Minn. L. Rev. 1 (1930).

[41] *Hazard* v. *Wight,* 201 N. Y. 399, 94 N. E. 855 (1911); *Topken, Loring & Schwartz, Inc.* v. *Schwartz,* 249 N. Y. 206, 163 N. E. 735 (1928); *Hoover Steel Ball Co.* v. *Schaefer Ball Bearings Co.,* 90 N. J. Eq. 164, 106 Atl. 471 (1919); *Hamor* v. *Taylor-Rice Eng. Co.,* 84 Fed. 392 (C. C. Del. 1897); *West Penn Chem. & Mfg. Co.* v. *Prentice, supra* note 22.

made when the corporation did have a sufficient surplus, can be enforced when the necessary surplus no longer exists.[42]

The methods of diversion of assets which we have just touched upon are by and large contrary to express statutory prohibitions, but they obviously do not exhaust the possibilities, nor is a statute essential to impose liability upon those guilty of an improper diversion of assets. Thus, it has been held that directors are liable for the sale to one of their number of property for less than its full value, the court stating that the doctrine which it applied does not depend on statute "but rather on principles inherent in the nature of corporations as artificial persons whose creditors can only enforce their debts by a resort to the property the corporation has acquired".[43]

---

[42] In Re Atlantic Printing Co., supra note 39; Keith v. Kilmer, 261 Fed. 733 (C. C. A. 1st 1919) cert. den. 252 U. S. 578, 40 S. Ct. 344, 64 L. Ed. 725; In re O'Gara & Maguire, Inc., 259 Fed. 935 (D. C. N. J. 1919); Grasselli Chem. Co. v. Aetna Explosives Co., 258 Fed. 66 (D. C. S. D. N. Y. 1918); In re Fechheimer Fishel Co., 212 Fed. 357 (C. C. A. 2d 1914) cert. den. 234 U. S. 760, 34 S. Ct. 777, 58 L. Ed. 1580; In Re Tichenor-Grand Co., 203 Fed. 720 (D. C. S. D. N. Y. 1913); Clark v. E. C. Clark Mach. Co., 151 Mich. 416, 115 N. W. 416 (1908). Cf. Keith v. Kilmer, 272 Fed. 643 (C. C. A. 1st 1921); Cross v. Beguelin, 252 N. Y. 262, 169 N. E. 378 (1929); First Trust Co. v. Illinois Central RR. Co., 256 Fed. 830 (C. C. A. 8th 1919). As to rights of creditors upon subsequent insolvency where the transaction was consummated while solvent, see Kaminsky v. Phinizy, 54 F. (2d) 16 (C. C. A. 5th 1931); Clapp v. Peterson, 104 Ill. 26 (1882); In Re Brockway Mfg. Co., 89 Me. 121, 35 Atl. 1612 (1896); Lebens v. Nelson, 148 Minn. 240, 181 N. W. 350 (1921); Wolff v. Heidritter Lumber Co., 112 N. J. Eq. 34, 163 Atl. 140 (1932); Tait v. Pigott, 32 Wash. 344, 73 Pac. 364 (1903); Marvin v. Anderson, 111 Wis 387, 87 N. W. 226 (1901).

[43] Wilkinson v. Bauerle, 41 N. J. Eq. 635, 644 (1886). See also

Short-term creditors, or those in a position promptly to mature the obligation and enforce its payment by the usual methods, are less dependent upon equitable relief [44] than the long-term creditor tied to a corporation for many years.[45] He can hardly be satisfied with a position entirely divorced of any power to prevent incompetent or improvident dissipation of the corporate assets. He is obliged to rely upon the intervention of equity or seek to bolster his legal position by private contract.[46] Necessarily, a very few typical illustrations must suffice. A bill by a mortgage bondholder to prevent the impairment of the mortgaged property by the improper sale of the property or of more bonds secured by the same mortgage has been sustained,[47] but it may be that directors who operate

Darcy v. Bklyn. & N. Y. Ferry Co., supra note 26. As to rights of a subsequent creditor, see Graham v. LaCrosse & M. R. R. Co., 102 U. S. 148, 26 L. Ed. 106 (1880).

[44] Assuming that they are in possession of current data as to the affairs of the corporation, otherwise the assertion of their legal rights is generally "too late".

[45] The specific creditor may of course sever the relationship by selling the evidence of indebtedness—if there exists a market therefor. From 1913 to 1932 the total indebtedness of industrial corporations increased 75% but their long term debt increased 150%, The Internal Debts of the United States (ed. Clark, 1933) 175.

[46] Frequently representatives of the security house that floats a bond issue are elected to the board to represent the bondholders. See O'Leary, Corporate Enterprise In Modern Economic Life (1933) 41–44. See Green v. People's Gas Light & Coke Co., 118 Misc. 1, 192 N. Y. S. 232, affd. 206 App. Div. 647, 198 N. Y. S. 917 (1923) for a case involving conflicting interests between a minority bondholder and a majority bondholder who, as majority stockholder, also controlled the debtor corporation. Cf. (Note) Protective Devices Available to the Preferred Stockholders (1927) 27 Columbia L. Rev. 587.

[47] Whitmore v. International F. & S. Co., 214 Mass. 525, 102 N. E.

mortgaged property in violation of the terms of the mortgage and depreciate its value are accountable only to the corporation and not to the bondholders.[48]

In *Hoyt* v. *DuPont de Nemours Co.*,[49] the corporation was enjoined, at the suit of a bondholder secured by a "charge" on all its assets, from using certain debentures received for its assets even though such use would have left the bondholder with twice as much security as he had before. Where the mortgage provides for a sinking fund the mortgagee may obtain an accounting in the event of non-compliance,[50] and a controlling stockholder has been held liable for the corporation's failure to maintain a sinking fund as agreed, the stockholder having profited by the use of the funds.[51] Extraordinary circumstances may induce a court to deprive a bondholder of clear contract rights. In *New Jersey National Bank* v. *Lincoln*

59 (1913). It was alleged that the corporation was insolvent and in default, but the court said "the bill is maintainable whether the principal be due or not, or whether the coupons be paid or unpaid".

[48] *Young* v. *Haviland*, 215 Mass. 120, 102 N. E. 338 (1913); *Hart* v. *Hanson*, 14 No. Dak. 570, 105 N. W. 942 (1905).

[49] 88 N. J. Eq. 196, 102 Atl. 666 (1917).

[50] *New York Trust Co.* v. *Michigan Traction Co.*, 193 Fed. 175 (D. C. W. D. Mich. 1912). The court recognized the right of a mortgagee to invoke the aid of equity to preserve the mortgaged property. We are not treating in this book the rights of secured creditors beyond the limited extent necessary briefly to indicate some types of control which a creditor may achieve by special contract.

[51] *Penn. Canal Co.* v. *Brown*, 235 Fed. 669 (C. C. A. 3d 1916), cert. den. 242 U. S. 646, 37 S. Ct. 240, 61 L. Ed. 543. The court recognized the right of a bondholder to insist that the debtor corporation receive a fair price upon a sale of its property.

Mortgage and Title Guaranty Company,[52] bonds
had been issued under a trust indenture under
which there were pledged real estate mortgages as
collateral. The indenture contained express and
precise provisions calculated to maintain the collateral at all times at a fixed value and free of de-
faulted mortgages. Due to the financial depression
and the resultant defaults in the mortgages, the
debtor corporation was unable to comply, and the
court authorized the trustee under the indenture to
join in an agreement substantially modifying the
indenture.[53] The decision is not without precedent [54]
but the earlier decisions indicate a greater reluctance on the part of courts to interfere with contract provisions.[55]

Not being vested with any active affirmative
right of control, a creditor may, when completely
pessimistic as to the possibilities of the current
management, prefer that the corporate affairs be
turned over to the control of a court and to that
end seek the appointment of a receiver. The corpo-

[52] 105 N. J. Eq. 557, 148 Atl. 713 (1930).

[53] The petition was opposed by only one small bondholder.

[54] See, *Baltimore City* v. *United Rys. Co.,* 108 Md. 64, 69 Atl. 436
(1908) ; *Leviness* v. *Consolidated Gas Co.,* 114 Md. 559, 80 Atl. 304
(1911) ; *Detroit* v. *Detroit United Ry.,* 226 Mich. 354, 197 N. W. 697
(1924) ; *Price* v. *Long,* 87 N. J. Eq. 578, 101 Atl. 195 (1917) ; *New
York State Rys.* v. *Security Trust Co.,* 135 Misc. 456, 238 N. Y. S.
354, *affd.* 228 App. Div. 750, 238 N. Y. S. 887 (1930).

[55] See, *Duncan* v. *Mobile & O. R. Co.,* 2 Woods 542, Fed. Cas. No.
4137 (C. C. S. D. Ala. 1876) ; *Fidelity Ins. T. & S. D. Co.* v. *United
N. J. R. R. & C. Co.,* 36 N. J. Eq. 405, (1883) ; *Clark* v. *St. Louis,
A. & T. H. R. R. Co.,* 58 How. Pr. 21 (N .Y. 1879) ; *Watt* v.
Railroad Co., 1 Brewster 418 (Pa. 1867). As to necessary parties,
see also, *Colorado & So. Ry. Co.* v. *Blair,* 214 N. Y. 497, 108 N. E.
840 (1915).

ration may be insolvent and the object liquidation.[56] But that subject is outside the scope of this book.[57]

Operating Receiverships.[58]

The general rule is that in the absence of statute,

[56] See 2 Clark, Receivers (2d Ed. 1929) Sec. 706.

[57] Our attempt at segregation is largely unrealistic and therefore unsuccessful. Litigation generally arises when the corporation is in financial difficulties. But we adhere in the thought that it may be possible, as it is important, to develop a set of preventive rights and powers. In the two concluding sections (on receiverships and reorganizations) our primary concern is with the not too insolvent corporation, *i.e.*, one with hope but little life.

[58] There are a number of interesting procedural questions involved in federal receivership suits which we shall not treat. Among the more important are: *Venue and the need for Ancillary proceedings,* see Judicial Code, Sec. 56 (28 U. S. C. A. Sec. 117); *Lion Bonding Co.* v. *Karatz,* 262 U. S. 77, 43 S. Ct. 480, 67 L. Ed. 871 (1923); *Great Western Min. & Mfg. Co.* v. *Harris,* 198 U. S. 561, 25 S. Ct. 770, 49 L. Ed. 1163 (1905); *Primos Chem. Co.* v. *Fulton Steel Corp.* 255 Fed. 427 (D. C. S. D. N. Y. 1918), 254 Fed. 454 (D. C. N. D. N. Y. 1918); *Gatch, Tenant & Co.* v. *Mobile & O. R. Co.,* 59 F. (2d) 217 (D. C. S. D. Ala. 1932); Laughlin, The Extraterritorial Power of Receivers, 45 Harvard L. Rev. 429 (1932). The burden of ancillary proceedings lead a Special Committee on Equity Receiverships of the Association of the Bar of the City of New York to recommend statutory changes, 1927 Year Book 299 (see also hearings on H. R. 9999, 10000, 71st Cong. 2d. Sess. before House Judiciary Committee, April 11, 1930). See General Order in Bankruptcy LI promulgated May 15, 1933. *Cf.* Bankruptcy Act. Sec. 77c (Act of March 3, 1933) as to powers of a "trustee" thereunder. *Conflict with other proceedings,* see *Gross* v. *Irving Trust Co.,* 289 U. S. 342, 53 S. Ct. 605, — L. Ed. — (1933); *Harkin* v. *Brundage,* 276 U. S. 36, 48 S. Ct. 268, 72 I. Ed. 453 (1928); *Matter of Paramount Publix Corp.* 64 F. (2d) 500 (C. C. A. 2d, 1933); *Moore* v. *Scott,* 55 F. (2d) 863 (C. C. A. 9th 1932); *Superior Oil Corp.* v. *Matlock,* 47 F. (2d) 993 (C. C. A. 10th, 1931); see also (Note) State Statutes and the Federal Equity Courts, 32 Columbia L. Rev. 688 (1932). *Disaffirmance or Adoption of contracts,* see *Samuels* v. *E. F. Drew & Co., Inc.,* 292 Fed. 734 (C. C. A. 2d 1923); *American Brake S. & F. Co.* v. *N. Y. Rys. Co.,* 282 Fed. 523 (C. C. A. 2d 1922) app. dis. 262 U. S. 736, 43 S. Ct. 704, 67

an unsecured, non-judgment creditor may not obtain the appointment of a receiver.[59] There are exceptions to this rule [60] but one—the federal equity consent receivership—has achieved such importance that it has verily become the "rule" and almost preempts the field.[61]

Much learning has been devoted to finding the precise legal source of this type of receivership in

L. Ed. 1207; *Menke* v. *Willcox*, 275 Fed. 57 (D. C. S. D. N. Y. 1921); Clark, *et al.*, Adoption and Rejection of Contracts and Leases by Receivers (1933) 46 Harvard L. Rev. 1111. *Receiver's Certificates*, see *Union Trust Co.* v. *Illinois Midland Ry. Co.*, 117 U. S. 434 (1886); *Von Boston* v. *United Rys.* 8 F (2d) 826, (C. C. A. 8th (1925), cert. den. 271 U. S. 665, 46 S. Ct. 475, 70 L. Ed. 1140; *Mercantile Trust Co.* v. *Tennessee Cent. R. Co.*, 291 Fed. 462 (D. C. M. D. Tenn. 1921); *Westinghouse E. & Mfg. Co.* v. *Brooklyn Rapid Transit Co.*, 260 Fed. 550 (C. C. A. 2d 1919); *American Brake Shoe & F. Co.* v. *Pere Marquette R. Co.*, 205 Fed. 14 (C. C. A. 6th 1913) cert. den. 229 U. S. 624, 33 S. Ct. 1051, 57 L. Ed. 1356; Thacher, Some Tendencies of Modern Receiverships, 4 Calif. L. Rev. 32 (1915). Labor Problems in the Judicial Operation of Properties (Note 1933) 33 Columbia L. Rev. 882.

[59] *Pusey & Jones Co.* v. *Hanssen*, 261 U. S. 491, 43 S. Ct. 454, 67 L. Ed. 763 (1923); *Hollins* v. *Brierfield Coal & Iron Co.*, 150 U. S. 371, 14 S. Ct. 127, 37 L. Ed. 1113 (1893); *Trustees Systems Co.* v. *Payne*, 65 F. (2d) 103 (C. C. A. 3d 1933); *Home Mtge. Co.* v. *Ramsey*, 49 F. (2d) 738 (C. C. A. 4th 1931); *Lee* v. *Riefler & Sons*, 43 F. (2d) 364 (D. C. M. D. Pa. 1930); *Pond* v. *Framingham & Lowell RR.*, 130 Mass. 194 (1881); *Adee* v. *Bigler*, 81 N. Y. 349 (1880). This is true even when the corporation is insolvent. Solvency is not necessarily a sufficient reason for the denial of a receivership even by a state court. See *Adams* v. *Farmers Natl. Bank* 167 Ky. 506, 180 S. W. 807 (1915), "gross" mismanagement. A secured creditor may obtain a receivership only if the very property mortgaged is jeopardized, *Hutson* v. *Long Bell Lumber Co.*, 1 F. Supp. 468 (D. C. W. D. Mo. 1932).

[60] The readiness with which courts have come to appoint receivers has recently called forth a rebuke by a state appellate court, *Tachna* v. *Pressed Steel Car Co.*, 112 N. J. Eq. 411, 164 Atl. 413 (1933).

[61] The Act of March 3, 1933 amending the Bankruptcy Law does not apply to corporations other than railroads.

old English Chancery practice,[62] but whatever the source it exists today, in many respects *sui generis.* Its development was made necessary by the fact that the bankruptcy courts, prior to the amendment of March 3, 1933, were not available to railroads[63] and it was made possible by the diversity

[62] See Kroeger, Jurisdiction of Courts of Equity to Administer Insolvents' Estates, 9 St. Louis L. Rev. 87 (1924); Glenn, The Basis of the Federal Receivership, 25 Columbia L. Rev. 434 (1925); Dodd, Equity Receiverships as Proceedings in Rem, 23 Ill. L. Rev. 105 (1928); (Note) The Propriety of Friendly Receiverships in the Federal Courts, 43 Harvard L. Rev. 1298 (1930); Jacobs, Problems in Federal "Receivership" Jurisdiction, 1 Mercer Beasley L. Rev. 29 (1932); (Note) Consent Receiverships Instituted by Non-Judgment Creditor, 41 Yale L. J. 1086 (1932). The Federal courts do not appoint receivers of individuals under the same circumstances as justify them in appointing receivers of corporations. See, *Zechial* v. *Firemen's Fund Ins. Co.,* 61 F. (2d) 27 (C. C. A. 4th 1916); *Davis* v. *Hayden,* 238 Fed. 734 (C. C. A. 4th 1916) cert. den. 243 U. S. 636, 37 S. Ct. 400, 61 L. Ed. 941 (1917); *Maxwell* v. *McDaniels,* 184 Fed. 311 (C. C. A. 4th 1910); Clark, Simple Contract Creditor Securing Appointment of Receiver, 1 Univ. of Cinn. L. Rev. 388 (1927). The Supreme Court has held that the conveyance by an individual of his property to a corporation for the purpose of procuring its administration in equity is "fraudulent in law", *Shapiro* v. *Wilgus,* 287 U. S. 348, 53 S. Ct. 145, 77 L. Ed. 149 (1932). But a receiver may be appointed of the assets of a proposed corporation which proves abortive, *Garland* v. *Wilson,* 289 Pa. 272, 137 Atl. 266 (1927). Clark (Receivers, 2d Ed. 1929, Vol. 1, pp. 228–230) is of the opinion that courts will ultimately appoint receivers of individuals under the same circumstances as they do in the case of corporations.

[63] Bankruptcy Act, Sec. 4. Although it was the financial distress of the railroads that gave the initial impetus to the practice, it is not confined to public utilities, *United States* v. *Butterworth-Judson Corp.,* 269 U. S. 504, 46 S. Ct. 179, 70 L. Ed. 380 (1926); *Price* v. *United States,* 269 U. S. 492, 46 S. Ct. 180, 70 L. Ed. 373 (1926); *First Natl. Bank* v. *Stewart Fruit Co.,* 17 F. (2d) 621 (D. C. N. D. Cal. 1927); *Union Trust Co.* v. *Jones,* 16 F. (2d) 236 (C. C. A. 4th 1926). Some of the practices which have grown up in receiverships, such as with regard to the priority of "six months claims", have not yet been extended beyond public utilities. 1 Clark, Receivers, (2d Ed. 1929) Secs. 676–677.

clause of the federal constitution.[64]

In 1888, the Supreme Court held[65] that an equity court might, as a matter of discretion in a proper case, on a bill by a judgment-creditor, appoint a receiver to operate a quasi-public corporation and that the creditor's failure to have issued execution was immaterial in the absence of an objection by the corporation. Two years later it extended the rule by holding that the corporation's objection that the plaintiff had an adequate remedy at law which he had not exhausted must be made seasonably.[66]

Prior thereto a federal court had appointed equity receivers of the Wabash on its own bill[67] and when the proceedings were thereafter indirectly before the Supreme Court, it did not condemn the practice.[68]

[64] United States Constitution, Art. III, Sec. 2. See, *supra* p. 20, note 32.

[65] *Sage* v. *Memphis and Little Rock RR. Co.*, 125 U. S. 361, 8 S. Ct., 887, 31 L. Ed. 694 (1888).

[66] *Brown* v. *Lake Superior Iron Co.*, 134 U. S. 530, 10 S. Ct. 604, 33 L. Ed. 1021 (1890).

[67] See *Wabash, St. L. & P. Ry. Co.* v. *Central Trust Co.*, 22 Fed. 272 (C. C. E. D. Mo. 1884); *Atkins* v. *Wabash, St. L. & P. Ry. Co.*, 29 Fed. 161 (C. C. N. D. Ill. 1886); *Central Trust Co.* v. *Wabash, St. L. & P. Ry. Co.*, 29 Fed. 618 (C. C. E. D. Mo. 1886).

[68] *Quincy, M. & P. RR. Co.* v. *Humphreys*, 145 U. S. 82, 12 S. Ct. 787, 36 L. Ed. 632 (1892). It is doubtful whether the Supreme Court would tolerate the practice today. See *Shapiro* v. *Wilgus, supra* note 62 at p. 356. The practice was however severely criticized by other courts, *State ex rel. Merriam* v. *Ross*, 122 Mo. 435, 25 S. W. 947 (1894), app. dis. 156 U. S. 478; *McIlhenny* v. *Union Trust Co.*, 80 Tex. 1, 13 S. W. 655, app. dis. 145 U. S. 641 (1890). See also *Jones* v. *Bank of Leadville,* 10 Colo. 464 (1887); *In Re Moss Cigar Co.*, 50 La. Ann. 789, 23 So. 544 (1898); *Kimball* v. *Goodburn,* 32 Mich. 10 (1875); *Jones* v. *Schaff Bros. Co.*, 187 Mo. App. 597 (1915);

The first direct ruling by the Supreme Court on consent receiverships, as we now know them, was made in 1908, when it sustained the equity receivership of the New York City transit lines.[69] It held that the objection that the plaintiff has no judgment may be waived,[70] that a creditor's receivership bill presents a justiciable "controversy" notwithstanding the defendant's admissions of the allegations and consent to the receivership, and that there is no "collusion" in such admission, consent, and the agreement of the parties to resort to the federal court.[71]

Its legality confirmed by this decision,[72] there developed during the succeeding twenty years a recognized and customary consent equity receivership

Chamberlain, New-Fashioned Receiverships, 10 Harvard L. Rev. 139 (1896) *Cf. Collins* v. *Central Bank*, 1 Ga. 435 (1846); *Petition of Kittanning Ins. Co.*, 146 Pa. 102, 23 Atl. 336 (1892).

[69] *Re Metropolitan Railway Receivership*, 208 U. S. 90, 28 S. Ct. 219, 52 L. Ed. 403 (1908). The lower court had noted the existence of "a multitude of precedents", *Penn. Steel Co.* v. *N. Y. City Ry. Co.*, 157 Fed. 440, 443 (C. C. S. D. N. Y. 1907).

[70] The waiver need not be express. See *Finney* v. *Continental Baking & Milling Co.*, 17 F. (2d) 107 (D. C. Ind. 1927), removal from state court; *Walker* v. *U. S. Light & Heating Co.*, 220 Fed. 393 (D. C. S. D. N. Y. 1915) consent in another district. Not all the state courts follow the federal practice. See *National Lumberman's Bank* v. *Lake Shore Machinery Co.*, 260 Mich. 440, 245 N. W. 494 (1932) and the note thereon 31 Mich. L. Rev. 100 (1933).

[71] This decision, together with that in *Atlantic Trust Co.* v. *Chapman* (208 U. S. 360) decided the same year holding that the liabilities of a receivership are not chargeable against the plaintiff, rendered use of the procedure adopted by the Wabash unnecessary.

[72] It left no doubt as to the *power* of the court, but the propriety of its exercise in any particular case is necessarily an open question. See *Kingsport Press, Inc.* v. *Brief English Systems, Inc.* 54 F. (2d) 497 (C. C. A. 2d 1931), cert. den. 286 U. S. 545, 52 S. Ct. 497, 76 L. Ed. 282.

practice in the federal courts.[73]

The theoretical justification for equity receivership seems sound enough even for industrial corporations to whom bankruptcy is available. "In bankruptcy nearly every case ends merely in liquidation, * * * the underlying thought, the compelling motive of equity receiverships is to save the business".[74]

The requisite technique for coming within the permissive language of the *Metropolitan* case was rapidly perfected. It involves procuring a willing non-resident creditor [75] with a claim for more than $3,000 [76] to act as plaintiff, the preparation of a bill which sufficiently indicates that the corporation is unable to meet its debts as they mature [77] and that there would be insufficient assets to meet the claims of creditors if they were all permitted to obtain

[73] From January 1, 1917 to December 1, 1923, the United States District Court for the Southern District of New York appointed equity receivers for 233 corporations having nominal assets of over $750,000,000, Equity Receiverships in United States Courts, an inquiry by F. L. Hopkins (The N. Y. World, 1924).

[74] Mayer, Federal Equity Receiverships, 6 Lectures on Legal Topics (1924) 161, 165. See also *Benton* v. *R. G. Peters Salt & Lumber Co.*, 190 Fed. 262, 265 (C. C. W. D. Mich. 1911); Kroeger, *supra* note 62 at pp. 200-201.

[75] See *Harkin* v. *Brundage, supra* note 58, at p. 50. A director of the corporation, if a creditor, may act, *Hutchinson* v. *Phila. & G. S. S. Co.*, 216 Fed. 795 (D. C. E. D. Pa. 1914). But the filing of a bill by a subsidiary corporation, 99% of whose capital stock is owned by the defendant, has been condemned and picturesquely described as "incestuous litigation", *Municipal Fin. Corp.* v. *Bankus Corp.*, 45 F. (2d) 902 (D. C. S. D. N. Y. 1930).

[76] *Lion Bonding Co.* v. *Karatz, supra* note 58.

[77] *i.e.*, "insolvency" in the equity sense.

judgments and levy executions [78] but that the corporation is "solvent".[79] The "complete administration" which the bill seeks is held sufficient compliance with the rule that a receivership must be incidental to some ultimate relief.[80] The preparatory work is done quickly and secretly [81] and when

[78] See *Luhring Collieries Co.* v. *Interstate Coal Dock Co.*, 281 Fed. 265, *aff'd.* 287 Fed. 711 (C. C. A. 2d 1923).

[79] *i.e.*, in the bankruptcy sense, Bankruptcy Act, Sec. 1 (15). See *American Can Co.* v. *Erie Preserving Co.*, 171 Fed. 540 *aff'd.* 183 Fed. 96 (C. C. A. 2d 1910). This is important. The appointment of a receiver, except on the ground of "insolvency", even with the consent of the corporation, is not an "act of bankruptcy" which would leave the way open to any creditor to file an involuntary petition in bankruptcy, *Nolte* v. *Hudson Navigation Co.*, 8 F. (2d) 859 (C. C. A. 2d 1925); *In re Edward Ellsworth*, 173 Fed. 699 (D. C. W. D. N. Y. 1909). *Cf. United States* v. *Butterworth-Judson Corp. supra* note 63; *Price* v. *United States, supra* note 63. Sections 74 and 77 of the Bankruptcy Act (added by amendment of March 3, 1933) permit the filing of a petition by a debtor who "is insolvent or unable to meet his debts as they mature".

[80] *Kingsport Press, Inc.* v. *Brief English Systems, Inc., supra* note 72, at p. 501; *Trustees System Co.* v. *Payne, supra* note 59. *Cf. National Lumberman's Bank* v. *Lake Shore Mach. Co., supra* note 70.

[81] For a vivid description of the preparations for a receivership and ancillary proceedings thereunder, see *May Hosiery Mills, Inc.* v. *F. & W. Grand 5-10-25 Cents Stores*, 59 F. (2d) 218 (D. C. Mont. 1932). See also New York Times, June 30, 1933, p. 34. If there is to be a receivership there is of course a legitimate need for haste and secrecy to prevent one creditor obtaining a preference by judgment or attachment. Unfortunately, it frequently is merely a race to make sure that the receivership will be under "friendly" auspices. For an indication of these "races" see *Christian* v. *R. Hoe & Co. Inc.*, 63 F. (2d) 221 (C. C. A. 2d 1933); *Matter of Paramount Publix Corp., supra* note 58. From their apparent eagerness to make sure that the receivers are appointed in "their" action, it would seem that attorneys have taken the remark that "there should be no 'friendly' receiverships" (*Harkin* v. *Brundage, supra* note 58, at p. 55) as the statement of a hope rather than a fact. It is said that telegrams have been left unopened by judges because they knew they contained information that a receiver had already been appointed by another court and would thus prevent the appointment of another, testimony

the bill is ready for filing there is also ready for simultaneous filing an answer admitting the allegations of the bill and consenting to, or joining in, the prayer for a receiver.[82] The receiver is then appointed without notice to any other creditor.[83]

of Mr. Blanc before House Judiciary Committee, *supra* note 58 at p. 20. Equity Rule 5 of the Southern District of New York requires the disclosure of all pending suits.

[82] At least to this extent the great majority of federal equity receiverships are prearranged. Standing alone it seems not to constitute illicit "collusion", *Metropolitan Railway Receivership, supra* note 69; *Kingsport Press, Inc.* v. *Brief English Systems, Inc., supra* note 72. In *Harkin* v. *Brundage, supra* note 58, there also appeared a conspiracy to oust the state court of jurisdiction and that the plaintiff was assured that it would not be involved in any expense. In *May Hosiery Mills, Inc.* v. *F. & W. Grand 5–10–25 Cent Stores, supra* note 81, the court found that the purpose of the receivership was not to aid the creditors but to aid the corporation escape some burdensome leases, *infra* note 88.

[83] Equity Rule 8 of the Southern District of New York provides that, except in the case of a public utility, a meeting of creditors should be held during the first 60 days of operations by the receiver. The receivership works no change in ownership and the corporate existence and functions continue, *Royal Indemnity Co.* v. *American Bond & Mortgage Co., supra* note 15; *cf. United States* v. *Whitridge*, 231 U. S. 144, 34 S. Ct. 24, 58 L. Ed. 159 (1913); *Michigan* v. *Michigan Trust Co.*, 286 U. S. 334, 52 S. Ct. 512, 76 L. Ed. 1136 (1932). The practice of appointing as co-receiver one of the officers of the defendant has been condemned, *May Hosiery Mills, Inc.* v. *F. & W. Grand 5–10–25–Cent Stores, supra* note 81, at p. 220. It must be noted that despite the refusal of the court in the cited case to appoint any ancillary receivers and its condemnation of the appointment of one Green, defendant's executive vice-president, as a co-receiver by the primary court (S. D. N. Y., E66-133, 1932), he was appointed ancillary co-receiver in 21 other jurisdictions (Receiver's Report, No. 1, July 1, 1932). The practice is of course defended on the ground that one familiar with the business is necessary for its successful operation. In deference to this reason it has been said that even an officer who had been guilty of mismanagement may be appointed receiver, *Fowler* v. *Jarvis-Conklin Mtge. Trust Co.*, 66 Fed. 14 (C. C. S. D. N. Y. 1894). Dewing, The Financial Policy of Corporations (1926) 952, cites a study by H. H. Swain,

Abuses developed[84] and brought forth vigorous condemnation by the Supreme Court calculated to restore equity operating receiverships to the status of the extraordinary instead of the usual.[85]

which showed that in 138 out of 150 railway receiverships from 1867 to 1897, old officers of the railroad were appointed as receivers or co-receivers. See also *American S. S. Co.* v. *Wickwire Spencer Steel Co.*, 42 F. (2d) 886, 891, *affd.* 49 F. (2d) 766 (C. C. A. 2d 1931).

[84] The most popular outcry has been against the patronage involved and the allegedly exorbitant allowances to receivers and their counsel. See Hopkins, *supra*, note 73. A Special Committee on Equity Receiverships of the Association of the Bar of the City of New York found that the costs in equity were higher than in bankruptcy but that the allowances in bankruptcy were too low, 1927 Year Book 299. It is also significant "that a careful review of the reported cases for the past ten years [1914-1924] discloses three instances only in which any security holder or creditor has taken exception to the fees or expenses of receivership", Rosenberg, Corporate Reorganization and the Federal Court (1924) XI. The aggregate cost of the large reorganization is very high. Thus the reorganization of the Chicago, Milwaukee & St. Paul cost more than $5,000,-000, *Chicago, Milwaukee & St. Paul Reorganization*, 131 I. C. C. 673, 699 (1928). It is also charged that receiverships are permitted to carry on much too long. "Indeed, such bills have come to afford a species of locus poenitentiae for the study of possibilities by creditors, shareholders, directors, receivers, and various self-appointed committees sitting under the chancellor's 'umbrella' and watching the weather outside", Hough, C. J., in *Manhattan Rubber Mfg. Co.* v. *Lucey Mfg. Co.*, 5 F. (2d) 39, 43 (C. C. A. 2d 1924). See also *Kingsport Press Inc.* v. *Brief English Systems, Inc., supra* note 72. This criticism somewhat overlooks the idea that equity receiverships were designed to permit reorganization and to prevent liquidation. The "weather" outside may be a most important element in the success of a reorganization. *Cf.* Equity Rule 8 of the Southern District of New York.

[85] *Harkin* v. *Brundage, supra* note 58 at p. 55; *Michigan* v. *Michigan Trust Co., supra* note 83, at p. 345; *Shapiro* v. *Wilgus, supra* note 62, at p. 356; *Johnson* v. *Manhattan Ry. Co.*, 289 U. S. 479, 53 S. Ct. 721,   L. Ed.   (1933). For a consideration of the effect of these "cautionary admonitions", see *Ex Parte Relmar Holding Co.*, 61 F. (2d) 941 (C. C. A. 2d 1932) cert. den 288 U. S. 614, 53 S. Ct. 405,   L. Ed.   (1933).

The equity courts themselves are endeavoring to correct some of the abuses. At least one court has adopted the procedure of appointing on an *ex parte* application only a temporary receiver and not making the appointment "permanent" until notice has been given to all parties in interest.[86] And if any objecting party establishes "the solvency of the defendant and its ability to meet its obligations currently accruing" the receivership will be terminated.[87] It has also been suggested that the purpose of the receivership must be to benefit creditors and not the defendant corporation.[88]

Equity receiverships have also been severely criticised because they have not achieved their avowed purpose—reorganization instead of liquidation. One investigator reported that a majority of the cases which he examined resulted in liquidation.[89] Another study disclosed that out of forty

[86] *Municipal Fin. Corp.* v. *Bankus Corp.*, *supra* note 75.

[87] *Christian* v. *R. Hoe & Co. Inc.*, 63 F. (2d) 218 (C. C. A. 2d 1933). See also *Mitchell* v. *Lay*, 48 F (2d) 79 (C. C. A. 9th 1930), cert. den. 283 U. S. 864, 51 S. Ct. 656, 75 L. Ed. 1469. *Cf. Union Trust Co.* v. *Jones*, *supra* note 63; *American Brake S. & F. Co.* v. *Pere Marquette R. Co.*, *supra* note 58. The objection must be made seasonably, *American S. S. Co* v. *Wickwire-Spencer Steel Co.*, *supra* note 83, objector stockholder of defendant.

[88] *May Hosiery Mills, Inc.* v. *F. & W. Grand 5-10-25 Cent Stores*, *supra* note 81. However, the receivership roundly condemned in the cited case was deemed proper in 29 jurisdictions and it proceeded in regular course until transferred to bankruptcy upon the recommendation of the equity receiver, *supra* note 83. The real objection was that the receivership was directed against a single class of creditors—the lessors. See Douglas and Frank, Landlord's Claims in Reorganizations (1933) 42 Yale L. J. 1003. For a number of instances where equity receiverships were had for purposes other than the direct benefit of creditors, see Dewing, *supra* note 83 at p. 945.

[89] Hopkins, *supra* note 73.

equity receiverships only one resulted in actual reorganization.[90] These statistics undoubtedly give an unfair picture because the same weight is given to small unimportant units as to the large and important ones.[91] The undue resort to equity may be because of excessive optimism or because of the lure of higher fees.[92] Recognizing the unwarranted strain imposed upon the system, determined efforts are being made to induce bankruptcy for those corporations which are palpably beyond rescue.[93] Whatever the weaknesses or abuses, the equity receivership is a method devised to achieve the socially desirable object of saving corporations only temporarily embarrassed, or of enabling those interested in them to realize their fair going-concern value rather than only scrap value. Accordingly, it is correctly regarded as merely a procedural step in reorganization.[94] It is an open question whether it is the best possible agency to

[90] Douglas and Weir, Equity Receiverships (1930) 4 Conn. B. J. 1.

[91] See Cravath, The Reorganization of Corporations, in Some Legal Phases of Corporate Financing, Reorganization and Regulation (1917) 154, for an indication of some of the successes of equity reorganization.

[92] *Supra* note 84.

[93] *Municipal Fin. Corp.* v. *Bankus Corp., supra* note 75; *Matter of Bankus Corp.*, 45 F. (2d) 907 (D. C. S. D. N. Y. 1930). The equity court is without power to compel bankruptcy, *Manhattan Rubber Mfg. Co.* v. *Lucey Mfg. Co., supra* note 84, but it has been sought to correct this by statute, see Hearings by House Judiciary Committee held April 11, 1930 on H. R. 9997, 71st Cong. 2d Sess.

[94] See Cravath, *supra* note 91; lecture on Foreclosure of Railroad Mortgages by Byrne in same volume; Cutcheon, Recent Developments in Federal Railroad Foreclosure Procedure, in Some Legal Phases of Corporate Financing, Reorganization and Regulation (1931) 79, 80; Rosenberg, *supra* note 84, p. 2; Dewing, *supra* note 83, p. 944.

operate embarrassed businesses and supervise their reorganization; it has its staunch defenders;[95] others prefer the bankruptcy court,[96] and still others, new administrative tribunals.[97] The method apparently most recently in favor with Congress is a combination of administrative and judicial action.[98]

[95] Mayer, *supra* note 74; Taft, Recent Criticism of the Federal Judiciary, 18 A. B. A. R. 237 (1895); Rosenberg, *supra* note 84, IX circa.

[96] Hough, C. J., in *Manhattan Rubber Mfg. Co.* v. *Lucey Mfg. Co.* *supra* note 84, p. 45. For an indication of the difficulties of reorganization in bankruptcy (except, of course, under the Act of March 3, 1933), see, *Acme Harvester Co.* v. *Beekman Lumber Co.*, 222 U. S. 300 (1911); *In re* Wayne Realty Co., 275 Fed. 955 (D. C. N. D. Ohio 1921); *In re Prudential Outfitting Co.*, 250 Fed. 504 (D. C. S. D. N. Y. 1918); *In re J. B. & J. M. Cornell Co.*, 186 Fed. 859, (D. C. S. D. N. Y. 1911); *In re Northampton Portland Cement Co.*, 185 Fed. 542 (D. C. E. D. Pa. 1911). But see 7 Remington, Bankruptcy, Sec. 3074.2.

[97] See Taft, *supra* note 95, p. 264; Rosenberg, *supra* note 95. This thought may underlie the remark by Mr. Justice Peckham, in the *Metropolitan Railway Receivership* case, *supra* note 69, that "a court is a very unsatisfactory body to administer the affairs of a railroad as a going concern". Administrative action, on the other hand, has not escaped criticism when it has been tried, see dissenting opinions of Commissioner Eastman in *Missouri-Kansas-Texas Reorganization*, 76 I. C. C. 84, 108 (1922); *Denver & Rio Grande Western Reorganization*, 90 I. C. C. 141, 156 (1924); *Missouri-Kansas-Texas Reorganization*, 99 I. C. C. 330, 332 (1925); *Chicago, Milwaukee & St. Paul Reorganization*, 131 I. C. C. 673, 701 (1928). See also Locklin, Regulation of Security Issues by the Interstate Commerce Commission (1925) Chap. X.

[98] Bankruptcy Act, Secs. 75, 77 (added March 3, 1933). This is no easy way out for "the relation between courts and administrative tribunals continues to be one of the most baffling problems", Powell, The Relation Between the Virginia Court of Appeals and the State Corporation Commission, 19 Virginia L. Rev. 433 (1933). See, Rodgers and Groom, Reorganization of Railroad Corporations Under Section 77 of the Bankruptcy Act (1933) 33 Columbia L. Rev. 582 *et seq.;* (Note) Supervision of Railroad Reorganization Expenses by

Whatever the auspices under which they may be promulgated, the basic problems inherent in reorganization will remain.[99]

Reorganization.[100]

The usual object of a reorganization necessitated by financial embarrassment is to rearrange the financial structure [101] without breaking up the business unit. To achieve this object, it is manifestly necessary to take away, in whole or part, from some their strict "legal" rights for the benefit of others. Primarily, the problem is economic and not legal.[102] In so far as it is legal, the basic ques-

the Interstate Commerce Commission, 40 Yale L. J. 974 (1931) condemning the concurrent jurisdiction of the courts and the Interstate Commerce Commission over railroad reorganizations.

[99] "Lawyers are apt to exaggerate their own importance and the significance of their legal machinery in determining the form and details of reorganization procedure, forgetful that a reorganization is primarily an adjustment of human motives and economic conditions, circumscribed rather than determined by the law", Dewing, *supra,* note 83, p. 932.

"Mere shift in the repository of power or change in the mechanics of courts goes for little or nothing", Bourquin, D. J., in *May Hosiery Mills, Inc.* v. *F. & W. Grand 5–10–25 Cent Stores, Inc., supra* note 81, p. 221.

[100] Probably the best available material on the legal aspects is to be found in the books cited *supra* notes 91, 94. See also Frank, Some Realistic Reflections on Some Aspects of Corporate Reorganizations, 19 Virginia L. Rev. 541 (1933) ; Rodgers and Groom, *supra* note 98. For a non-legal study by a lawyer of a large railroad receivership, see Lowenthal, The Investor Pays (1933).

[101] Generally, so as to reduce fixed charges, raise new capital, and fund past due or early maturities.

[102] "The letter of the railroad mortgage bond has come to be nothing more than mere legal verbiage, but if the property covered by the mortgage has earned its charges, the mortgage is allowed to remain and the bondholders are not asked to make sacrifices. If, on

tions involved relate to the relative priorities to which the different classes of "old" securities are entitled in the reorganized corporation, and the respective rights of the minority, or dissenting, holders of a particular class as against the majority thereof who are in favor of a proposed reorganization plan.

The first of these questions centers on compliance with the rule of the *Boyd* case.[103] It, in substance, is that upon reorganization the stockholders may not receive any rights or interests in the reorganized corporation in preference to the creditors,[104] and that when, in pursuance of a reorgani-

the other hand, the property behind the mortgage has failed to earn its charges the bondholders are forced to accept a lessening, perhaps a total extinction of their rights to demand a fixed income. They may object, but they are powerless to resist, except by acquiring the actual property itself at foreclosure sale; and the failure of their property to earn its charges prior to the receivership gives little promise that its earnings would be better after the bondholders themselves have exercised the letter of their legal rights * * *". Dewing, *supra* note 83 at pp. 996–997.

[103] *Northern Pacific Ry.* v. *Boyd*, 228 U. S. 482, 33 S. Ct. 554, 57 L. Ed. 931 (1913). The decision might have been predicted on the basis of *Railroad Co.* v. *Howard*, 7 Wall. 392 (U. S. 1868) and *Louisville Trust Co.* v. *Louisville, etc. Ry.*, 174 U. S. 674, 19 S. Ct. 827, 43 L. Ed. 1130 (1899), but see the contrary lower federal, and state, court decisions cited in the *Boyd* opinion at p. 503. The view that the "sale" is a mere "form" for effecting a transfer to the reorganized corporation was also not new, see *Walker* v. *Whelen*, 4 Phila. 389 (Pa. 1861).

[104] The principle may be broader and may mean "that the relative priorities of the old securities, senior to the most junior securities which continue to have any interest in the property, must not be inequitably disturbed", Swaine, Reorganization of Corporations: Certain Developments of the Last Decade (1927) in Some Legal Phases of Corporate Financing Reorganization and Regulation (1931) 142 and the same author in Corporate Reorganization and the Federal Court, *supra* note 84, at p. 104. This would not neces-

zation plan which provides for the stockholders [105] but not for the creditors, the property is sold to the "new" corporation, a creditor may follow the assets.[106] The Supreme Court, however, qualified

sarily be so if the *Boyd* decision was only an application of the rule against fraudulent conveyances (Glenn, The Law of Fraudulent Conveyances (1931) 300), although it has been suggested that the same result could be reached by a court of equity on some broad notion of "fairness", Frank, *supra* note 100. See, *Guaranty Trust Co.* v. *Missouri Pac. Ry. Co.*, 238 Fed. 812 (D. C. E. D. Mo. 1916); *New York Trust Co.* v. *Continental & Comm. Trust & S. Bank*, 26 F. (2d) 872 (C. C. A. 8th 1928) cert. den. 278 U. S. 644, 49 S. Ct. 80, 73 L. Ed. 538; *In re Howell*, 215 Fed. 1 (C. C. A. 2d 1914), cert. den. 235 U. S. 703, 35 S. Ct. 205, 59 L. Ed. 205.

[105] "There is no moral turpitude, nor is there any illegality in the making and performing of an agreement between the bondholders secured by mortgages, the stockholders, and the unsecured creditors of an insolvent mortgagor, that there should be a foreclosure and sale of the mortgaged property to or for the benefit of a new corporation in which all the members of the three classes shall be permitted at the option of each of them to take the bonds or stock of the new corporation in substantial proportion to the respective ranks and equities of the classes", *St. Louis-San Francisco Ry. Co.* v. *McElvain*, 253 Fed. 123, 133 (D. C. E. D. Mo. 1918). The right of a stockholder to receive securities in the reorganized corporation arises not out of his status as stockholder but solely under the Plan of Reorganization and he must therefore receive them pursuant thereto if at all, *Dow* v. *Iowa Central Ry. Co.*, 144 N. Y. 426, 39 N. E. 398 (1895). Where he is not a party to the reorganization agreement (Bondholders') but only a beneficiary thereunder he has no standing to sue for its modification but must accept or reject it in toto, *Miller* v. *Dodge*, 28 Misc. 640, 59 N. Y. S. 1070 (1899). In *United Water Works Co.* v. *Omaha Water Co.*, 164 N. Y. 41, 58 N. E. 58 (1900) it was held that under the Plan the Bondholders' Committee was not authorized to allot common stock in the "new" corporation to the preferred stockholders of the "old".

[106] The right exists in favor of all who hold "unsatisfied claims", *Pierce* v. *United States*, 255 U. S. 398, 41 S. Ct. 365, 65 L. Ed. 697 (1921) fine; *Safety Car Heating & Lighting Co.* v. *U. S. Light & Heating Co.* 2 F. (2d) 384 (D. C. W. D. N. Y. 1924) patent infringement claim; *Howard* v. *Maxwell Motor Co.*, 269 Fed. 292, *affd.* 275 Fed. 53 (C. C. A. 2d 1921) lease; *cf. Kansas City Terminal Ry. Co.*

the rule as follows:[107]

"This conclusion does not, as claimed, require the impossible and make it necessary to pay an unsecured creditor in cash as a condition of stockholders retaining an interest in the reorganized company. His interest can be preserved by the issuance, on equitable terms, of income bonds or preferred stock. If he declines a fair offer he is left to protect himself as any other creditor of a judgment debtor, and, having refused to come into a just reorganization, could not thereafter be heard in a court of equity to attack".

Despite the mental distress which the *Boyd* decision caused reorganization lawyers,[108] it must be accepted as controlling. The problem is to make certain, beyond peradventure, that the reorganiza-

v. *Central Union Trust Co.*, 28 F. (2d) 177 (C. C. A. 8th 1928) cert. den. 278 U. S. 655, 49 S. Ct. 179, 73 L. Ed. 564 executory contract, but see *Okmulgee Window Glass Co.* v. *Frink*, 260 Fed. 159 (C. C. A. 8th 1918) cert. den. 251 U. S. 563, 40 S. Ct. 342, 64 L. Ed. 415. *Cf. Equitable Trust Co.* v. *United Box Board & Paper Co.*, 220 Fed. 714 (D. C. N. J. 1915). The right may be lost by laches, *Waller* v. *Texas & Pac. Ry. Co.*, 245 U. S. 398, 38 S. Ct. 142 (1918) ; *St. Louis & San Francisco RR. Co.* v. *Spiller*, 274 U. S. 304, 47 S. Ct. 635 (1927). The measure of recovery is considered in *Mountain States Power Co.* v. *A. L. Jordan Lumber Co.*, 293 Fed. 502 (C. C. A. 9th 1923) cert. den. 264 U. S. 582, 44 S. Ct. 217, 68 L. Ed. 860, but see Mr. Swaine's comments thereon, *supra* note 104, at pp. 174–175.

[107] 228 U. S. 482, 508.

[108] See Cravath, *supra* note 91, at p. 197; Cutcheon, An Examination of Devices Employed to Obviate the Embarrassments to Reorganizations created by the *Boyd* Case (1927) in Some Legal Phases of Corporate Finance Reorganization and Regulation (1931) 35.

tion is "just" and that the terms offered the creditors are "fair" and "equitable".

What is "just, fair and equitable" is, of course, so completely dependent upon the details and circumstances of the particular case that nothing beyond the broadest generalities are available for guidance.[109] The following may be ventured:

(1) The stockholders may receive securities in the "new" corporation worth more than the amount they are assessed as a condition of participation.[110]

(2) The securities offered to the creditors need not be superior in rank or grade to those which the stockholders may obtain; the priorities may be adjusted in the amount of securities given to each or in the amount of the assessment imposed on each.[111]

(3) Where the creditor is offered two or more alternatives, it is sufficient if only one is

[109] See generally, Bonbright and Bergerman, Two Rival Theories of Priority Rights of Security Holders in a Corporate Reorganization, 28 Columbia L. Rev. 127 (1928); Swaine, *supra* note 104, at pp. 148–160; Buscheck, A Formula For the Judicial Reorganization of Public Service Corporations (1932) 32 Columbia L. Rev. 964.

[110] *Jameson* v. *Guaranty Trust Co.*, 20 F. (2d) 808 (C. C. A. 7th 1927) cert. den. 275 U. S. 569, 48 S. Ct. 141, 72 L. Ed. 431; *P. R. Walsh Tie & Timber Co.* v. *Missouri Pac. Ry. Co.* 280 Fed. 38 (C. C. A. 8th 1922) cert. den. 260 U. S. 743, 43 S. Ct. 164, 67 L. Ed. 491.

[111] *Kansas City Ry.* v. *Central Union Trust Co.*, 271 U. S. 445, 455, 46 S. Ct. 549, 70 L. Ed. 1028 (1926). For the application of the principles in the same case see 28 F. (2d) 177 (C. C. A. 8th 1928) cert. den. 278 U. S. 655, 49 S. Ct. 179, 73 L. Ed. 564. See also *Temmer* v. *Denver Tramway Co.*, 18 F. (2d) 226 (C. C. A. 8th 1927).

fair.[112]

(4) The fairness of the reorganization must be determined by the chancellor in the "exercise of an informed discretion concerning the practical adjustment of the several rights",[113] and he should "avoid artificial scruples" but look for "substantial justice".[114]

But how to procure the *timely* approval of the chancellor so as to put to rest the specter of the *Boyd* case?[115] The typical equity receivership of the kind above discussed is ordinarily promptly consolidated with a foreclosure suit brought by the first mortgagee (commonly a corporate-trustee under a trust-mortgage securing the mortgage bonds). In due course the mortgagee procures a judgment of foreclosure and sale and is in position to wipe out all junior security-holders.[116] At this stage, economic realities impinge upon legal theory. The first mortgagee does not want to foreclose all junior interests because it is from them that the needed new capital is most readily obtained. Nobody but the bondholders,

[112] *Kansas City Terminal Ry. Co.* v. *Central Union Trust Co.*, 28 F. (2d) 177, 188 (C. C. A. 8th 1928) cert. den. *supra* note 111.

[113] *Kansas City Ry.* v. *Central Union Trust Co., supra* note 111.

[114] *Kansas City Ry.* v. *Guardian Trust Co.*, 240 U. S. 166, 178, 36 S. Ct. 334 (1916). It seems that reorganization plans are "uniformly sanctioned" by the courts, see Weiner, Reorganization Under Section 77: A Comment (1933) 33 Columbia L. Rev. 834, 846; Tracy, Corporate Foreclosures (1929) 350.

[115] Cutcheon, *supra* note 108; *Swaine, supra* note 104, pp. 142-148.

[116] For a discussion of some procedural problems in connection with sales in equity under the Federal Judicial Code, see Israels, Reorganization Sales, 32 Columbia L. Rev. 668 (1932).

because of the right to use the bonds in payment, can reasonably bid for the property at a foreclosure sale, and hence the sale, instead of being a means of realizing in cash the fair value of the property sold, becomes an idle ceremony whereby title is transferred to those who represent the majority-bondholders.[117]

Prior to the *Boyd* case, the courts adopted the practice [118] of inserting in the foreclosure decree an "upset price", that is, the minimum price at which the court would confirm the sale.[119] Its object was, of course, to protect the mortgagor from a sale at an inadequate price. In effect it is a weapon in the hands of the court in a conflict between assenting and dissenting mortgage bondholders because a low upset price means a small cash distribution to the bondholders who stay out of the reorganization and a high upset price means a large cash distribution to them with the resultant burden upon the reorganization.[120]

With the enunciation of the doctrine of the *Boyd* case, "fairness" achieved by such indirection became clearly insufficient. A direct judicial determi-

[117] The set-up is frequently much more complicated and requires the adjustment of conflicting claims to the mortgaged property and, in railroad receiverships, the problem of divisional liens is no simple one.

[118] It is discretionary, *American S. S. Co.* v. *Wickwire Spencer Steel Co., supra* note 83, at p. 895.

[119] Spring, Upset Price in Corporate Reorganizations, 32 Harvard L. Rev. 489 (1919).

[120] Weiner, Conflicting Functions of the Upset Price in a Corporate Reorganization, 27 Columbia L. Rev. 132 (1927). See also Colin, Why Upset Price? An Argument for Reorganization by Decree (1933) 28 Illinois L. Rev. 225.

nation of "fairness" became essential.[121] This required a marked change in the attitude theretofore assumed by receivership courts as to their "neutrality" with respect to reorganization plans,[122]

[121] Where there is a foreclosure sale the determination is ordinarily made in connection with the confirmation of the sale pursuant to provisions inserted in the foreclosure decree, *Kansas City Terminal Ry. Co.* v. *Central Union Trust Co., supra* note 112, at p. 185; *St. Louis-San Francisco Ry. Co.* v. *McElvain, supra* note 105; Swaine, *supra* note 104 p. 146 note 34. Sometimes the determination is made before, see *Guaranty Trust Co.* v. *Missouri Pacific Ry. Co.,* 238 Fed. 812 (D. C. E. D. Mo. 1916); *Guaranty Trust Co.* v. *Chicago, M. & St. P. Ry.,* 15 F. (2d) 434 (D. C. N. D. Ill. 1926); *Sullivan* v. *St. Louis-San Francisco Ry. Co.,* 263 N. Y. Supp. 396 (1933). In *Industrial & General Trust Ltd.* v. *Tod,* 180 N. Y. 215, 73 N. E. 7 (1908) it was held that under the deposit agreement there considered, the committee was impliedly bound to submit a reorganization plan before foreclosure sale so that the depositors might avail of the right to withdraw in time to act. The foreclosure decree is no adjudication of the rights of the parties to a reorganization agreement *inter sese, Fuller* v. *Venable,* 118 Fed. 543 (C. C. A. 4th 1902). The sale may, of course, be in equity and without a mortgage foreclosure, *Habirshaw Electric Cable Co.* v. *Habirshaw Electric Cable Co., Inc.,* 296 Fed. 875 (C. C. A. 2d 1924), cert. den. 265 U. S. 587, 44 S. Ct. 633, 68 L. Ed. 1193. The sale may be "private", *Stokes* v. *Williams,* 226 Fed. 148 (C. C. A. 3d 1915), cert. den. 241 U. S. 681, 36 S. Ct. 728, 60 L. Ed. 1234. As to whether a sale is necessary in order to cut off the rights of security holders who do not participate in the reorganization, see *Phipps* v. *Chicago, R. I. & P. Ry. Co.* 284 Fed. 945 (C. C. A. 8th 1922), cert. granted, 261 U. S. 611, dismissed by stipulation, 262 U. S. 762; *Coriell* v. *Morris White, Inc.,* 54 F. (2d) 255 (C. C. A. 2d 1931), *revd. sub. nom.* National Surety Co. v. Coriell, 289 U. S. 426, 53 S. Ct. 678 (1933); *Harding* v. *American Sumatra Tobacco Co.,* 14 F. (2d) 168 (D. C. N. D. Ga. 1926).

[122] In 1894, Circuit Judge Lacombe required "absolute neutrality" on the part of a "receiver as between conflicting plans of reorganization" *Fowler* v. *Jarvis-Conklin Mtge. Co.,* 63 Fed. 888, 890, (C. C. S. D. N. Y.). In 1918, after the Circuit Court of Appeals had sustained his order in the *Aetna Explosives Company* receivership (252 Fed. 456), Judge Mayer appointed a reorganization committee and upon its failure to agree personally promulgated a plan of reorganization, Rosenberg, *supra* note 84, 62–63. More recently Judge Mack directed

and some modification of technique, but the most difficult problem was to assure the binding effect of the decree. The matter is still beclouded with uncertainty.

When the property of the corporation is sold to a new corporation all the old creditors and security-holders are effectually barred by the decree con-

a trustee in bankruptcy to assist in the organization of a bondhold-ers' committee and to supervise the drafting of the deposit agree-ment, *In re G. L. Miller & Co., Inc.*, (U. S. D. C. S. D. N. Y. 1926). In practice the tie-up is frequently most close. In the *Missouri-Kansas-Texas Reorganization*, 99 I. C. C. 330, 336 (1925), it was noted that "the reorganization managers acted substantially as a board of directors for the receivers in all matters affecting the man-agement and operation of the property during the period of the receivership". The notion of judicial "impartiality" persists, see *In re International Match Corp.*, 59 F. (2d) 1012 (D. C. S. D. N. Y. 1932). The foreclosure of very large real-estate mortgage bond issues has recently presented the state courts with analogous situations and they seem to have gone even further than the federal courts in their direct attack on the fairness of reorganization plans, see *Clinton Trust Co.* v. *142–144 Joralemon Street Corp.*, 237 App. Div. 789, 263 N. Y. Supp. 359 (1933); *Bergelt* v. *Roberts*, 144 Misc. 832, 258 N. Y. Supp. 905 *affd.* 236 App. Div. 777 (1932); *Bank of Manhattan Trust Co.* v. *Ellda Corp.*, 147 Misc. 374, 265 N. Y. S. 115 (1933). See also Carey and Brabner-Smith, Studies in Realty Mortgage Foreclosures: V Reorganization (1933) 28 Illinois L. Rev. 1; *People* v. *S. W. Straus & Co., Inc.*, N. Y. L. J. May 2, 1933 p. 2644. It has however been held that a separate plenary suit is necessary in order to procure an injunction against the consummation of a reorganiza-tion, *Empire Trust Co.* v. *Bim's Realty Corp.*, N. Y. L. J. Nov. 23, 1932, p. 2323. In *Clinton Trust Co.* v. *142–144 Joralemon Street Corp.*, the court suggested that equity has another indirect weapon of control in its power to direct the foreclosing trustee to purchase the property for the benefit of *all* bondholders. See *First National Bank* v. *Neil*, 137 Kans. 436, 20 Pac. (2d) 528 (1933) and the authorities there cited; Leesman, Corporate Trusteeships and Receiverships (1933) 28 Illinois L. Rev. 238, 259–261. See also Chapter 729 of the New York Laws of 1933 granting such power by statute; *cf.* the Michigan Statute held unconstitutional as to dissenting bondholders in *Detroit Trust Co.* v. *Stormfeltz Loveley Co.*, 257 Mich. 655, 242 N. W. 227 (1932).

firming the sale, because, in the absence of a violation of the *Boyd* doctrine, they may not follow the assets and the "right" against the old corporation —left without assets—is valueless.[123] Recognizing the empty formality of the sale in a reorganization, courts have attempted to do without it. The outstanding case is *Phipps* v. *Chicago, R. I. & P. Ry. Co.*[124] The Circuit Court of Appeals for the Eighth Circuit there held that a court of equity having possession of property may authorize its transfer to a reorganized corporation and restrain creditors from pursuing the property except pursuant to the plan of reorganization thus compelling them to accept securities under the reorganization plan if the court deems the terms fair. The decision was defended[125] and criticised.[126] The Supreme Court granted certiorari[127] but was unfortunately prevented from passing on its merits.[128] In the cited case the Court held the decree binding on a creditor who filed a claim, but in a related case[129] it also

---

[123] As to the rights of receivership creditors, see *Texas & Pacific Ry. Co.* v. *Bloom,* 164 U. S. 636, 17 S. Ct. 216, 41 L. Ed. 580 (1897).

[124] 284 Fed. 945 (C. C. A. 8th 1922). See also *American Brake Shoe & Foundry Co.* v. *Pittsburgh Rys. Co.,* 296 Fed. 204 (D. C. W. D. Pa. 1918) where a receivership was terminated without sale and the court enjoined creditors from prosecuting their claims for ten months, the corporation being required to comply with certain conditions in the interim.

[125] Rosenberg, *supra* note 84, 124. See also *Colin, supra* note 120.

[126] See Swaine, *supra* note 104, 167–172; *Harding* v. *American Sumatra Tobacco Co., supra* note 121.

[127] 261 U. S. 611, 43 S. Ct. 363, 67 L. Ed. 826 (1923).

[128] Dismissed per stipulation, 262 U. S. 762, 43 S. Ct. 701, 67 L. Ed. 1221 (1923).

[129] *Chicago, R. I. & P. Ry. Co.* v. *Lincoln Horse & Mule Comm. Co.,* 284 Fed. 955 (C. C. A. 8th 1922).

held it binding upon one who did not.

In a little known and uncited case [130] the Supreme Court held that a receivership court is without jurisdiction to enter such a decree as against persons not parties to the suit.

The latest ruling on the question is by the Circuit Court of Appeals for the Second Circuit [131] which held that creditors may not be required to accept securities for their claims and are entitled to cash—ordinarily their proportionate share of the proceeds of a judicial sale, but that a dissenting creditor is not always entitled to insist upon a sale and in lieu thereof may be required to accept his proportionate share in cash based on an appraisal of the property. The Supreme Court reversed, without passing on these questions, because the lower court approved the reorganization plan on insufficient evidence.[132]

Whether the procedural problems are solved by statute or by judicial legislation, the conflict of interest between those who approve and those who disapprove a proposed plan of reorganization will remain.[133] It is important that any procedure

[130] *International Ins. Co.* v. *Sherman,* 262 U. S. 346, 43 S. Ct. 574, 67 L. Ed. 1018 (1923). Receivership on stockholders' bill based on mismanagement, court approved of a reorganization plan and barred "annuity certificate" holders who did not join in plan within twenty days from asserting any claim. Held, without jurisdiction as to non parties.

[131] *Coriell* v. *Morris White, Inc.,* 54 F. (2d) 255 (C. C. A. 2d 1931).

[132] *National Surety Co.* v. *Coriell, supra* note 121. The court also was apparently dissatisfied because the value was fixed one year later. The valuation has also been criticised as being merely liquidating value, see Frank, *supra* note 100, pp. 716–718.

[133] "The inevitable outcome of it all is compromise. An adjustment

adopted make adequate provision for the present-
ment of their respective views to the tribunal
whose decree will bind them.[134]

There is a very strong feeling that the wishes of
the majority should govern,[135] but there is real
danger that blind adherence to any such rule may
permit the working of injustice. The individual
security-holder is not in a position to pass upon the
merits of a proposed reorganization or effectively
to express any views thereon even if he has any.[136]

is reached partly on the basis of the constructive power of the majority, and partly through the weight of obstructive tactics at the
hands of the minority", W. Z. Ripley, Railroads: Finance and Organization (1915) 390.

[134] For a discussion of proceedings before the Interstate Commerce Commission, see Harvey, Rights of Minority Stockholders (2d
Ed. 1929).

[135] *Jameson* v. *Guaranty Trust Co., supra* note 110, at p. 815;
Fearon v. *Bankers' Trust Co.,* 238 Fed. 83 (C. C. A. 3d 1916); Cor-
porate Reorganization—an Amendment to the Bankruptcy Act—a
Symposium (1933) 19 Va. L. Rev. 317; (Note) 42 Yale L. J. 387
(1933); Seiff, Corporate Reorganizations: Defects and a Remedy,
67 U. S. Law Rev. 75 (1933); Act amending Federal Bankruptcy
Act approved March 3, 1933; Delaware Gen. Corp. Law, Sec. 5 (9);
Kentucky Statutes, Sec. 771a; *Gates* v. *Boston & N. Y. Air Line
RR. Co.,* 53 Conn. 333, 5 Atl. 695, app. dis. 122 U. S. 646 (1885);
Gilfillan v. *Union Canal Co.,* 109 U. S. 401 (1883); *Canada So. Ry.
Co.* v. *Gebhard,* 109 U. S. 527 (1883). *Cf. Mather* v. *Cinn. Ry. Tun-
nel Co.,* 3 Ohio C. C. 284 (1888); *Landis* v. *West Penn Ry. Co.,* 133
Pa. 579, 19 Atl. 556 (1890); *Keane* v. *Moffly,* 217 Pa. 240, 66 Atl.
319 (1907).

[136] An individual security holder will ordinarily not be permitted
to intervene (*Penn. Steel Co.* v. *N. Y. City Ry. Co.,* 160 Fed. 222—
C. C. S. D. N. Y. 1908), but a committee, or even more than one for
good reason, will be, *Penn. Steel Co.* v. *N. Y. City Ry. Co.,* 181 Fed.
285 (C. C. S. D. N. Y. 1910). "In my opinion, the recognition by the
court of any bondholders', stockholders' or creditors' committee in
receivership proceedings should be conditioned upon the submission
to the court of the terms of the deposit agreement and further modification of or approval by the court and that such provisions, not

In practice, therefore, the majority vote is simply that of the "protective" committee, or of the reorganization committee, with whom a majority of the securities of a particular class have been deposited.[137] This might be deemed quite sufficient if

merely as to compensation but also as to creditors' rights of withdrawal, ratification of reorganization plans and many other matters as the court may deem proper in the circumstances of the particular case", Circuit Judge Mack, as Arbitrator, in *Central Hanover Bank & Trust Co.* v. *Ulster & Delaware Railroad Co.*, U. S. D. C. S. D. N. Y. E. 61–329, April 8, 1932. Intervention is "discretionary", *Guaranty Trust Co.* v. *Chicago, M. & St. P. Ry.*, *supra* note 121; *cf.* *Central Trust Co.* v. *Chicago, R. I. & P. Ry. Co.*, 218 Fed. 336 (C. C. A. 2d 1914). Stockholders will not be permitted to intervene in a foreclosure merely to assert defenses which the receiver can assert, *Conley* v. *International Pump Co.*, 237 Fed. 286 (D. C. S. D. N. Y. 1915). In a strict foreclosure, that is, one proceeding without the aid or agreement of the stockholders, the stockholders have no standing to attack the reorganization, if the value of the property is less than the liabilities, *American S. S. Co.* v. *Wickwire Spencer Steel Co.*, *supra* note 83. Ordinarily bondholders will be permitted to intervene only when the trustee acting for them also represents conflicting interests or is guilty of bad faith, *Guaranty Trust Co.* v. *Chicago, M. & St. P. Ry. Co.*, *supra* note 121; *Clinton Trust Co.* v. *142–144 Joralemon Street Corp.*, *supra* note 122. In *Guaranty Trust Co.* v. *Chicago, M. & St. P. Ry. Co.*, it was held that the mere fact that the trustee was depositary for a committee and one of its officers was secretary of the committee was not sufficient. *Cf. Central Trust Co.* v. *Chicago, R. I. & P. Ry. Co.*, 218 Fed. 336 (C. C. A. 2d 1914). See also *Fidelity Trust Co.* v. *Washington-Oregon Corp.*, 217 Fed. 588 (D. C. W. D. Wash. 1914). One need not be a party in order to be heard, *Investment Registry, Ltd.* v. *Chicago & M. E. Ry. Co.*, 212 Fed. 594 (C. C. A. 7th 1913). Section 77 of the Bankruptcy Act has been criticised for according to dissenters too generously the right to be heard, Rodgers and Groom, *supra* note 98, at pp. 590–592. Dissenters are, however, given "little real protection", *ibid.* at p. 589; see also, Weiner, *supra* note 114; Frank, *supra* note 100, at pp. 708–711.

[137] See generally, Rodgers, Rights and Duties of the Committee in Bondholders' Reorganizations, 42 Harvard L. Rev. 899 (1929); (Note) Bondholders' Committees in Reorganization, 41 Harvard L. Rev. 377 (1928). See Chap. V, *supra*.

deposit bespoke an actual choice and agreement. In truth, the practical and psychological factors are such that the security-holder deposits without much consideration of the merits.[138] The necessary result is that the court must be "vigilant to see, on the one hand, that a dissenter be not permitted to create a manouvering value in his bonds by opposing confirmation, and on the other, that the majority does not use its power * * * to oppress a helpless minority."[139]

The right of the minority to be treated equally with the majority[140] is not sufficiently assured by an offer of formal equality. The majority may be

[138] *Investment Registry Ltd.* v. *Chicago & M. E. Ry. Co.*, supra note 136, at p. 611; Isaacs, Business Security and Legal Security (1923) 37 Harvard L. Rev. 201, 208–9; Commissioner Eastman dissenting in *Chicago, Milwaukee & St. Paul Reorganization*, 131 I. C. C. 673, 702–703 (1928); *Industrial & Realty Fin. Corp.* v. *S. W. Straus & Co., Inc.*, N. Y. L. J. Sept. 21, 1932 p. 1039. Mr. Frank goes so far as to say that majority approval should have "no probative value whatever", supra note 100, at p. 714.

[139] *Investment Registry Ltd.* v. *Chicago & M. E. Ry. Co.*, supra note 136, at p. 610; to the same effect, *Palmer* v. *Bankers' Trust Co.*, 12 F. (2d) 747, 754 (C. C. A. 8th 1926), where the court also stated that in weighing the claims of dissenters it would consider whether they bought the securities "pending the reorganization and for the purpose of speculating thereon".

[140] *Southern Pacific Co.* v. *Bogert* 250 U. S. 483, 39 S. Ct. 533, 63 L. Ed. 1099 (1919). *Cf. North Amer. Co.* v. *St. Louis-San Francisco Ry. Co.*, 28 F. (2d) 174, 175 (D. C. E. D. Mo. 1926) mod. and aff. sub. nom. *Kansas City Terminal Ry. Co.* v. *Central Union Trust Co.*, 28 F. (2d) 177 (C. C. A. 8th 1928) cert. den. 278 U. S. 655 holding that the fact that the reorganization committee purchased claims from certain creditors thus giving them better terms was no objection, but see *Investment Registry, Ltd.* v. *Chicago & M. E. Ry Co.*, supra note 136, where the court refused to confirm a sale because the committee had "chilled" the bidding by purchasing a large block of bonds which might have been used by a competing bidder.

motivated by private intangible considerations beneficial only to them [141] and the minority must therefore be given an opportunity not only to attack any discrimination against them but also the plan itself. Otherwise the dangers of a *pro forma* approval are too great.

A minority committee is generally at a great disadvantage because it is ordinarily organized to oppose a committee already in the field which was organized under the sponsorship either of the corporation or the investment bankers who sold the securities. The committee is wholly powerless to act if it is in no position to circularize the security-holders to solicit their deposits or proxies. It is essential therefore that the committee have their names and addresses. In a few recent cases the aid of the court has been sought to procure such lists. [142]

---

[141] Such as retaining control of the corporation, or the good will of the investment bankers who floated certain of the securities. In *National Surety Co.* v. *Coriell, supra* note 121, Mr. Justice Brandeis said (at p. 437):

"The creditors who approved of the plan of reorganization appeared to be actuated in their recommendations and desires by considerations not applicable to the dissenting creditors. For the bank creditors, unlike the others, were to a large extent secured by the pledge of assets and may, moreover, have received preferences which would be held invalid if bankruptcy proceedings were instituted. The assenting merchandise creditors were interested not merely as creditors but as sellers of goods; and it appeared that at least some were far more interested in expected profits from future sales than in possible dividends on their existing claims."

[142] *Bergelt* v. *Roberts, supra* note 122; *In re International Match Corp., supra* note 122; *Industrial & Realty Fin. Corp.* v. *S. W. Straus & Co., Inc. supra* note 138. See also *Hart* v. *Wiltsee*, 19 F. (2d) 903 (C. C. A. 1st 1927) cert. den. 275 U. S. 559, 48 S. Ct. 419,

Relief has been granted and denied. It would seem that the sound rule should be that the minority committee may compel disclosure when the information is in the possession of, or has been procured from, a person owing fiduciary obligations to all the security-holders of the class, such as the corporation itself,[143] the trustee under a mortgage indenture, a receiver,[144] or the investment bankers who floated the issue, but not when the information is in the possession of the majority committee as the result of its own efforts and expense.

72 L. Ed. 426; *People* v. *S. W. Straus & Co. Inc.*, 149 Misc. 38 (N. Y. 1933).

[143] By an application of the rule that the relationship between a debtor corporation and its bondholders is not that of trust (*supra*, p. 173, Note 25) such relief has been denied against the debtor corporation (*Marx* v. *Merchants' National Properties, Inc.*, 148 Misc. 6, 265 N. Y. S. 163 (1933). It would seem that a court could where the corporation is in financial difficulties find a trust relationship. (See, *supra* p. 174, Note 26.)

[144] *People* v. *S. W. Straus & Co. Inc.*, *supra* note 142.

CHAPTER VIII.

CLOSE CORPORATIONS

As the law has lagged behind in its adaptation to the newer developments in the organization of world-wide corporations, so it lags behind in failing to recognize the real differences which exist between a corporation having thousands of widely scattered stockholders disinterested in its management and one having a few stockholders actively engaged in its affairs and dependent upon it not only for dividends but also for salaries. By and large the statutes of this country do not differentiate between them.[1] In attempting to do equity between stockholders, the courts have at times felt obliged to heed such important differences as whether a stock has a ready market[2] or whether there is available to stockholders any public source of information as to its affairs,[3] but on the whole they have attempted to apply to all corporations

---

[1] But see, [Federal] Securities Act of 1933, Secs. 3(8) b, 4(1); New York General Corporation Law, Sec. 103. In Europe, the "private" corporation is an wholly distinct type. (*e.g.* England—see Palmer, Company Law (13th Ed. 1929) Chap. XXXVII). Compare Pennsylvania "Partnership Associations" (Purdon's Pa. St., Title 59, Chap. 3).

[2] See *Raynolds* v. *Diamond Mills Paper Co.,* 69 N. J. Eq. 299, 309–310, 60 Atl. 941, 945 (1905); *Hiscock* v. *Lacy,* 9 Misc. 578, 30 N. Y. S. 860 (1894).

[3] See *Matter of Wygant,* 101 Misc. 509, 513–514, 167 N. Y. S. 369 (1917). See also *supra* p. 57, note 14 and text.

the same rules.[4] The major resultant vice is that the minority stockholder owning 49% of the stock of a close corporation is in the same helpless position, with respect to control, as the owner of less than 1% of the stock of some large corporation [5]— indeed, because there does not even exist the possibility of cooperation with other stockholders, in a weaker position.

This result flows most directly from the literal application of the statutory rule that the management of a corporation is vested in its board of directors and not in its stockholders,[6] and from the legal obstacles thrown about attempts to control the board by contract.[7]

When the intention is to divide control equally between two stockholders, it is possible to perpetuate such equal control by the initial election of an evenly divided board.[8] Aside from the danger

[4] While proof of those factors which induce courts to "disregard the corporate fiction" may be easier when there are only a few stockholders, it seems that the number of shareholders is not controlling. See Wormser, The Disregard of the Corporate Fiction and Allied Corporate Problems (1929) 79–83; *cf.* Anderson, Limitations of the Corporate Entity (1931) Secs. 70–86, 322.

[5] The stockholders in a close corporation owe to each other no greater fiduciary obligations than do those in a large corporation. *Claude Neon Lights, Inc.* v. *Federal Electric Co., Inc.*, 135 Misc. 113, 236 N. Y. S. 692, *aff'd.* 227 App. Div. 696, 236 N. Y. S. 767 (1929). Where a proper case for equitable intervention is made out, the court may give greater attention, especially on discretionary matters, to the protests of a substantial minority stockholder than to those of a very small stockholder. See *supra* pp. 151–152.

[6] *E.g.*, New York General Corporation Law, Sec. 27; Uniform Business Corporation Act, Sec. 31.

[7] *Supra*, pp. 31–32.

[8] This will, by reason of the fact that most statutes fix the minimum number of directors at three, consist of at least four directors

of possible disloyalty on the part of one or more of the "dummies" elected to the board in order to comply with the statutory requirements as to the minimum number of directors,[9] the weakness of such a set-up is that it may prevent functioning of the corporation in the event of a deadlock and thus compel receivership and dissolution.[10] Even when control is not equally divided, some protection can be given to the minority, at least to the extent of preserving the status-quo while the initial board is in office, by providing that the board shall act only by unanimous vote.[11] This does not, however, prevent the election of an wholly unfavorable board by the majority stockholder.[12] Where the statute provides that directors shall be chosen by a plurality vote the charter may not stipulate for an unanimous vote,[13] nor, in the absence of a permissive statute, may the by-laws fix minimum requirements for a quorum at stockholders' elections.[14]

—two "dummies". The arrangement assumes the continuing loyalty of the "dummies".

[9] See Jackson v. Hooper, 76 N. J. Eq. 592, 75 Atl. 568 (1910); *People ex rel. Stauffer* v. *Bonwit Bros.*, 69 Misc. 70, 125 N. Y. S. 958 (1910); Baumgarten v. Nichols, 69 Hun 216, 23 N. Y. S. 592 (1893).

[10] See New York General Corporation Law, Sec. 103.

[11] *Levine* v. *Mayer*, 86 Misc. 116, 149 N. Y. S. 112 (1914).

[12] This can be prevented by providing for cumulative voting or by dividing the voting stock into classes, each entitled to elect a certain number of directors.

[13] *Matter of Boulevard Theatre & Realty Co.*, 195 App. Div. 518, 186 N. Y. S. 430, affd. 231 N. Y. 615, 132 N. E. 910 (1921).

[14] *Matter of Rapid Transit Ferry Co.*, 15 App. Div. 530, 44 N. Y. S. 539 (1897); *Matter of Keogh, Inc.*, 192 App. Div. 624, 183 N. Y. S. 408 (1920). See N. Y. Stock Corporation Law, Sec. 55. It

The measure of protection afforded by the devices indicated can in some aspects, such as with respect to employment by the corporation and possibly with respect to dividends, be somewhat increased by appropriate agreements with the corporation and the other stockholders.[15] The other major modification of the corporate structure generally desired in close corporations is the preservation of the *delectus personae* characteristic of partnerships but not of corporations.[16] To this end various restrictions upon the alienability of the stock is sought to be imposed by provisions in the certificate of incorporation, the by-laws, and in private agreements among the stockholders. In so far as these restrictions consist essentially of prior options to purchase exchanged among the stockholders they are valid,[17] but no general statement as to the validity of restrictions contained in the charter or by-laws can safely be made. It depends upon the controlling statutes, the form and "reasonableness" of the restriction, and the attitude of the court towards the desire to preserve the right to choose one's fellow-stockholders.[18]

is permissible, however, to provide that the *number* of directors shall be changed only by unanimous consent, *Ripin* v. *U. S. Woven Label Co.*, 205 N. Y. 442, 98 N. E. 55 (1912).

[15] See Chapter III, notes 16, 44–47, and text. See also *Kritzer* v. *Chloral Chemical Co.*, 238 App. Div. 611, 265 N. Y. S. 224 (1933).

[16] Corporations have the right to choose their initial subscribers. See *Starrett* v. *Rockland Co.*, 65 Me. 374 (1876); *Jackson* v. *Sabie*, 36 N. D. 49, 161 N. W. 722 (1917).

[17] *Scruggs* v. *Cotterill*, 67 App. Div. 583, 73 N. Y. S. 882 (1902).

[18] The cases are annotated in 65 A. L. R. 1159. In *Barrett* v. *King*, 181 Mass. 476, 479, 63 N. E. 934 (1902), then Chief Justice Holmes

A reasonable degree of safety can be achieved for the minority stockholder in a close corporation by the skillful use of all or some of the devices mentioned supplemented by contracts. The need for such elaborate machinery to achieve a comparatively simple objective seems unwarranted and arises from the absence of appropriate statutes and from conflicting judicial attitudes as to the close corporation. While on the one hand the validity of close—even one-man—corporations organized to achieve limited liability,[19] prevent the accrual of dower,[20] or "come within" the usury laws,[21] have been sustained, certain courts seem to feel that there is something akin to illegality in the attempt to achieve corporate immunity as to outsiders while retaining internally the partnership form of doing business.[22] The classic expression of this point of

said, "Stock in a corporation is not merely property. It also creates a personal relation analogous otherwise than technically to a partnership. [This is only true as to close corporations, see *supra* pp. 44–5.] Notwithstanding decisions under statutes, like *In re Klaus*, 67 Wis. 401, there seems to be no greater objection to retaining the right of choosing one's associates in a corporation than in a firm." This attitude is far from universal.

[19] *Elenkrieg* v. *Siebrecht*, 238 N. Y. 254, 144 N. E. 519 (1924); *Werner* v. *Hearst*, 177 N. Y. 63, 69 N. E. 221 (1903); *Demarest* v. *Flack*, 128 N. Y. 205, 28 N.E. 645 (1891); Canfield, Scope and Limits of the Corporate Entity Theory (1917) 17 Columbia L. Rev. 128, 141.

[20] *Poillon* v. *Poillon*, 90 App. Div. 71, 85 N. Y. S. 689 (1904).

[21] *Jenkins* v. *Moyse*, 254 N. Y. 319, 172 N. E. 521 (1930).

[22] See *Jackson* v. *Hooper, supra* note 9; *Seitz* v. *Michel*, 148 Minn. 80, 181 N. W. 102 (1921); *Boag* v. *Thompson*, 208 App. Div. 132, 203 N. Y. S. 395 (1924); *Thomashefsky* v. *Edelstein*, 192 App. Div. 368, 182 N. Y. S. 707 (1920) *Schuster* v. *Largman*, 308 Pa. 520, 162 Atl. 305 (1932).

view is found in *Jackson* v. *Hooper*:[23]

"The law never contemplated that persons engaged in business as partners may incorporate, with intent to obtain the advantages and immunities of a corporate form, and then, Proteuslike, become at will a copartnership or a corporation, as the exigencies or purposes of their joint enterprise may from time to time require. * * * They cannot be partners *inter sese* and a corporation as to the rest of the world".[24]

It is submitted that the time is ripe for a sharper division of corporation law into two parts, one dealing with the large publicly-owned corporations and the other with close corporations.[25] This can perhaps be best accomplished by a statute expressly authorizing, under appropriate safeguards, the incorporation of limited liability companies whose management and control shall be vested directly in the stockholders and whose internal affairs may be regulated by private contract among the owners. Short of this the courts should not refuse, except under the compulsion of mandatory statutes,

[23] *Supra* note 9, at pp. 662–3.

[24] Why not? It is difficult to see how the general public or corporate creditors are benefitted by permitting the owner of 51% of the stock to oust the owner of 49% from all voice in the management.

[25] See, Weiner, Legislative Recognition of the Close Corporation (1929) 27 Michigan L. Rev. 273; Spellman, Corporate Directors (1931) Sec. 9; Frank, Some Realistic Reflections on Some Aspects of Corporate Reorganizations (1933) 19 Va. L. Rev. 541, 554.

to see the differences inherent in the two types of corporations, merely because they both, in obedience to prevailing statutes, happen to be set-up in the same outward molds.

TABLE OF CASES

INDEX

247

[Index prepared by Mr. Abraham Porter]

www.ingramcontent.com/pod-product-compliance
Lightning Source LLC
Chambersburg PA
CBHW030717250326
R18027900001B/R180279PG41599CBX00011B/13